D0985702

THE CHRIST OF FAITH
AND THE
JESUS OF HISTORY

Lives of Jesus Series

LEANDER E. KECK, *General Editor*

THE CHRIST OF FAITH
AND THE
JESUS OF HISTORY

A Critique of Schleiermacher's *Life of Jesus*

by

DAVID FRIEDRICH STRAUSS

*Translated, edited,
and with an
Introduction by*

Leander E. Keck

FORTRESS PRESS
Philadelphia

This book is a translation of *Der Christus des Glaubens und der Jesus der Geschichte: Eine Kritik des Schleiermacherschen Lebens Jesu* (Berlin: Franz Duncker, 1865).

COPYRIGHT © 1977 BY FORTRESS PRESS

All rights reserved. No part of this publication may be reproduced, stored in a retrieval system, or transmitted in any form or by any means, electronic, mechanical, photocopying, recording, or otherwise, without the prior permission of the copyright owner.

Library of Congress Catalog Card Number 75–37152
ISBN 0–8006–1273–6

4487F76   Printed in U.S.A.   1–1273

FOREWORD TO THE SERIES

In a time when a premium is placed on experimentation for the future and when theological work itself values "new theology," the reasons for reissuing theological works from the past are not self-evident. Above all, there is broad consensus that the "Lives of Jesus" produced by our forebears failed both as sound history and as viable theology. Why, then, make these works available once more?

First of all, this series does not represent an effort to turn the clock back, to declare these books to be the norm to which we should conform, either in method or in content. Neither critical research nor constructive theology can be repristinated. Nevertheless, root problems in the historical-critical study of Jesus and of theological reflection are perennial. Moreover, advances are generally made by a critical dialogue with the inherited tradition, whether in the historical reconstruction of the life of Jesus or in theology as a whole. Such a dialogue cannot occur, however, if the tradition is allowed to fade into the mists or is available to students only in handbooks which perpetuate the judgments and clichés of the intervening generation. But a major obstacle is the fact that certain pivotal works have never been available to the present generation, for they were either long out of print or not translated at all. A central aim, then, in republishing certain "Lives of Jesus" is to encourage a fresh discovery of and a lively debate with this tradition so that our own work may be richer and more precise.

Titles were selected which have proven to be significant for ongoing issues in Gospel study and in the theological enterprise as a whole. H. S. Reimarus inaugurated the truly critical investigation of Jesus and so was an obvious choice. His *On the Intention of Jesus* was reissued by the American Theological Library Association in 1962, but has not really entered the discussion despite the fact that questions he raised have been opened again, especially by S. G. F. Brandon's *Jesus and the Zealots*. Our edition, moreover, includes also his previously untranslated discussion of the resurrection and part of D. F. Strauss's evaluation of Reimarus. That Strauss's *Life of Jesus* must be included was clear from the start. Our edition, using George Eliot's translation, has taken account of Strauss's shifting views as well. Schleiermacher's *Life of Jesus* has been translated, partly because it is significant for the study of Schleiermacher himself and partly because he is the wellspring of repeated concern for the inner life of Jesus. One of the most influential expressions of this motif came from Wilhelm Herrmann's *The Communion of the Christian with God*, which, while technically not a Life of Jesus, emphasizes more than any other work the religious significance of Jesus' inner life. In fresh form, this emphasis has been rejuvenated in the recent work of Ernst Fuchs and Gerhard Ebeling who concentrate on Jesus' own faith. Herrmann, then, is a bridge between Schleiermacher and the present. In such a series, it was also deemed important to translate Strauss's critique of Schleiermacher, *The Christ of Faith and the Jesus of History*, for here important critical issues were exposed. Probably no book was more significant for twentieth-century study of Jesus than Johannes Weiss's *Jesus' Proclamation of the Kingdom of God*, for together with Albert Schweitzer, Weiss turned the entire course of Jesus-research and undermined the foundations of the prevailing Protestant theology. From the American scene, Shailer Mathews's *Jesus on Social*

Institutions was included. There can be no substantive dialogue with our own theological tradition which ignores his work, together with that of Shirley Jackson Case. Case's *Jesus: A New Biography* was originally planned for inclusion, but its availability in two other editions has made that unnecessary. Finally, Alfred Loisy's *The Gospel and the Church* has been added to the series, partly for its intrinsic merit and partly because this was the most important contribution from the Roman Catholic tradition; both Catholics and Protestants will profit from this trenchant reply to Harnack's *What is Christianity?* Doubtless other works could have been included with justification; however, these will suffice to enliven the theological scene if read perceptively.

In each case, an editor was invited to provide an introductory essay and annotations to the text in order to assist the reader in seeing the book in perspective. The bibliography will aid further research, though in no case was there an attempt to be comprehensive. The aim is not to produce critical editions in the technical sense (which would require a massive apparatus), but a useable series of texts with guidance at essential points. Within these aims the several editors enjoyed considerable latitude in developing their contributions. The series will achieve its aim if it facilitates a rediscovery of an exciting and controversial history and so makes our own work more fruitful.

The present volume is translated (for the first time) and edited by Leander E. Keck, Professor of New Testament and currently Chairman of the Division of Religion of the Graduate School at Emory University. After earning his B.A. at Linfield College in McMinnville, Oregon, he received his theological education at Andover Newton Theological School and a B.D. degree in 1953. His doctoral program included a year's study at Kiel and Göttingen; he received his Ph.D. from Yale University in 1957. After two years at Wellesley College, he taught New Testament at Vanderbilt University (1959–72) before going to Emory. His recent book *A Future for the Historical Jesus* (Abingdon, 1971) and his editorship of the Lives of Jesus Series indicate his longstanding concern with historical and theological issues in the study of Jesus.

CONTENTS

PREFACE

Given the general low esteem into which book reviews have fallen, the value of translating a century-old review of Schleiermacher's *Life of Jesus* is not self-evident. Nonetheless, I have long been persuaded not only that we have much to learn from previous Lives of Jesus, but that entering into this particular discussion by Strauss can be rewarding; this is especially true in light of the publication of the Lives of Jesus by Strauss and Schleiermacher.

Even though Peter C. Hodgson's introduction to Strauss's *Life of Jesus Critically Examined* traced the life and thought of Strauss up to the fourth edition of 1840, it seemed wise to provide an overview of Strauss's total career in order to put his lifelong debate with Schleiermacher into context. In doing so, Hodgson's work on F. C. Baur, no less than on Strauss, has been of major help. Moreover, in 1971 Hodgson and I shared a highly useful seminar on Strauss; one of the students in that seminar, Mr. James Duke, was of special help in combing the collected works of Strauss for references to Schleiermacher.

The move to Emory University and the weight of other responsibilities have slowed progress on the manuscript, but they allowed time for a wider reading and extended reflection—enough to nurture the conviction that generally we have not yet understood precisely enough the role of Strauss, and the ideas which he embodied, in the nineteenth- and twentieth-century culture of the North Atlantic community.

For example, much to be desired is a perceptive analysis of the interaction between the work of Strauss and German church politics, and its fallout upon Protestantism and Catholicism in Great Britain and America as well as in Germany. Perhaps the series will stimulate others to undertake such a task.

I want also to share with the reader my deep appreciation for the manifold assistance of Lelah Rotch, and of my wife, Janice, who typed a chaotic manuscript of the translation while I was Visiting Professor at the Union Theological Seminary in the Philippines in 1971. This volume is dedicated to the faculty and students there as a gesture of gratitude for memorable hospitality.

LEANDER E. KECK

ABBREVIATIONS

(for details, see Select Bibliography below, pp. cvii–cxii)

Primary Sources

AB	Eduard Zeller, ed., *Ausgewählte Briefe von David Friedrich Strauss*
Briefwechsel	Adolf Rapp, ed., *Briefwechsel zwischen Strauss und Vischer*
Geischer	Hans-Jürgen Geischer, ed., *Der Christus des Glaubens und der Jesus der Geschichte*
GL	*Die Glaubenslehre*
GS	Eduard Zeller, ed., *Gesammelte Schriften von David Friedrich Strauss*
LD	"Literarische Denkwürdigkeiten"
LJGP	*The Life of Jesus for the German People*
LJCE	*The Life of Jesus Critically Examined*
Märklin	*Christian Märklin*
ZA	"Zum Andenken meiner guten Mutter"
ZfB	*Zwei friedliche Blätter*

ABBREVIATIONS

Secondary Sources

Brazill	William J. Brazill, *The Young Hegelians*
Harris	Horton Harris, *David Friedrich Strauss and His Theology*
Hausrath	Adolf Hausrath, *David Friedrich Strauss und die Theologie seiner Zeit*
Hillerbrand	Hans J. Hillerbrand, *A Fellowship of Discontent*
Müller	Gotthold Müller, *Identität und Immanenz: Zur Genese der Theologie von David Friedrich Strauss*
Sandberger	Jörg F. Sandberger, *David Friedrich Strauss als Theologischer Hegelianer*
Zeller	Eduard Zeller, *David Friedrich Strauss in seinem Leben und Schriften*
Ziegler	Theobald Ziegler, *David Friedrich Strauss*

EDITOR'S INTRODUCTION

Some great books have the capacity to focus the questions of the day so that everyone must deal with them; others rise to greatness only when they are discovered years later. Strauss's *The Life of Jesus Critically Examined*[1] is among the former; the works of Kierkegaard are among the latter. Strauss's *The Christ of Faith and the Jesus of History* belongs to neither group.

It is, nonetheless, an important work—perhaps more important for us late twentieth-century theologians than for our forebears a century ago. When it was published, the theological world was tired of Strauss and thought it had left him behind. We, on the other hand, are discovering that we are not yet finished with him. Not that we are on the verge of a Strauss-renaissance. Rather, we are not yet finished with him because the questions with which he grappled did not pass from the scene with him. In 1840 Bruno Bauer, not yet the notorious Hegelian of the left, asserted that theology must be "engaged in answering the questions that Strauss has raised."[2] A century later, Karl

1. This was the title of Strauss's *first* Life of Jesus, published in 1835. The fourth edition, translated by George Eliot, has been republished in the Lives of Jesus Series with a critical introduction and notes by Peter C. Hodgson (Philadelphia: Fortress Press, 1972). All references to *The Life of Jesus Critically Examined* are to this new edition (hereafter cited as *LJCE*). Strauss's *second* Life of Jesus, published in 1864, was called *The Life of Jesus for the German People* (hereafter cited as *LJGP*).

2. William J. Brazill, *The Young Hegelians*, p. 168 (hereafter cited as Brazill).

Barth said much the same thing.[3] How is it that after the richest, freest and most diverse body of theological scholarship, we still face this task?

The Christ of Faith and the Jesus of History yields important clues because in it Strauss brings to a head issues which had dominated his theological work. When read in light of Strauss's career—if one may use the term with a certain looseness in his case—this book illumines major issues of modern Christian theology, especially in its Protestant form. The future of Christianity (and particularly of Christian theology) in the modern world, the relation of the Jesus of history to the Christ of theology, the character of the Gospels and the historical accuracy of what they report about Jesus, the possibility of getting at "Jesus as he really was," and the relevance of such a Jesus for modern man—these issues would not let Strauss go. Moreover, Strauss's career permits us to see modern theology in relation to the intellectual and social upheavals of the nineteenth century. Though a loner, Strauss was also part of the self-conscious effort of left-wing Hegelians to discard traditional Christianity with its transcendent God. Conversely, the storms which broke around him illumine the forces of ecclesiastical and political reaction to the effort. Finally, in being an acute critic of the work of others without being able to construct a viable alternative to what he had dismantled, in holding radical theological ideas while remaining a socially conservative middle-class intellectual, and in precisely grasping theological ideas while lacking a personal relation to any religious community where those ideas were rooted, Strauss the Protestant theologian is remarkably contemporary. Considerations such as these make this book an

3. *David Friedrich Strauss als Theologe.* Barth wrote this piece on the one hundredth anniversary of Strauss's forced retirement at Zürich. Its substance is contained in Barth's chapter on Strauss in *Protestant Thought: From Rousseau to Ritschl.*

aperture into our pivotal past where certain present theological struggles are grounded.

Albert Schweitzer said that to understand Strauss one must love him.[4] But Strauss does not come through as a lovable person. Nor was he a tragic figure, as Barth rightly saw, for no inevitable fate was his—although he was capable of thinking so. He was a brilliant, sensitive, cantankerous, willful Swabian who delighted in infuriating his critics and who repeatedly irritated his closest friends. Not surprisingly, sympathetic biographers tend to exonerate him and critics to damn him, frequently neglecting to see the man and his work as a whole. In order to facilitate a more balanced perspective we shall first sketch his life and work; then we shall outline the fluctuations in the long quarrel with Schleiermacher so as to set the present book in context. Finally, we shall reflect briefly on the significance of the issues upon which this quarrel kept turning.

THE TRUE CRITICISM OF STRAUSS IS HIS HISTORY[5]

Who was David Friedrich Strauss? The Judas of our time, said his colleague and former teacher.[6] One admiring

4. Albert Schweitzer, *The Quest of the Historical Jesus*, trans. W. Montgomery, p. 68.

5. An allusion to Strauss's dictum that "the true criticism of dogma is its history;" see below, p. xxxiii.

6. C. A. Eschenmayer, *Der Ischariotismus unserer Tage* (Tübingen, 1835). Eschenmayer had introduced Strauss to clairvoyance and hypnotism. After retirement, Eschenmayer joined forces with a tippling tailor to expel or convert demons; later he regarded the *LJCE* as proof for the existence of demons. See Adolf Hausrath, *David Friedrich Strauss und die Theologie seiner Zeit* (hereafter cited as Hausrath). In 1837 Eschenmayer published *Konflict zwischen Himmel und Hölle* (Tübingen und Leipzig: Verlag der Buchhandlung Zu-Guttenberg, 1837). In the addendum he portrayed a special place in hell where the "mythicists" cry, "Great is the Goddess Idea of Berlin!" Judas Iscariot baptizes them in the name of Hegelian categories, and finally Strauss receives the prize for having done the most to destroy

biographer claimed he was the German counterpart to Voltaire,[7] while another conceded he was "a pathological phenomenon."[8] An English theologian labeled him "the Frankenstein of the Hegelian philosophy."[9] Balanced portrayals and assessments of Strauss will continue to elude us, partly because his contradictory traits contended with one another throughout his life,[10] and partly because assessing his significance requires us to see his work as a whole in relation to his times.

Misfortune and unhappiness hounded him, having caught his scent even before he was born. At least he thought so, for he never could rid himself of the belief that his melancholy and "total lack of joy in life" stemmed from the fact that he had been conceived during the period of mourning for a brother who died at the age of eight.[11] (A sister had died previously; of the two brothers born after David Friedrich only one survived.) He was not the only unhappy theologian of the day. His Danish contemporary Kierkegaard also lived with disappointment and bitterness; yet he

Christianity. Strauss's review of Eschenmayer, written in 1838, is found in *Charakteristiken und Kritiken*, pp. 355–76. Apparently the Judas-epithet generated a legend that Strauss was red-haired, as was Judas in iconographic tradition! See Theobald Ziegler, *David Friedrich Strauss*, 2:726, n. 1 (hereafter cited as Ziegler).

7. Ziegler, 2:763.

8. Hausrath, 2:390.

9. A. M. Fairbairn, *The Place of Christ in Modern Theology* (New York: Scribner's, 1903), p. 214.

10. Ziegler (2:757–58) characterized him as a man of reason who was also softhearted and sensitive; though angry, his mood was one of melancholy rather than rage; a revolutionary in theology, he was conservative in politics and morals. Though an individualist and an esthete, he valued social and national questions more than the sufferings and joys of individuals. A relentless critic, he was sensitive to criticism; at times eager for companionship and delightful company, he was lonesome, shy, and happiest when alone with his books.

11. Eduard Zeller, ed., *Ausgewählte Briefe von David Friedrich Strauss*, no. 84 (hereafter cited as *AB*).

left a drastically different legacy. To this day, Kierkegaard is probed for his constructive position while Strauss is read for his destructive criticism, even though the former was also critical and the latter tried to be constructive. Because Strauss's public work is inseparable from his private fortunes, we must see his life as a whole if we would assess his work.

The Meteoric Career

On January 27, 1808, David Friedrich was born into the home of a merchant in Ludwigsburg, near Stuttgart. Though his father would have preferred intellectual pursuits, custom had required him to enter the family retail business—in which the circumstances of the times and his own disposition conspired against his success. After the defeat of Napoleon, lowered tariffs made English goods cheaper on the continent and the elder Strauss, as stubborn as his son was to be, refused to lower prices on merchandise already stocked, and so ceased to be competitive.[12] Moreover, his mind was on his bees and his books; on walks he loved to take the works of classical authors whom he read in Latin.[13] Fritz, as David Friedrich was called, was not close to his father, though he attributed his own ability to turn a phrase to his father's facility in this regard. The young Strauss became devoted to his mother, an uneducated but cheerful, solid *Hausfrau* who spoke only Swabian; her interest in religion was practical and, unlike her husband's, not concerned with doctrine. Later, Fritz saw himself as cultivating what he had inherited from his mother while trying to expel traits from his father.

12. Ziegler, 1:10.

13. Strauss, "Zum Andenken an meine gute Mutter," *Kleine Schriften* (Bonn: Emil Strauss, 1898³), pp. 88 ff. (hereafter cited as *ZA*). Strauss wrote this essay on the occasion of his daughter's confirmation, and read it to Georgine and young Fritz (*AB*, no. 369).

Fritz was a somewhat delicate child whose exclusion from the rough and tumble boys' games encouraged his intellectual and poetic gifts, and portended his lifelong role as a sensitive and easily hurt outsider.[14]   At thirteen he graduated from the local school and earned a scholarship through competitive examinations, which involved translating German into Latin, Greek, and Hebrew as well as composing Latin verses.[15]   Although he was determined to pursue a theological vocation,[16] we know virtually nothing of his religious convictions at the time, or of his confirmation.[17]   It is precarious to attribute his later views to a rebellion against childhood religion.

Barely a teenager, Strauss entered the Protestant preparatory school (the *Seminar*) at Blaubeuren, near Ulm. Once a monastery, it now housed forty to fifty students and five instructors, among whom were F. H. Kern (1790–1842) and F. C. Baur (1792–1860).   In this isolated and cheerless setting where the pretheological students wore black,[18] Strauss developed into a student of great promise for later work at the University of Tübingen.   The years at Blau-

14. According to the memory of his boyhood playmate and lifelong friend Friedrich Vischer, in "Strauss und die Württemberger" (1838), which was included in Vischer's *Kritische Gänge* (Stuttgart, 1861–73), 1:84.   The characterization is repeated by Eduard Zeller, *David Friedrich Strauss in seinem Leben und Schriften*, p. 9 (hereafter cited Zeller), and by Adolf Kohut, *David Friedrich Strauss als Denker und Erzieher* pp. 13–14.   Strauss himself portrayed his boyhood in more positive terms (*ZA*, p. 91).

15. Ziegler, 1:15–16; 18, n. 1.

16. *ZA*, p. 971.

17. Ziegler, 1:16.

18. Ziegler, 1:20–21.   In the biography of his classmate Märklin, Strauss describes the cloistered life in which the days began at 5:30 A.M. (*Christian Märklin. Ein Charakterbid aus der Gegenwart* [hereafter cited as *Märklin*], included in Eduard Zeller, ed., *Gesammelte Schriften von David Friedrich Strauss* [hereafter cited as *GS*]).

beuren were formative,[19] for here he came under Baur's influence. Baur's first important work, on symbolism and myth in antiquity, was written during these years, and he presented the material to his classes.[20] The instruction in the Christian religion, on the other hand, was among his least effective pedagogical experiences.[21]

At Tübingen the curriculum for theological students called for two years of philosophy, philology, and history, followed by three years of theology proper. But the philosophy which was taught bored Strauss and his friends, so they taught each other what was required and turned their interests elsewhere. They joined a circle of romantics, and Strauss himself wrote a short drama in this vein.[22] The group came under the influence of Jakob Boehme and the mystical tradition; Schelling was read avidly. Cultivating the immediacy of truth, they could not understand why Kant asked epistemological questions.[23] The desire for immediate experiencing of supernatural truth led the group, encouraged by Eschenmayer (see above, note 6), to spiritualism.[24] The

---

19. Gotthold Müller emphasizes the importance of Blaubeuren for Strauss's development, though this would have been true only for the early period (*Identität und Immanenz. Zur Genese der Theologie von David Friedrich Strauss*, p. 39 [hereafter cited as Müller]).

20. F. C. Baur, *Symbolik und Mythologie, oder die Naturreligion des Altertums*, 2 vols. (Stuttgart: J. B. Metzler, 1824–25).

21. Ziegler, 1:34.

22. Printed in Müller, pp. 279–310, with notes and commentary. Years later Strauss admitted that had he discovered a talent for poetry or writing he would have left philosophy and theology alone ("Literarische Denkwürdigkeiten" in *Kleine Schriften*, 8; 60 [hereafter cited as *LD*]; also in *GS* 1).

23. Müller, p. 40.

24. They visited a clairvoyant, who, among other things, inaccurately predicted that Strauss would never become an unbeliever. He was disappointed to hear later that she no longer even remembered him (Müller, p. 42).

man who led him out of this swampy interest was Schleiermacher, who had himself moved through romanticism.[25]

In July 1826, when a post became vacant on the theological faculty, 124 students (was Strauss among them?) petitioned the faculty to invite Baur to fill it.[26] By the time Strauss began his theological study, both Baur and Kern had moved to Tübingen, and Baur became Strauss's mentor. Strauss heard Baur's lectures on church history, the history of dogma, symbolics, Acts, and 1 Corinthians.[27] In systematics, J. C. L. Steudel so much represented the supernaturalist orthodoxy that Strauss endured his lectures for but a month; moreover, he was an outspoken opponent of Schleiermacher, to whom Strauss (with Baur's encouragement) was then looking for guidance. But Strauss's allegiance to Schleiermacher, the liberator from supernaturalist orthodoxy,[28] was short-lived. In the summer of 1829, Strauss and his friends began privately studying Hegel's *Phenomenology*.[29] In 1828, Strauss submitted (to the Catholic theological faculty) an essay on the resurrection of the flesh, and he won the prize. Later he wrote a friend that although he had "proved" with full conviction the resurrection of the dead, when he put in the last period he nonetheless knew there was nothing to the whole thing.[30]

25. Strauss was attracted by the aesthetic form of Schleiermacher's *Speeches* and *Soliloquies* (*LD*, p. 12).

26. Müller, p. 174, n. 33.

27. Zeller, p. 23.

28. Müller, pp. 215–22.

29. Müller, pp. 45–46. Stimulated by Schneckenburger's lectures on modern philosophy, the group met on Sunday mornings across the street from the house of Steudel, whom they frequently encountered as he left for church (*Märklin*, p. 225). See Jörg F. Sandberger, *David Friedrich Strauss als theologischer Hegelianer* (hereafter cited as Sandberger), whose recent analysis of Strauss's understanding of Hegel includes previously unpublished letters to Märklin.

30. Strauss later regarded this essay as a milestone (*AB*, no. 39). Brazill (p. 105) rightly calls this hindsight, not current awareness.

After passing his examinations in the summer of 1830, he became *Vikar* in the village church at Kleiningersheim, near Ludwigsburg.[31] Here he preached and gave catechetical instruction, as was the custom, but remained for only nine months because in the summer of 1831 he was invited to teach at the preparatory school at Maulbronn. Among the students whom he instructed in Latin, history, and Hebrew was Eduard Zeller, who became a lifelong friend and posthumous editor of his works. Strauss remained only until fall, when he decided to go to Berlin to study directly with Schleiermacher and Hegel. Simultaneously he applied for his doctorate in philosophy and funds for his Berlin study. But he needed a dissertation! He requested that the philosophical faculty accept his essay on the resurrection of the flesh, and asked a professor to get the essay from the files and to submit it for him. Two days later Strauss submitted a totally new work instead; as it turned out, the earlier work could not be found anyway. The new work was a twenty-eight-page study on the theme "The Restoration of All Things," which had been written in the spring as an ecclesiastical requirement and already accepted as such.[32] Strauss received his degree and travel funds (but not support money) and had the diploma mailed to him in Berlin.

On November 15, Dr. Strauss presented himself to Schleiermacher, who told him that cholera had claimed Hegel the previous night. Tradition has it that Strauss blurted out, "But it was for him that I came here!" Schleiermacher

31. Despite his deep interest in Hegel, Strauss was an active participant in "practical theology" during his last year in Tübingen, and earned a prize in preaching and catechetics. In 1830 he was chosen to preach the opening sermon for the three hundredth anniversary of the Augsburg confession (Hausrath, 1:47, 51). Hausrath includes the sermon which, curiously, affirms Jesus' resurrection—which he had "proven" in the essay of 1828, though no longer believing it himself (see above, note 30).

32. The "dissertation" was found only recently, and has been published by Müller, who traces the influences upon it.

was less than pleased.[33]   Though disappointed, Strauss remained in Berlin until late spring.   He became acquainted with Frau Professor Hegel and with Hegel's students, made excerpts of their notes of Hegel's lectures, and began a life-long friendship with W. Vatke, a Hegel-oriented instructor in Old Testament.   Strauss not only attended Vatke's lectures and discussed his ideas with him, but was a frequent guest in his home, where the host's piano playing awakened Strauss's enduring love for music.[34]   Strauss also attended Schleiermacher's lectures and preaching, though it took him some time to appreciate their style.   It was through Schleiermacher that he first saw the pedagogical possibilities of lecturing from notes instead of reading a manuscript, as was Baur's custom.[35]   Unfortunately, Schleiermacher was not lecturing on the life of Jesus, but Strauss secured two sets of student notes and transcribed what he wanted.   During these six months Strauss projected his three-part program:[36] first, the positive part, which was to be "an objective presentation of the life of Jesus according to the Gospels, a description of the way Jesus lives subjectively in the faithful, and the mediation of these two aspects in the second article of the Apostles' Creed"; second, the negative or critical part,

33. The story, including Schleiermacher's reaction, continues to be repeated, even though Ziegler insisted that it was a legend; Schleiermacher did, of course, inform Strauss of Hegel's death (Ziegler, 1:94). See also the important letter to Märklin of the same day (AB, no. 4).

34. Ziegler (1:98) emphasizes the significance of this friendship.   Vatke's *Die Religion des Alten Testaments*, also in a Hegelian vein, appeared in 1835, a few months after Strauss's *Life of Jesus.*

35. See the letter to Grüneisen quoted by Ziegler (1:100–01). For additional comments on Schleiermacher's lecture style, see below, pp. 11–13.

36. Ziegler (1:131) insists that the impulse did not come from Schleiermacher but from Strauss's own attempt to apply Hegel's distinction between image (*Vorstellung*) and concept or idea (*Begriff*) to theology.   This problem had been central to Strauss for some time, and is clearly evident in the correspondence with Märklin from the time at Kleiningersheim onward. See also Sandberger, pp. 42–48.

which would mostly "annul the life of Jesus as history"; and third, a constructive part, which "would reestablish dogmatically what has been destroyed critically."[37] With this plan in mind and notes from Schleiermacher's lectures in hand, Strauss evidently saw no need to remain in Berlin for the summer term of 1832, even though Schleiermacher announced that he would lecture on the life of Jesus—as it turned out, for the last time.[38] Ironically, notebooks from these lectures were the basis of Rütenik's posthumous edition of Schleiermacher's *Life of Jesus* of 1865,[39] to which the present Strauss volume is a response.

In May 1832 Strauss returned to Tübingen to be a tutor at the *Stift*, a residential college for theological students.[40] Strauss not only guided theological students in the *Stift* but exercised his right to lecture in the University. His lectures were totally within the philosophical faculty.[41] Zeller, who heard them, said they were like welcome rain in the desert; more than a hundred students attended.[42] Though Schneck-

37. Strauss, *Streitschriften*, no. 3, pp. 57–60, cited from Hodgson's introduction to *LJCE*, p. xxiii. Strauss went on to say that in the actual writing of the *Life of Jesus*, "the first part fell away, the third became a mere appendix, and the second grew into the real body of the book." The first part appeared in *LJGP*.

38. Ziegler, 1:104–05. I fail to see why Ziegler insists that Strauss's departure shows that he had not yet planned to write his own Life of Jesus.

39. Friedrich Schleiermacher, *The Life of Jesus*, trans. S. MacLean Gilmour and ed. Jack C. Verheyden, Lives of Jesus Series (Philadelphia: Fortress Press, 1975).

40. He used the return trip to further his interests. At Leipzig, he discussed Hegel and Schelling with Weisse; at Jena he came to know Hase who had published a Life of Jesus in 1819 (although apparently they did not discuss it); at Heidelberg he met Daub, whom he was to portray in an essay several years later (see below, note 57) (Ziegler, 1:105–06).

41. He lectured on the history of philosophy since Kant, on Plato's *Symposium*, and on the history of moral philosophy; he outlined his tasks in a letter to Vischer (*AB*, no. 37). The manuscripts of these lectures are now being edited for publication. For a preliminary resumé see Sandberger, pp. 66–74.

42. Ziegler, 1:116.

enburger had introduced Hegel three years before, it was in Strauss that Hegel found his expositor and enthusiastic advocate. Little did Strauss suspect that these happy semesters would be his sole experience in the classroom.

Despite this success, Strauss ceased lecturing after three semesters and devoted himself to the first part of his program, *The Life of Jesus*.[43] He worked intensely and with a sure instinct for what he wanted to say.[44] Within a year the manuscript (over fourteen hundred printed pages) was finished. In fact, it took the publisher as long to manufacture the book as it took Strauss to write it.[45] Strauss refocused the issues in German Protestant theology.[46] Not

43. It is not altogether clear why he stopped lecturing. Ziegler (1:118 ff.) insists that his colleagues in the philosophical faculty became jealous, and voted that henceforth students could not get academic credit for lectures given by tutors at the *Stift*. This is disputed; Maier insists that Strauss could have gone into philosophy had he desired to do so. Strauss never complains of the philosophical faculty. (Heinrich Maier, ed., *Briefe von David Friedrich Strauss an L. Georgii*, p., n. 1).

44. His copious note-taking is evidenced by the vast amount of literature which he mastered and assessed. For the bibliography of works used see *LJCE*, pp. 803–10. Strauss also published a review of three studies of Matthew and wrote a review of Hase's *Leben Jesu*; the review was rejected, however (*LD*, pp. 4–5). The Matthean studies are included in *Charakteristiken und Kritiken*, pp. 235–85; for an analysis of the reviews see Sandberger, pp. 74–81.

45. Volume 1 appeared at the beginning of June, 1835; volume 2 appeared in November, 1835, although it is dated 1836.

46. In 1847 F. C. Baur insisted that one must regard Strauss's book "as a *product of its time*, and . . . in the *then* existing stage of criticism it was not only a possible but also a necessary phenomenon . . . its chief merit lay not in the knowledge which it brought to light, but in the lack of knowledge of which it made men conscious" (*Kritische Untersuchungen über die kanonischen Evangelien* [Tübingen: L. F. Fues, 1847], pp. 48–52, quoted from Peter C. Hodgson, *The Formation of Historical Theology*, pp. 75–76 [hereafter cited as *Formation*]; Hodgson's italics). A few years later Baur observed, "The Straussian *Life of Jesus* was the spark through which the long-accumulated fuel burst into bright flame" (*Kirchengeschichte des neunzehnten Jahrhunderts*, ed. Eduard Zeller [Tübingen: L.

that what he said was wholly new—as his introduction shows, many before him had spoken of the mythical element in the Gospels, and had conceded that certain stories and motifs were not historical. But no one had yet brought the various lines of criticism together into a clear and comprehensive position; never before had anyone marched relentlessly through all the material to show just how much myth, and how little solid history, the Gospels appear to contain.[47] Moreover, the clear and eloquent German reinforced his argument. Probably no other theological work has ever caused such a sensation. Years later Strauss himself called it "an inspired book," by which he meant that "the author took into himself the strongest developing forces of theological science of the time, and out of this momentum, the book emerged."[48] He regarded it as his best book—and he was right.[49]

F. Fues, 1862], p. 363; reprinted in 1970 by Fromman Verlag in Stuttgart). Brazill (p. 98) shows that this was seen already in 1838 by Edgar Quinet ("De la Vie de Jésus par le Docteur Strauss," *Revue des deux Mondes* 15 [1838]:587–88); Quinet's review is translated and included in Beard's *Voices of the Church* (see note 50).

47. Horton Harris argues that as late as 1832 Strauss himself had seen only the presence of mythic material in the Gospels, and that he did not discover the comprehensive interpretation until he returned to Tübingen. Then he read an anonymous article, "Die verschiedenen Rücksichten in welchen und für welche der Biograph Jesu arbeiten kann" (*Kritisches Journal der neuesten theologischen Literatur* 5 [1816]:225–45). This, Harris claims, provided the key he needed. The project envisaged in Berlin was Hegelian but not mythic. After reading this article, it became both mythic and Hegelian. (*David Friedrich Strauss and his Theology*, pp. 46–47, especially ch. 23 [hereafter cited as Harris]). That the understanding of myth had no inherent relation to Strauss's use of Hegel has been argued before by Christian Hartlich and Walter Sachs (*Der Ursprung des Mythosbegriffes in der modernen Bibelwissenschaft*, pp. 122–25). But Sandberger (pp. 91–102) argues, rightly I think, that from the start Strauss had correlated myth (as understood by "the mythical school" associated with Gabler, Heyne, and G. L. Bauer) with Hegel's *Vorstellung* (image).

48. *LD*, pp. 4, 62.

49. For an excellent discussion see Hodgson's introduction, *LJCE*.

Reaction was swift and relentless.[50]   Within a month the government asked Strauss for a position paper; ten days later he replied, to no avail.   On August 3 he was relieved of his post and transferred to the lyceum in Ludwigsburg for the fall.   He received permission, however, to remain in Tübingen as a private scholar in order to finish writing the second volume.   In November he moved into virtual exile.

Actually, exile would have been better, for it would have

50. For details see Ziegler 1, ch. 4, which quotes the relevant texts, including Strauss's response to the government.   See also Hans J. Hillerbrand, *A Fellowship of Discontent*, pp. 137–41 (hereafter cited as Hillerbrand).   For a discussion of the polemics which flowed from theologians see Hausrath, 1:184–202 (pp. 189–90 provide a bibliography).   In Munich, the government forbade public libraries to lend the book.   In Berlin the government considered suppressing the book, but Neander successfully counseled against this action (Hausrath, 1:193).   A local pietist showed how the obscure number 666, mentioned in the Book of Revelation, could be computed so as to yield "Strauss" (Hausrath, 1:233); the end of the world was to occur in 1836! For American reactions at the time see Jerry Wayne Brown, *The Rise of Biblical Criticism in America, 1800–1870, The New England Scholars* (Middletown, Conn.: Wesleyan University Press, 1969), ch. 9, in which reviews are cited.   H. B. Hackett favorably reviewed the massive book by A. Ebrard (1842) which set forth procedures which any reader could follow to refute Strauss ("Critique on Strauss's *Life of Jesus*," *Bibliotheca Sacra* 2 [1845]:48–79).   Brown wrongly implied that Strauss was ignored in Britain; in 1840, W. H. Hill published a lengthy critique in the *Christian Advocate*, followed by a series of defenses of the early chapters of Matthew and Luke (*Observations on the Attempted Application of Pantheistic Principles to the Theory and Historic Criticism of the Gospel* [Cambridge: Deighton, Bell, 1854; reprinted 1861]).   Moreover, five years later J. R. Beard edited a volume of essays, *Voices of the Church in Reply to Dr. D. F. Strauss*, etc. (London: Simpkin, Marshall & Co., 1845); the introduction refers to previous efforts to deal with Strauss. The volume includes also a translation of a tract pseudonymously published in Tübingen in 1837, "The Fallacy of the Mythical Theory of Dr. Strauss, Illustrated from the History of Martin Luther and from the Actual Mohammedan Myths of the Life of Jesus." The translation of the original German title is "Extracts from the Book *The Life of Luther Critically Examined* by Dr. Casuar (Mexico, 2836)"! In 1850 Henry Rogers published *Reason and Faith* (London: Longman, Brown, Green & Longmans); Beard's book was applauded, and the appendix (pp. 93–123) dealt specifically with Strauss, as did the bulk of the main essay.

removed him from the storm. As it was, he was not only cut off from library resources and colleagues but, living with his parents, was in continual conflict with his father over the book and its controversies.[51] After a year he gave up his position and moved to Stuttgart, made revisions for the second edition,[52] and attacked three vociferous critics in the *Streitschriften*.[53] Soon thereafter he undertook the third edition, famous for its concessions and for a move in the direction of Schleiermacher, which will be discussed below.[54] When it was ready for the press in December, 1837, he wrote to Zeller that he hoped never to write theology again.[55] At this time he contributed pieces to the new journal of the left-wing Hegelians, the *Hallische Jahrbücher*, edited by Arnold Ruge. But he soon broke off his relationship with the journal and its circle.[56] The next two years saw him publish minor reviews, a piece on Schleier-

---

51. These were exacerbated by someone who kept sending his father hostile newspapers clippings (*ZA*, p. 102).

52. For the differences between the first and second editions see Hodgson's introduction, pp. xxiv–xxv. The preface to the second edition is included on pp. lv–lvi.

53. According to Adolf Rapp, in April, 1837 Strauss asked Baur and an attorney to read the piece against Menzel before publication—the former to check the content, the latter to check for possible libel (*Briefwechsel Zwischen Strauss und Vischer*, 1:29 [hereafter cited as *Briefwechsel*]). Strauss devoted one pamphlet to J. C. L. Steudel and one to C. A. Eschenmayer (see above, note 6) and W. Menzel, a Stuttgart editor; a third responded to reviews in three journals. For an analysis see Sandberger, pp. 112–40.

54. For a discussion of these changes and their significance see Hodgson's introduction, *LJCE*, pp. xxxvi–xliii. The preface to the third edition is on pp. lvi–lviii; the new concluding section to the third edition is on pp. 798–802. Hodgson's annotations (pp. 785–98) make it possible for the first time to compare in detail the shifts in Strauss's views.

55. *AB*, no. 33.

56. Brazill, pp. 119–20. For a discussion of this journal and its importance see ch. 2.

macher and Daub,[57] and two conciliatory essays.[58] In this period from 1837 to 1840, he moved toward appropriating traditional Christianity.[59] Later he regretted these conciliatory efforts, admitting that he had written both the third edition and the minor pieces while in shock at finding himself virtually alone.[60]

Disappointment turned to bitterness over the "Zürich affair."[61] In 1839, after several unsuccessful attempts, the Zürich liberals, led by Hitzig, obtained for Strauss an invitation to become Professor of Theology at the recently established university.[62] He accepted the invitation but never

57. "Schleiermacher und Daub," *Charakteristiken und Kritiken*, pp. 3–212; originally in *Hallische Jahrbücher für deutsche Wissenschaft und Kunst*, 1839.

58. "Über Justinus Kerner" and "Über Vergängliches und Bleibendes im Christentum." The latter appeared in the Hamburg journal *Freihafen* 1, no. 3 (1836): 1–48. These essays were published together as *Zwei friedliche Blätter* (hereafter cited as *ZfB*).

59. The preface to *ZfB* (dated March 15, 1839) asserts that he did not regard Christianity as the religion which taught that there is but a single moment when the division between God and man was overcome, but as the religion of their unification throughout. Consequently, the more completely this unification of God and man occurs, the more perfectly Christianity actualizes itself. Therefore, the contemporary—or Hegelian—world view is more Christian than the early Christian one (*ZfB*, p. xxxii).

60. Zeller, p. 50. In 1838 Strauss visited Heidelberg. He was pleasantly surprised to find that theologians were not afraid to associate with him, and that outside of Württemberg he had also a positive reputation (*Briefwechsel*, 1:69; Ziegler, 1:261–62). Otherwise he felt like a pariah. On February 25, 1838 he complained to his friend Märklin that the world had developed such a distorted picture of him that he often wanted to change his name. "I am so fed up with the nonsense of being regarded as the symbol of unbelief, which certainly is the farthest from my real nature." (*Briefwechsel*, 1:41).

61. For a fuller account see Hillerbrand, pp. 143–46; Hausrath, 1:341–95 (*Beilagen* 15–23 include Strauss's letter to Hitzig); and Harris, pp. 123–33.

62. The conciliatory gestures in the third edition of *LJCE* as well as in the *ZfB* encouraged Hitzig to press for a positive decision (Hausrath, 1:347–48). Hitzig's memo to the faculty is included in the *Beilagen*, as are other relevant texts.

became professor, for the appointment caused such a furor[63] that the authorities were compelled by law to retire him and pay him a pension.[64] This proved to be his last opportunity to enter academic life; after this series of events, Strauss remained permanently hostile to theologians.[65] The pain was compounded by the death of his mother in the same year;[66] two years later his father also died. In 1840 he produced the fourth edition of the *Life of Jesus* (see above, note 1) and took back the concessions he had made in the third edition.

Strauss now withdrew even more to his books, lived alone in Stuttgart, and shunned social contact, though he avidly attended the theater and concerts. He threw his energies into writing the second part of his original plan, a critical history of dogma.[67] On the basis of his dictum, "the

63. Some Zürich pietists, he complained, even sent him hate mail—unstamped! (*AB*, no. 60).

64. Accepting the legally specified half salary (one thousand Swiss francs) also caused consternation (Ziegler, 1:307–08). According to Adolf Rapp, he used the pension for worthy causes (*Briefwechsel*, 1:90). For a general picture of Strauss's financial resources see Ziegler, 2:362–63, and Harris, p. 149.

65. Ziegler, 1:324. Hausrath (1:417) observes that this growing bitterness, directed toward theology itself as well as toward theologians, grew ever more pathological. In Berlin, Hengstenberg (his bitter foe, the editor of the *Evangelische Kirchenzeitung*) saw the Zürich agitation against Strauss as one case when *vox populi* was truly *vox dei*.

66. For eighteen years, since leaving for Blaubeuren, he had corresponded regularly with his mother. In 1858 he still had all her letters (*ZA*, p. 98). For his reaction to her death, including his inability to affirm life after death, see *AB*, no. 66.

67. *Die christliche Glaubenslehre, in ihrer geschichtlichen Entwicklung und im Kampfe mit der modernen Wissenschaft dargestellt* (Tübingen, 1840–41) (hereafter cited as *GL*). Hillerbrand (p. 146) appears to think that Strauss was merely trying to salvage the preparations he had made for the Zürich lectures; but this work had been in his mind from the start. Moreover, he had begun reading for it as early as 1838, as his letter to Baur of November 9 clearly states. See Ernst Barnikol, "Der Briefwechsel zwischen Strauss and Baur," *Zeitschrift für Kirchengeschichte* 73 (1962: 107, no. 11.

true criticism of dogma is its history,"[68] Strauss argued that historical circumstances produced the dogmas, and that these in turn produced contradictions which more or less dissolved them.[69] Moreover, the emergence of the modern world antiquated the whole theological tradition; in light of this fact the differences between Protestant and Catholic theology were insignificant. Significantly, Strauss now gave up Hegel's view that philosophy and theology have identical content but different expression. He saw that for Hegel the human and the divine are essentially identical in Christ, but in Christian dogma Christ unites, without assimilation, the two natures. If this is so, he surmised, then Hegel's philosophy does not say the same thing as Christian doctrine.[70] From now on, religion and philosophy are opposed.[71] Accordingly, Strauss gave up trying to produce a theology which accommodated the Christian theological tradition to the modern mind.[72] Still he did not yet explicitly reject Christianity (as he understood it). This important work has never received the same attention as the *Leben Jesu*, partly because Strauss's views were no longer novel, and partly because Feuerbach's *The Essence of Christianity*, which also appeared in 1841, was more constructive, for it not only dissolved Christian doctrine (as did Strauss) but accounted for the origin of dogmas in man's needs. For the

---

68. *GL*, 1:71.

69. Emanuel Hirsch observes that Strauss shifted the whole struggle over Christian doctrine to the ground of historical research. (*Geschichte der neueren evangelischen Theologie*, 5:517).

70. *GL*, 1:29–30.

71. Later he observed that Feuerbach's early writings had persuaded him to change his mind (*LD*, p. 14).

72. Max Huber is incorrect when he contends that the early Strauss must be seen as a mediating theologian—one who intended so to relate theology and science that neither was compromised (*Jesus Christus als Erlöser* [Winterthur: P. G. Keller, 1956], pp. 81, 116).

next twenty-three years, Strauss ceased to publish theology.[73]

The decade from 1831 to 1841, which had begun so auspiciously in the Tübingen lecture halls, ended with his expulsion from the academic world for which he was well suited, and the momentary happiness he had enjoyed as a tutor was squelched by growing alienation and bitterness. What to do next? Not being a professor, he had no obligation to express himself continuously or to clarify or modify his position through research and conversation with colleagues.[74] As a loner, he was free to pursue whatever interested him—if only he could find something that summoned his energies!

The Ex-Theologian

The decade from 1841 to 1851 also began on a higher level than it ended. In 1842 he married a singer, Agnese Schebest,[75] whom he met in the cultured circles of Stuttgart which he had penetrated.[76] The marriage was a disaster.[77]

---

73. Exploring possible reasons why Strauss failed to become a theologian is the aim of the richly documented article by Hans Geisser, "David Friedrich Strauss als verhinderter (Züricher) Dogmatiker" (*Zeitschrift für Theologie und Kirche* 69 (1972):214–58).

74. In retrospect, he wrote that his interest in theology declined largely because he had no professional future (*LD*, p. 15). But more was involved. He confided to a friend that he had to be angry to write and that he had spent his wrath (Zeller, p. 63). Furthermore, painstaking research and data-gathering bored him; his real joy was shaping the material to express himself (*LD*, pp. 6–7).

75. Strauss had had a strange courtship with a Tübingen innkeeper's daughter. For details, not without humor, see Adolf Rapp's account and Strauss's own letters (*Briefwechsel*, 1:47 ff.). It is odd that Strauss should switch his interest from this undistinguished girl to a famous diva such as Agnese Schebest. For a sketch of her personality, background, and career see Hausrath, 2:35–45.

76. When Strauss began to move in musical circles, he even wrote a libretto for an opera! (*LD*, p. 15).

77. For details see Ziegler, 2: ch. 6; *Briefwechsel*, 1:177 ff.; and Hillerbrand, pp. 149–50. Strauss's biographers speak of Agnese's jealousy and

After five stormy years, they separated without divorce. Agnese, with the daughter Georgine and the infant son Fritz, moved back to Stuttgart. After four years, in 1851, Strauss managed to reverse the arrangement so that he had the children and Agnese had the visiting rights. Even so, relations remained strained until Agnese died in 1870.[78] On top of the misery which the separation caused came his alienation from his mentor Baur. In 1847, the same year as the separation, Baur published his own work on the Gospels, in which he appeared to repudiate Strauss's work.[79] Understandably, Strauss called 1847 "one of the worst times of my life."[80] He had not been able to concentrate; the muses would not come to a married Strauss. But in 1847 he did produce a biography of the Swabian poet Schubart, as well as a satirical piece.[81]

Then came 1848, the year of revolution. He declined to run for representative to the Frankfurt Assembly, where intellectuals tried to unite the "German nation."[82] He did

---

possessiveness—but Strauss too was jealous. In the early years of separation she sought friendship and solace in the home of Strauss's friend, Justinus Kerner. When Strauss learned of this, he tried to forbid every act of hospitality! (Kohut, p. 38).

78. There was repeated tension over the children; when Strauss lived in Cologne, Agnese came to visit a child who was ill, but Strauss refused to let her into the house (*Briefwechsel*, 2:57).

79. *Kritische Untersuchungen über die kanonischen Evangelien.* The fascinating relationship between Baur and Strauss is traced by Hodgson (*Formation*, pp. 73–84).

80. *LD*, p. 16.

81. "Der Romantiker auf dem Thron Cäsaren," now in *Kleine Schriften.* He compared Julian the Apostate, who vainly sought to restore paganism, to Friedrich Wilhelm IV of Prussia and his current efforts to restore orthodoxy. For the historical context, epitomized by the Prussian government's suppression of the journals of the left-wing Hegelians, see Brazill, pp. 83–94.

82. The Frankfurt Parliament contained forty-nine professors and lecturers and fifty-seven schoolmasters; at least three-fourths of its members had been to universities (Lewis Namier, *1848: The Revolution of the Intellectuals* [Garden City: Doubleday Anchorbooks, 1964], p. 106, n. 4).

agree to run for the Württemberg legislature, but the populace in the countryside was not about to be represented by the famous infidel. Nevertheless, in Ludwigsburg, which elected its own representative by indirect ballot, he won hands down. In three months, his resignation was called for. Politically Strauss was a conservative and pro-Prussian monarchist.[83] In opposing the left, he found himself allied in politics with his enemies in theology: Menzel, the church, and the nobility. Two days before Christmas he resigned.[84] His career as a man of public affairs was even shorter than his career as an academic. At forty, he was a pensioned professor without having taught, a husband and father without wife and children at home, and an ex-politician without a constituency. So he returned to being a free-lance writer, restlessly moving from city to city, partly to get away from his wife and partly to seek an environment in which he could find himself.

In Munich, where he frequented the art galleries, he wrote a newspaper column and minor pieces for an encyclopedia.[85] Unable to appreciate the Bavarians, he was dreadfully lonesome, especially at first. But he learned a bit of Italian, and in the spring of 1851 he traveled to Italy.[86] In

83. He said that if he had to choose between princely and popular despotism, he would unhesitatingly prefer the former (Zeller, pp. 72 ff.). He wrote to Vischer, "a nature such as mine was happier under the old police state, when at least order reigned in the streets. . . . Toward this outpouring of the spirit on every lad and maid, toward this wisdom from the gutter, I can only adopt an attitude of bitter irony and scorn" (*Briefwechsel,* 1:213, cited from Brazill, p. 121). Brazill thinks his conservative middle-class attitude was reinforced by the left-wing Hegelian ideology, according to which the emergent state was not to rest on the consent of the governed but on the absolute spirit's self-expression which it embodied (Brazill, pp. 39–43).

84. For details, see Ziegler, 2: ch. 7. Strauss recounts this episode without bitterness in *LD,* pp. 18–22. Six of his campaign speeches were published; for details, see Hausrath, 2:107–81.

85. *LD,* p. 23. For details of the Munich period see Hausrath, 2:185–207.

86. Excerpts from his travel diary are quoted in Ziegler, 2:473 ff.

the fall he took the children and moved to Weimar; the next summer they went to Cologne, where his brother Wilhelm was a sugar manufacturer. But he detested the city, and three years later, in 1854, moved to Heidelberg, where he remained six years. With young Fritz in the boarding school near Maulbronn and his daughter at a school in Heidelberg,[87] Strauss found a measure of stability and regained some productivity.

It was here that he discovered his talent for writing biography.[88] To write biography, Strauss said, he had to empathize with his heroes. They, in turn, must be oriented toward freedom of the spirit and opposed to despots and clerics.[89] In 1857 he produced a significant biography of Ulrich von Hutten, a Reformation figure.[90] So successful was this work that the next year he considered writing a series of literary biographies of figures ranging from Klopstock and Lessing to Goethe and Schiller, but nothing came of it. When he was urged to follow his *Hutten* with a biography of Luther, he began reading for it, but soon discovered that his own requirements for biographical writing made the job impossible for him to undertake. He had no stomach for a man, he wrote, who regarded himself as a lost sinner who was saved only by faith in Christ's blood.[91] Hutten was

87. According to Adolf Rapp, Strauss put the children in schools partly to make it impossible for his wife to see him if she were to visit the children (*Briefwechsel*, 2:70).

88. For an assessment of Strauss as biographer and a discussion of how his biographical skills developed, see Ziegler, 2: ch. 8; see also the essay by Kuno Fischer, "Über David Friedrich Strauss," *Gesammelte Schriften*.

89. *LD*, p. 31.

90. *Ulrich von Hutten* was published in 1858; the preface was written in 1857. Strauss had access to the sources gathered by Eduard Bocking, who later published them. For a recent assessment of Strauss's work see the bibliographic note in Hajo Holborn, *Ulrich von Hutten and the German Reformation*, trans. Roland H. Bainton (New York: Harper and Row Torchbooks, 1966; originally published in 1937 by Yale University Press).

91. *LD*, p. 41; *AB*, no. 356.

as close to the Reformation as Strauss could get with comfort.[92]

As the end of the 1850s neared, it appeared that Strauss had found himself in biographical writing and literary criticism, and that he was through not only with theologians but with theology as well. In fact, he asked that his theological library be shipped to Heidelberg to be sold, for he expected never to read those books again.[93] Nonetheless, in the 1860s Strauss returned to theology. In discerning what led to this change we understand something of this complex and unhappy man, who could neither be a practicing theologian nor give up theology permanently.

The Return to Theology

Apparently, three factors joined to lead him back to theology. First, *The Life of Jesus* was virtually out of print. Presumably this fact raised the question of a reprinting or a revision. Moreover, 1860 would mark the twenty-fifth anniversary of the first edition, and this might have suggested an updating. Apparently Strauss shared such thoughts with his friends Vatke in Berlin and Gervinus, the historian, in Heidelberg, who urged a scholarly revision of the fourth edition.[94] But this would require massive reading in the critical literature of the last two decades, more theological literature than Strauss could endure. Such a revision would also commit him to writing for theologians, of whom he had had his fill. Nonetheless, the time seemed ripe for a return to *The Life of Jesus.*

Secondly, after publishing his biography of Hutten, he began to translate his speeches. The publisher asked that the introduction relate the significance of Hutten to the

92. *AB*, no. 364.
93. May 30, 1858 to Ernst Rapp (Ziegler, 2:554–55).
94. *AB*, no. 409.

contemporary situation, and so Strauss commented on mid-nineteenth-century Catholicism and Protestantism.[95] His caustic remarks signalled what was to come. He argued that Protestantism had betrayed itself, for it had exchanged its principle of personal inner conviction as the ultimate ground of truth for bondage to creed and the Bible.[96] Still, this Protestant principle survived in German classical literature (Lessing, Goethe, Schiller), although it is unthinkable in Catholicism. The pious who warn against the destructive influence of this literature are right, said Strauss, for none of these authors were Christians. So we must decide whether to go to hell with them or to heaven with the orthodox like Hengstenberg.

The name of Hengstenberg evidently encouraged the free flow of Strauss's bile, for the remainder of the introduction is a self-vindication against the widespread assumption that his *Life of Jesus* had been controverted. The fact that Baur showed that much Gospel material was not the spontaneous product of Christian piety, but was deliberately created because of party strife in the church, surely does not overturn Strauss's claim that the material is not history; the orthodox have no reason to rejoice, says Strauss. Also, Baur's work on the Fourth Gospel does go beyond what he had said in *The Life of Jesus*, but this too supports his view that this Gospel is not a historical source. In the face of these developments and the emergence of historical consciousness in the popular mind, theology acted like some businessmen facing bankruptcy: it swindled customers and borrowed whatever it could from various creditors. Contemporary theology is a charade, Strauss contends. The-

---

95. *Briefwechsel*, 2:156; Ziegler, 2:464 ff.

96. Introduction to *Gespräche von Ulrich von Hutten*, now included in *Ulrich von Hutten*; also in *GS* (7:537–62). Note how Strauss understands the classical Protestant view of the "inner witness of the Holy Spirit."

ological education encourages students to seek only what they can appropriate without destroying their faith, not to ask, Is it true? Church leaders vulgarize Schleiermacher by separating piety completely from theology, and prop up the hollow tree with new churchiness.[97] The fact is that the educated no longer believe the church dogma, though they believe that they believe. Nor do the clergy. Are we still Christians? Strauss says he does not know, but the name does not really matter.[98] We shall be true Protestants only if we are honest.

The concluding paragraph of this introduction to the speeches of Hutten is so significant in Strauss's return to theology that it should be quoted.

> The theme in which I have landed makes old times new for me. Just in these days it is a quarter of a century since my *Life of Jesus* first went into the world. The theologians will scarcely celebrate the twenty-fifth anniversary of this book, even though unnoticed it first helped more than one of them toward all sorts of nice thoughts, then to office and dignity. . . . I myself could even despise this book for it has done me much harm (and justly! cry the pious). It locked me out of public teaching activity, for which I had desire and perhaps also talent; it tore me out of natural relationships and drove me into unnatural ones; it made my life solitary. And yet, I reflect, what would have become of me had I been silent about the word that was laid on my soul, if I had suppressed the doubts which worked in me? Then I bless the book. . . . And so I attest on its anniversary, that it was written out of a compulsion, with honorable purpose, without passion or ulterior motives, and that I wish that all its opponents, when they write against it, were equally free from ulterior motives and fanaticism. I

97. Hausrath (2:31–46) provides a description of the sad state of church theology of the time.
98. In his last work, *The Old Faith and the New*, he will answer this question with a resounding *no!* (see below, p. xlvii).

also attest that it has not been controverted, but only further developed, and that if it is seldom read any longer, this stems from the fact that it has been absorbed by the development of the times, and has penetrated all views of contemporary science. I finally attest that in the whole twenty-five years in which the content has been treated, not a line of significance has been written in which its influence is not to be recognized.

The third factor at work in Strauss's return to theology was just the sort that would provoke him. In the summer of 1858 he visited his long-time friend Ernst Rapp, who was pastor in Münkheim. On Sunday, Strauss naturally went to church with the Rapp family. To his consternation and Rapp's pain, this created a furor which brought the wrath of the ecclesiastical establishment upon his poor friend. Strauss was helpless, for anything he said could only make things worse for Rapp.[99]

Evidently these three factors combined to set Strauss in motion to write what became *The Life of Jesus for the German People*.[100] In the preface he remarked that he no longer cared whether theologians read it or not;[101] he was now appealing to the educated public.

99. *LD*, pp. 43 ff.; *Briefwechsel*, 2:151–52; Ziegler, 2:356 ff.

100. *Das Leben Jesu für das deutsche Volk bearbeitet* (hereafter cited as *LJGP*). Harris (pp. 191–99) also sees the confluence of these three factors; our conclusions were reached independently.

101. He admitted to Vischer that this remark must be taken with a grain of salt, and added, "I know that they [the theologians] hear me and [I] also speak so that they should hear me" (*AB*, no. 464). He regarded the popular book as a way of attacking theologians from the rear rather than frontally (*AB*, no. 410). While he was writing, his hostility toward theologians and clerics was fanned by his disgust at a funeral. He came home and wrote instructions that no clergyman was to be present at *his* funeral (*Briefwechsel*, 2:176). Later he apparently rewrote the instructions (see below, note 145). Strauss's anticlericalism was expressed sharply in the book's preface: "Whoever wants to rid the church of its clerics must first rid religion of the miraculous." Carl Beck, a pious orthodox critic, welcomed this honest disclosure of what was really at stake in biblical

He began preparation without knowing whether to revise or start afresh.[102]   When he reread *The Life of Jesus* he discovered that it had become a strange book for him, so removed from theology had he become.[103]   He discovered that though he had kept abreast of the work of Baur and his students, he had much catching up to do because he had become a dilettante.[104]   But he knew how to turn his preparation to publishing advantage.[105]   He not only read the more recent literature, but went back to the eighteenth century[106] to read H. S. Reimarus, with whom the modern critical study of Jesus began.   In 1861 he published "Brockes und Reimarus."[107]   A year later he published a full-length monograph on Reimarus, summarizing the argu-

criticism, and contrasted Strauss's present openness with his earlier claim (*Streitschriften*, 1:20) that he had not sought to undermine Christianity in his first *Life of Jesus* ("Kritische Anzeige von 'Strauss, *Das Leben Jesu für das deutsche Volk bearbeitet,*'" *Theologische Studien und Kritiken* 38 [1865]:74–81).

102. On December 6, 1860 he wrote Vischer that he expeced to revise the *Life of Jesus* by drawing on the work of Baur and his students, and then also to write a popular book (*Briefwechsel*, 2:166).   By January 29, 1861 he had made up his mind: he would not turn the *Life of Jesus* into a patchwork.   But he also complained that he had no one with whom he could discuss the work, and that his eyes were bothering him (*Briefwechsel*, 2:170).   Strauss had long been nearsighted, and now his lifelong reading took its toll.   In the fall of 1860 he went to Berlin for an operation, which helped moderately.

103. *AB*, no. 441.

104. *LD*, pp. 35, 61; see also *AB*, no. 419.

105. On March 21, 1861 he published "F. Chr. Baur und seine Bedeutung für die deutsche Theologie" in *Die Zeit* (Frankfurt), *Beilage* 3.   In 1863 came "Schleiermacher und die Auferstehung Jesu" in *Zeitschrift für wissenschaftliche Theologie*.

106. In 1860 he reviewed Röpe's book, which defended Pastor Götze's attack on Lessing, in *Grenzbote* (*Briefwechsel*, 2:160, n. 115).   In 1861 he published an essay on Lessing's "Nathan the Wise," originally a public lecture given for the support of the German fleet.

107. Brockes, a poet with seemingly orthodox views (Reimarus, too, was orthodox in public), was one of the persons to whom Reimarus had shown his secret manuscript, "Apology for Rational Worshippers of God."

ment of Reimarus's secret manuscript and assessing his significance.[108] In 1863 Ernst Renan's *Life of Jesus* appeared in France; far from discouraging him,[109] this appeared to spur him on in the hope of being able to do for literate Germans what Renan had done for literate Frenchmen (see the preface). Apparently he did. *The Life of Jesus for the German People* appeared at the beginning of 1864; in six months a reprint was necessary. But he did not match Renan's success in writing in an easy, popular style; although much critical analysis had been omitted, Strauss still demanded a good deal from the reader.[110] For one thing, stung by Baur's insistence that the criticism of the Gospels must precede criticism of Gospel stories, Strauss led the readers through a discussion of the Gospels and their criticism. What was really new in his work, however, was that now Strauss sketched what he believed could be known of Jesus' life[111] and was no longer content to expose what could not be regarded as historical.[112] Because the book was not received as well as he had expected, being over-

108. The section in which Strauss assessed the significance of Reimarus has been made available in English for the first time in *Reimarus: Fragments,* ed. Charles H. Talbert, Lives of Jesus Series (Philadelphia: Fortress Press, 1970), pp. 44–57. Strauss's admirable summary of the massive manuscript remains unsurpassed.

109. Ziegler (2:590) insists, rightly I think, that Strauss was not motivated to publish by jealousy (he had already been at work for over three years); rather, he was persuaded that, despite similarity in stance, he had a different point of view, especially with regard to Renan's uncritical use of the Fourth Gospel.

110. He admitted that the style was still heavy; he viewed Book Two as the heart of the book, and insisted that this could not be popularized more (*AB,* no. 464). Because his eyes were troubling him, he had to dictate the book, and this did not facilitate an easy style.

111. Eight years later, however, in *Der Alte und der neue Glaube,* he changed his mind: nothing reliable could be known (see below, p. lxxviii).

112. Ziegler (2:605) notes that Strauss had become an outstanding biographer, and thus was challenged by the task of writing a biography of Jesus. But Strauss himself never refers to this motivation.

shadowed by other works like those of Holtzmann, Schenkel (see next paragraph), and Renan, Strauss blamed the public's lack of discrimination.[113] He was, naturally enough, bitterly attacked.[114] He deserved it in part, having ignored the import of recent studies of the Synoptic problem which showed that Mark was used by Matthew.

Once, while he was writing this book, he thought it would be his last work.[115] How wrong he was! Before the year was out, Strauss showed that he could not avoid a battle with theologians; but this time Strauss was the aggressor, spoiling for a fight. During 1864 Daniel Schenkel, an ecclesiastical official who was also a professor at Heidelberg, published a book on Jesus.[116] This work represented a moderate, mediating position—something Strauss could not tolerate.[117] To the conservatives, on the other hand, the

113. He penned the following lines:

> Das Publicum ist eine Kuh,
> Die grast und grast nur immer zu;
> Kommt ein Blum' ihr vor der Nas',
> Die nimmt sie mit und sagt nicht: Was?
> Ist ihr wie anderes futter auch,
> Beschäftigt das Maul and füllt den Bauch.

(Hausrath, 2:285)

114. Hausrath (2:288) reports that one polemicist wrote that he prayed that Strauss should remember his more pious youth and repent lest he die with Judas's question on his mind: where can one buy the best rope? Still, the book was no longer shocking, even if it shocked Yale's church historian, George Fisher, into suggesting a more apt title, *Conjectures Concerning the Life of One Jesus by a Disbeliever in the Authenticity of the Gospels and the Existence of God.* (George Fisher, *Essays on the Supernatural Origin of Christianity* [New York: Scribner's, 1887³], p. 430). With better hindsight, Karl Barth observed that had Strauss written of Jesus in 1835–36 as he did now (see below, pp. lxxii–lxxvi), he would not have lost his post (*David Friedrich Strauss als Theologe*, p. 18).

115. Letter to Vischer, November 29, 1861 (*Briefwechsel*, 2:173).

116. *Das Charakterbild Jesu* (Wiesbaden: C. W. Kreidel, 1864).

117. He once expressed his contempt for mediating theology by comparing it with *Wurst* (sausage): Orthodoxy provides the meat, Schleiermacher the *Speck* (fat), and a dash of Hegel the spice. Already Lessing, he noted, found this *Wurst* unpalatable (Kohut, pp. 85–86).

book appeared so radical that Schenkel's dismissal was called for. In July, a counterprotest succeeded in vindicating him. Instead of hailing this as a step in the right direction, Strauss wrote in September that Schenkel did not deserve defense.[118] The same year, 1864, saw the publication of Schleiermacher's *Leben Jesu* lectures, and in Berlin Strauss promptly wrote his critique (the present volume). In order to fill out the book and make it worth the price, he slightly modified his attack on Schenkel and included it.[119]

There was also a certain logic in this, for the dispute with Schenkel signals much of what appears in *The Christ of Faith and the Jesus of History.* Schenkel said he feared that the public might infer from Strauss's inclusion of the article that, though they were both under fire, Strauss had rejected his overtures to make common cause. Strauss was furious enough to produce one of his finest polemical writings, *Die Halben und die Ganzen*,[120] which attacked both Schenkel and his old enemy Hengstenberg. The latter, said Strauss, had viewed the first *Life of Jesus* as if it were the beast from the abyss, and now regarded the second *Life* as already superseded by allegedly new discoveries. Strauss went to work with a relish, demolishing this contention and treating his opponent with contempt and sarcasm. He boasted to Vischer that writing these polemical pieces revived his spirit and made him feel young again;[121] he regarded this work as

118. "Der Schenkelsche Handeln in Baden" (*National Zeitung*, September 24, 1864 [Hausrath, 2:291, 327]). Hausrath is severely critical of Strauss for allowing his desire for revenge against Schenkel to place him in the same camp with Hengstenberg. Strauss's desire for revenge stemmed partly from 1852 when Schenkel, then at Heidelberg, had been active in the agitation against Strauss's friend, the philosopher Kuno Fischer. See Albert Schweitzer, *Quest of the Historical Jesus*, pp. 123, 208–9.

119. *LD*, p. 58.

120. Hausrath (2:334–35) reports that during his brief political career in 1848 the phrase used in this title ("the half-hearted and the thorough") had been used against Strauss himself.

121. *Briefwechsel*, 2:198; see also *LD*, p. 58.

his best polemical writing.[122]   Strauss was right: he had to be angry in order to write.

Strauss did not return to theology in the 1860s under stabilized personal circumstances.   This decade, too, was painful.   It began with an operation on his eyes in Berlin during the fall of 1860 (see above, note 102).   From Berlin he returned to Heilbronn to be near Fritz, who was in the gymnasium there; Georgine managed the house.   But in 1863 Fritz went to the University of Tübingen, and in 1864— the year of the new *Life of Jesus* and the piece against Schenkel—Georgine married.   Once more Strauss had to rearrange his life.   He returned to Berlin, where he wrote *The Christ of Faith*.   In the spring of 1865 he moved from place to place again: Heidelberg, Baden, Munich, Bonn, and finally to Darmstadt in the fall.[123]   There he remained for seven years (1865–72), except for the winter of 1867–68 when he fled to Munich.

The escape to Munich reminds us of Strauss's futile quest for domestic tranquility, for he found it necessary to run away from love.   He had fallen in love with a widow, who returned his affection.   But Agnese, being Catholic, refused to give him a divorce.   Since he could not bear the thought of a clandestine love and lived by the mores of the mid-nineteenth century rather than those of the mid-twentieth, he fled to Munich.   Whereas the first half of the decade had been highly productive despite many moves, he published little in the second half due to this frustration.[124]   From 1867 onward his pain was assuaged, interestingly, by a remarkable friendship with another woman, Princess Alice of Eng-

---

122. *LD*, p. 62.
123. It was here that he began, on February 2, 1866, to keep a journal, the "Literarische Denkwürdigkeiten," in which he reflected upon his literary career. The last entry is dated December 27, 1872.
124. For details see Ziegler, 2:667 ff.

land,[125] and her husband, Prince Ludwig of Hesse.[126] In this period he began reading Voltaire,[127] and produced six lectures which he read to the Princess on successive evenings. When he published them he dedicated the book to her.[128] The work was a success,[129] requiring three editions in two years.

Strauss had strong opinions about German nationalism, and saw hope only in the leadership of Prussia—a point which alienated him from his friend Vischer. Catholic Austria could never lead the German nation, he thought. Not surprisingly, when war with France broke out in 1870 he defended the German cause in an exchange of letters with Renan, which he published in the press.[130]

The original theological project, it will be recalled, included a constructive part—"to reestablish dogmatically what had been destroyed critically." This had not yet been done. During his work on Voltaire he began to think of this task.[131] He read Schopenhauer and Darwin in preparation, and began writing in 1871; in October 1872 his theo-

125. For details see Ziegler, 2:652 ff.

126. Strauss wrote Vischer that he came to respect the prince because he had deliberately undermined the Anglican religious instruction which his daughter received (*Briefwechsel*, 2:248).

127. In 1840 he wrote his brother of his distaste for Voltaire (*AB*, no. 78). According to Ziegler, it was Voltaire's correspondence with Frederick the Great that sparked the new appreciation. Strauss eventually read the entire corpus (Ziegler, 2:652).

128. *Voltaire: Sechs Vorträge.* There is some uncertainty regarding the date of the lectures. In the *LD* Strauss says he began the oral presentations on December 9, 1860, but in the published text he speaks of December 9, 1861. Hausrath (2:264, n. 1) argues that the latter is correct.

129. Zeller (pp. 98–100) regards this as Strauss's finest biographical work, comparable only to Goethe's *Dichtung und Wahrheit.*

130. The correspondence appears in *GS* 1. For circumstances attending the correspondence see *LD*, pp. 72 ff, and Ziegler, 2:661 ff.

131. The journal entry date November 19, 1867 expresses both his desire to write his theological testament and his doubts as to whether he still had the capacity to do so (*LD*, pp. 61–62). Two weeks later he wrote Zeller that his theological interest was exhausted and that his eyesight seemed to preclude undertaking any new work (*AB*, no. 487). On June 18, 1868

logical testament appeared.[132] He sought to articulate the stance of those whom Bishop James Pike was later to call "Christian alumni." He structured the book around four questions. The first, Are we still Christians? he answered negatively; in response to the second, Do we still have religion? he insisted that it depends on the definition of religion. That is, if religion is anything other than reverence for the God immanent in the universe, the answer is *No*; if it reveres the panentheist God, *Yes*. He would have agreed with the statement of his friend Vischer, who said, "Since I no longer believe, I have, for the first time, become religious."[133] In answering the third, How do we understand the world? he appealed to Darwinism[134] and rejected the Hegelian dialectic of nature and spirit for a thoroughgoing materialism.[135] In discussing the fourth, How do we order our lives? he appealed to the morality of middle-class intellectuals. It is little wonder that this book came to be regarded as his least successful writing.[136]

---

he wrote Vischer that now it was not a matter of making Christianity rational but of setting it aside completely. But no one would listen! (*Briefwechsel*, 2:262).

132. *Der alte und der neue Glaube. Ein Bekenntnis.*

133. Brazill, p. 169.

134. "Only Darwin liberates us from the idea of creation; we philosophers always wanted to get away from it, but only Darwin has shown us where the carpenter made the exit" (*AB*, no. 509). Harris (p. 248) claims that Strauss was the first theologian to champion Darwinism. According to Werner Elert, Darwin was popular in the 1860s in Germany. *The Origin of Species* was translated in 1860, and the entire edition (twelve hundred and fifty copies) was sold the first day; the second printing (three thousand copies) sold almost as fast. Continental intellectuals saw it as documentation of what Schelling had postulated—the unity of all nature. (Werner Elert, *Der Kampf um das Christentum*, p. 195).

135. Strauss did not see himself as abandoning Hegel, because his lifelong fight had been against dualism and a transcendent God. Brazill (pp. 130–31) sees this clearly.

136. The book evoked a quip: "[The *Glaubenslehre*] has the same resemblance to a system of dogmatics as a cemetery has to a city" (F. Lichtenberger, *History of German Theology in the Nineteenth Century*, ed. and trans. W. Hastie [Edinburgh: T. & T. Clark, 1889], p. 329).

It succeeded, however, in provoking another controversy. The book sold well—six editions in as many months. But even the liberals sought to distance themselves from Strauss;[137] his friends were silent,[138] and Nietzsche said the book was senile at birth.[139] Strauss was shocked and hurt by the response. He regarded the work as articulating *his* views; his opponents, however, saw it as an attack on *theirs*. Fighter though he was,[140] battles never really toughened his skin. But now he no longer had the will to fight back. To a friend he wrote that in this difficult time he heard only the chant, "Samson, the Philistines are upon you!" and yet his hair had not grown sufficiently.[141] Yet on the occasion of the second edition he wrote:

> Up, old warrior, leave regrets
> And gird your loins!
> In storm you began,
> In storm you are to end.[142]

137. In 1873, Schenkel published the fourth, revised edition of *Das Charakterbild Jesu*, and in the foreword wrote an extended critique of Strauss's recent book, noting with evident satisfaction that even the liberals had repudiated it. Further, with unconcealed delight, he called Strauss the "half-hearted unbeliever" (Strauss had called Schenkel the "half-hearted critic" [see above, note 120]) because he retained an aura of piety for the All.

138. Ziegler (2:724–25) notes that the two who were sympathetic, Kuno Fischer and Eduard Zeller, remained silent. Ziegler himself responded to Strauss's critics. By this time Strauss's relationship with his lifelong friend Vischer was strained. When Strauss learned that Vischer was writing a response to the book, he assumed that an antagonistic review would be published. Actually Vischer wrote over fifty pages of response and mailed the packet, together with a conciliatory cover letter—but Strauss refused to open it!

139. "David Strauss, the Confessor and the Writer," *Thoughts Out of Season*, part 1, trans. A. M. Ludovici in O. Levy, ed., *The Complete Works of Friedrich Nietzsche* (New York: Russell and Russell, 1964), 4:1–97.

140. Zeller reports that Strauss had always appropriated the lines, "Say that I was a man, and that means to be a fighter" (*AB*, p. v).

141. Zeller, p. 112.

142. Ibid.

Still, the foreword to the fourth and subsequent editions was rather subdued. He said his desire was not to attack others but to distinguish what one can say and cannot say. He looked forward to a time when he would be understood, but realized that he would not live to see it. He was wrong and he was right—wrong in that the book has not been accepted; right in that in a little over a year he would be buried.

In October 1872 he left Darmstadt for Ludwigsburg, and closed out his life where it began.[143] Soon after the new year began, he became ill and aged rapidly. Though in great pain, he remained remarkably cheerful. To stay that way, he ceased reading what was written about him, and left letters urging his conversion unread. Instead he read what he liked, wrote verses for Georgine's twins, and corresponded with friends.[144] During his last days he was reading Plato's *Phaedo* in Greek. In January 1874 he underwent an exploratory operation, but nothing could be done. On February 8 he died in his son's arms.

Earlier instructions for his burial (see above, note 101)[145] were carried out: burial in a simple fir casket, no clergymen, and a sum of money given for the poor. Accordingly, on February 10, without the traditional tolling of the bell or participation of a minister, he was buried in the presence of his family and friends.[146] But even this provoked a con-

143. Ziegler points out that Strauss spent five-sixths of his life in Swabia; he insists that Strauss can be understood only as a Swabian (Ziegler, 1:ix). Gotthold Müller also emphasizes this parochial character.

144. In 1873 Ernst Rapp alone received seventy-two letters from Strauss (Ziegler, 2:736).

145. Harris (p. 257–58) publishes, for the first time, Strauss's "Last Will and Testimony with Regard to my Burial," dated June 22, 1873. Evidently Strauss put in writing what he had said before.

146. Zeller's illness kept him away, and estrangement prevented Vischer from attending. Yet ten years later, when a plaque was dedicated at the house where Strauss had been born, it was the seventy-six-year-old Vischer who made the speech. Even then, Vischer said he felt that Strauss's ghost did not welcome him (*Briefwechsel*, 2:301).

troversy, for local pietists protested at what was said at the grave.[147]

STRAUSS'S CRITIQUES OF SCHLEIERMACHER

The Christ of Faith can be understood properly only in the context of Strauss's shifting views of Christology and of the historical Jesus. These changes alternatively brought him closer to Schleiermacher and distanced him from the Berlin theologian. Accordingly, our task now is to trace the lineaments of Strauss's quarrel with Schleiermacher. Because his stance toward Schleiermacher was derived from F. C. Baur, we must begin with Baur's influence on Strauss.

Baur's Influence

At Blaubeuren, Baur bequeathed to the young Strauss a love of history and a passion for understanding it in light of philosophy. Baur asserted, "Without philosophy, history remains for me eternally dead and mute."[148] It was with this point of view that Baur captivated Strauss. Baur's admission implies that the task of philosophy is to enliven historical facts, to give them coherence, validity, and significance. But *which* philosophy? Despite the oft-repeated view that Baur was a Hegelian,[149] at Blaubeuren Baur had not yet known Hegel's thought. Rather it is to the idealist

147. For a portrait of Württemberg pietism in Strauss's day see Hausrath, 1:217–62.

148. Baur, *Symbolik und Mythologie*, 1:xi (see above, note 20), quoted from Müller, p. 187. Müller (p. 175) argues that Strauss's "dissertation" is largely a paraphrase and condensation of Baur.

149. Hodgson has shown that Baur first studied Hegel just before and during the time Strauss was writing his *Life of Jesus*, i.e., after Baur's basic direction had been established. Though for a subsequent brief period Baur identified himself with Hegelians, he wrote, "I am not a disciple of any philosophical system . . . but likewise I have the conviction that there is a great deal for theology to learn from Hegel" (*Formation*, p. 65; see also pp. 22–24 and 54–66).

tradition, and especially to Schelling,[150] that we must look.

What Baur found in Schelling was an alternative to supernaturalism and rationalism, namely, the dictum that "history as a whole is a continuous, gradually self-disclosing revelation of the absolute," and that in Christianity the universal is viewed as history.[151] On this basis the Christ-event becomes the locus at which this process is disclosed. Historical events can be understood properly only from the standpoint of the absolute's self-expression; every particularity is a detail in the cosmic process. Christ is not an event in which God becomes man, but an event which discloses that God and man are essentially identical, since human history is the disclosure of the divine, the absolute, or the ideal. Here religious interest in Christ becomes indistinguishable from philosophical interests. Baur was able to say, not surprisingly, "Philosophy and religion have the same content, the absolute, and all doctrines of religion belong also to the content of philosophy,"[152]—a point made also by Schelling and Hegel, and one which Strauss eventually rejected. What Strauss learned from Baur can be identified as: (1) a conviction that contemporary philosophy offered a fruitful alternative to the worn-out issues of supernaturalism and rationalism, (2) a predilection for treating theological issues in terms of philosophy, a philosophy committed to overcoming the "extraneousness" of God to the world by positing their dialectical identity, and (3) a conviction that the truth of Christianity could be expressed in terms of this idealist philosophy.

From Baur, Strauss also learned an appreciation for

---

150. Baur had studied Schelling while a student in Tübingen, and continued to do so at Blaubeuren. For details of Baur's reliance on Schelling see Müller, pp. 180–82, where other literature is noted; see also *Formation,* pp. 9–11, 15 and 146.

151. Müller, p. 182.

152. *Symbolik und Mythologie,* 1:98, quoted from Müller, p. 190.

Schleiermacher and, even more importantly, acquired a dissatisfaction with his theology at precisely the point at which it conflicted most with idealist philosophy—Christology. While writing the *Symbolik* Baur read with enthusiasm the first edition of Schleiermacher's *The Christian Faith* (1821–22) (see below, note 217), in which he found liberation from supernaturalism's extraneous God and externally grounded truth (miracles and inspired scripture), and from rationalism's inability to deal constructively with the reality of the Christian church and its actual history. Schleiermacher's emphasis on pious self-consciousness, mediated by the church, was the answer to both, for now the truth of Christianity was not "inserted" into human history but was seen as the actualization of what is deepest in the human self. The church was no longer the distorter of the pristine truth which Jesus taught, but the historical mediator of the redemption made available in Jesus. Nonetheless, Baur detected a flaw which he described in a letter to his brother:

> If the major elements which concerned the person of the Redeemer are themselves derived from religious self-consciousness,[153] then the outward history of Jesus could be taken as a history of the internal development of religious self-consciousness [in general], and I could think of the Redeemer only as a certain form and potency of self-consciousness which would therefore appear in an outward historical form only because the natural development of self-consciousness must necessarily so form itself once in its highest perfection. Therefore, Christ is in every man, and the outward appearance of Jesus is not the original fact [from which Christian consciousness is derived].[154]

The signal which Baur sent privately to his brother was presented publicly in Baur's inaugural lecture at Tübingen in

153. Schleiermacher asserted the redemptive significance of Christ because Christian piety knows itself dependent on him—at least this is how Baur understood him.

154. Quoted from *Formation*, p. 14.

1827; this, in turn, stated seminally what would be developed in subsequent work.[155] Baur scored Schleiermacher for not accounting adequately for his (correct) concentration on Christ. First, Baur believed that the structure of *The Christian Faith* frustrated Schleimermacher's aim, for by starting with an analysis of the inherent, human sense of dependence, he made pious self-consciousness the real content of dogmatics. But on what basis then did consciousness of redemption derive from the historical event of Christ? Secondly, Baur pointed out that because in Christology Schleiermacher began with the "ideal Christ"—the Christ who is known in the experience of redemption—he could do no more than *assert* that this ideal, archetypal Christ was simultaneously the historical Jesus, the starting point for Christian self-consciousness; he was unable to *show* that this is the case. Not on traditional dogmatic grounds could he show it, for Schleiermacher was indifferent to the doctrine of the virgin birth, by which the tradition had accounted for Jesus' distinctiveness; he opted for a historical, nonsupernaturalist view, which by definition cannot show what is needed dogmatically. Nor could he prove his assertion on philosophical grounds, for there is no necessity that the ideal, archetypal Christ be actualized in history in a single individual in order to activate human self-consciousness into its redeemed state. Furthermore, it is impossible that the ideal Christ is actualized in a single historical person, for this would annul his historicity.[156] Baur's third point was

155. *Formation*, p. 17. The analysis here is indebted to Hodgson (*Formation*, pp. 43–54), who draws on Baur's various discussions of Schleiermacher.

156. Carl E. Hester III rightly observes that Baur, to be followed by Strauss, (wrongly) equated Schleiermacher's archetype with Hegel's idea of divine-human unity, in his dissertation "Schleiermacher in Tübingen: A Study in Reaction." Yet it would be more accurate to speak of Schelling and the idealist tradition, since in 1827 Baur did not know Hegel's work. Heinz Liebing also saw that Baur misread Schleiermacher at the decisive point ("Ferdinand Christian Baurs Kritik an Schleiermachers Glaubenslehre," *Zeitschrift für Theologie und Kirche* 54 [1957]: 235).

that while Schleiermacher saw correctly the significance of Jesus as the founder of Christianity, he reasoned wrongly: one cannot understand historical mediation by reasoning from effects to their cause, but only by reasoning from the cause toward the effects, for there is no historical necessity that the effects stem from one cause, or from this particular one. As Hodgson summarizes, Schleiermacher "fails to provide for the *possibility* of an authentically historical Jesus . . . [and] he fails to provide for the *necessity* of the historical Jesus." Fourthly, Baur also linked Schleiermacher with early Christian gnosticism.[157] Doubtless Strauss heard the inaugural lecture in which these criticisms were expressed; these same points (except for the link with gnosticism) reappeared eight years later in Strauss's own *Life of Jesus* and in the subsequent *Streitschriften*.[158]

Finally, Baur introduced Strauss to the idealist understanding of myth. Especially influential may have been Schelling's work on myths and legends, in which he asserted that philosophical myths present ideas in visual, palpable form, and hence are not expected to be taken at face value as factual history, but are expected to persuade one of their truth. Even if a philosophical myth should rest on reliable historical tradition, this conjunction of idea and history transforms the historical event into a philosophical myth because now the event serves a higher truth. On this basis, the incarnation is the mythological expression of the idea that God and man are one, and is not a report of what

157. Hester points out that Baur did not express himself on Schleiermacher again until after the latter's death in 1834. But in 1835 Baur published his *Die christliche Gnosis* and repeated his charges, adding that Schleiermacher's work lacked straightforwardness and that it was an example of unsuccessful mediating theology. Hester observes that Baur was actually aiming his remarks at Schleiermacher's followers ("Schleiermacher in Tübingen," pp. 45–46, 70–71).

158. Schleiermacher visited Tübingen in the fall of 1830, largely to meet Steudel and Baur, whose criticisms were known to him. This visit was the focal point of Hester's dissertation.

occurred at a point in time. Such views of myth and history did not originate with Schelling;[159] nonetheless, it was Schelling who helped Baur find his way, so that in his *Symbolik* Baur could say that myth is "the most perfect form in which the ideas of the absolute make themselves palpable [*Versinnlichen*]." Whereas a symbol is a static image, myth is a "visual presentation of an idea by means of an action."[160] Having drunk this wine, it is understandable why Strauss in Tübingen found the water of Steudel's supernaturalism too flat to drink and also turned to Schelling.[161]

Through Schleiermacher to Hegel

As we have seen, in Tübingen Strauss also became, albeit for a brief time, a Schleiermacher enthusiast.[162] Like Baur,

159. "Über Mythen, historiche Sagen und Philosopheme der ältesten Welt" (1793). The originality of Schelling's views is contested by Hartlich and Sachs, who assert that Schelling depended on Heyne and Eichhorn (Hartlich and Sachs, *Der Ursprung des Mythosbegriffes in der modernen Bibelwissenschaft*, p. 57).

160. Cited from Müller, p. 192.

161. Müller claims that it was through Schelling (and not Hegel) that Strauss was turned against the prevailing orthodoxy, and that Schelling persuaded him that there was nothing to the dogma of the resurrection of the flesh (the subject of his prizewinning essay of 1828) (Müller, pp. 213–15).

162. Schleiermacher's impact was positive in two ways. The first concerned his theological method. "He did not urge us . . . to break with our previous principle and to surrender to a new one, the authority of a revelation; rather our own human consciousness remained the principle, as before." (*Märklin*, p. 50; see Müller, pp. 218–19). The second concerned Strauss's self-discovery. "Now I came to know entirely new powers within me. . . . Only from that point onward did the right thrust come, yes real passion in my study; from this time onward I really learned for the first time, and also made such remarkably rapid progress that in a very short time I advanced beyond my older colleagues to whom I had looked up for all these years. . . . Now, even if I had no clear consciousness of it at the time, the gaping hole in my ability was filled, . . . a surrogate was found for creative fantasy [an allusion to his romanticism], . . . my previously divided being was unified. This surrogate consisted in the gift of a dialectical thinking which I had discovered within me" (*LD*, p. 12). He refers here to Schleiermacher's *Speeches* and *Soliloquies*.

he read Schleiermacher with chiefly philosophical questions in mind and, doubtless stimulated by Baur's inaugural
lecture, was soon disappointed. It was then, it will be
recalled, that Strauss and his friends discovered Hegel's
Phenomenology and became captivated by his distinction
between *Vorstellung* (image or representation) and *Begriff*
(concept or idea). Hegel had claimed that the latter transcended the former; in the dialectical movement of spirit,
the concept took up within itself the real meaning of the
image or representation and captured its meaning on a
higher, more adequate level. Here was the solution to his
problem with Schleiermacher, for Strauss equated theology
with the image or representation, and philosophy with the
concept. Whereas Schleiermacher failed to hold philosophy
and theology together,[163] Strauss inferred from Hegel that
philosophy transcended theology. That is, philosophy so
adequately captured the real truth of theology that the traditional theology could be left behind. What bothered Strauss
now was the core of the Christian theology, the whole
Gospel story of Jesus. Was this a representation or was
it a concept? Strauss and his friends took the Hegel "in
the liberal sense";[164] that is, they inferred that the story
was a representation of a truth that was better expressed in

163. "The study of Schleiermacher's *Glaubenslehre*, far from satisfying us
scientifically [i.e., philosophically], instead gave us double motivation to
press ahead where the master . . . had set boundary posts; the eternal
peace, which he was proud to have made between philosophy and theology,
appeared to us only as a fragile cease-fire, and we found ourselves advised
to prepare for war. But how much still was lacking in our philosophical
armament was again evident in the reading of Schleiermacher's dogmatics"
(*Märklin*, p. 223).

164. *AB*, no. 39. Later, in a reply to Zeller's review of his *Glaubenslehre*,
Strauss denied Zeller's claim that religion and philosophy can have parallel
relations to the same subject matter, as do art and philosophy. Art, says
Strauss, has its own appropriate medium, but not religion, for religion
deals with ultimately alien material—representations, which are reducible
to ideas (*AB*, no. 132).

philosophical concepts. On this basis, once one had grasped the philosophical concept which was expressed in the representation, the representation itself was no longer necessary. Philosophy needed no longer be coordinated with theology, as Schleiermacher had thought, but could supersede it. Schelling and the idealists, through Baur, had taught Strauss to look for the idea expressed in the myth; now Hegel suggested to him that one must look for the concept in the representation (in the Gospel story).

Although Strauss had found a way toward a Christology based on the Christ-idea rather than on the Christ-event, another issue came to the fore—eschatology. Could the traditional Christian doctrine of election, which spoke of a pretemporal decision to separate the saved from the unsaved, and of eschatology in which this separation was fulfilled, be understood in idealist terms which regarded the world and history as the self-manifestation of the divine? Strauss addressed this issue in his "doctoral dissertation"[165] (see above, p. xxiii). Strauss began by specifying the goal of all religion as that of harmonizing perceived contradictions between the divine and the human, the infinite and the finite; regularly this resolution had been put into the future and had so become an object of hope. But Strauss was a monist; accordingly, he construed his topic, "The Restoration of All Things," not as a reconstitution of creation in which the difference between God and the world is restored to its proper relationship, but as the restoration of primal identity. In other words, this monist reading of the idealist idea of primal identity is taken to be the concept in the biblical representation of "the restoration of all things."

Schleiermacher, who would probably have received major attention even if the assignment had not required it, had

---

165. Strauss had been assigned two problems: to determine whether 1 Cor. 15:21–58 and related texts prove an absolute "restoration of all things," and to assess Schleiermacher's views on this topic.

himself wrestled with questions of election and eschatology, and had affirmed the eventual conversion of all mankind. But Strauss was dissatisfied with Schleiermacher's efforts to reinterpret this biblical motif, and claimed that Schleiermacher's own view of God's relation to evil made his reinterpretation unnecessary. If Schleiermacher could hold that for God evil does not really exist and that what men call evil is really the not-yet-good, then the restoration of all things cannot be a future act of God but must be eternally present to God. But how can all religion perceive a current contradiction while for God the resolution is eternally present? Strauss simply asserted that the Hegelian theologian Marheinecke had suggested the solution: "This is the restoration of all things, that the goal of religion is also its beginning." That is, in religion one is not only aware of the contradiction, but one also participates in the eternal life of God. Strauss then appealed to Hegel directly, saying that his philosophy shows how the contradictory present can be understood to be without contradiction. Eternal damnation can be affirmed because evil is always impotent and doomed, and the restoration of all things can be affirmed because no being is without participation in the good. Thus there is no need of a temporal resolution. In this way, Strauss misused Hegel to overcome his dissatisfaction with Schleiermacher's duality by asserting an atemporal, philosophical view of God and evil. Repeatedly, from that point onward, Strauss scored Schleiermacher for trying to combine traditional Christian views with a modern philosophical standpoint. For Strauss it had to be one or the other but not both.

When Strauss proceeded to write *The Life of Jesus*, he was convinced that the central truth of Christianity was the divine incarnation in humanity as a whole, not in a single historical figure. To clear the way for the Christology he hoped to write, he first needed to show that the traditional

Christology, based on the historicity of the Christ-event, *could not* be sustained critically any longer; then he could show that it *should not* be attempted any longer since the truth of the matter lay elsewhere.[166]   Accordingly, Strauss had little interest in analyzing the Gospels in order to locate solid history.   Critics who down to the present have denounced Strauss for having virtually no history of Jesus left when he finished,[167] and for not feeling any regrets, were largely correct but beside the mark.   Strauss did what *he* set out to do, not what others thought should have been done.[168]

Accordingly, he hoped to make it impossible for theology to continue as before.   He exposed first the untenability of the supernaturalist interpretation, then that of the rationalist; the former dissolved real history by supernatural intervention, and the latter distorted the text by eliminating the miraculous.   By insisting on their mythical quality, the character of the stories can be maintained and, by the use of Hegel's distinction of representation and concept, the mythic material can be transcended without loss for theology, because the true meaning of the incarnation does not require a historical event.   In the preface to the first volume Strauss wrote, "The essence of the Christian faith is perfectly inde-

---

166. The formal similarity between Strauss's undertaking and Bultmann's position is clear.   See Rudolf Bultmann, "The Primitive Christian Kerygma and the Historical Jesus," in Carl E. Braaten and Roy A. Harrisville, eds., *The Historical Jesus and the Kerygmatic Christ* (Nashville: Abingdon, 1964).   For Bultmann, of course, the alternative to theological concern for the history of Jesus is the kerygma—the Word of God—not an idea.

167. Strauss did not deny that something historically factual could be ascertained; Hodgson has compiled these "positive results" (*LJCE*, pp. xxxi–xxxvi).

168. Barth saw this clearly (*David Friedrich Strauss als Theologe*, p. 25).   But Brazill's statement (p. 107) is misleading: "Strauss intended to discover the degree to which the historical basis of the Gospels could be accepted."   A similar failure to see the issue from Strauss's point of view appears in Harris, pp. 43 ff.

pendent of his [my] criticism. The supernatural birth of Christ, his miracles, his resurrection and ascension, remain eternal truths, whatever doubt may be cast on their reality as historical facts."[169]

Strauss turned Baur's definition of "philosophical myths," derived from the "mythical school," into "evangelical myths"—stories which express early Christian ideas of Christ.[170] In identifying what is mythic he used negative and positive criteria:[171] negatively, that is unhistorical which contradicts physical or psychological laws of cause and effect, or which contradicts another account of the same alleged event; positively, if the idea expressed in the narrative accords with ideas of Christ which are found in Christian circles, then the narrative can be regarded as a precipitate of those ideas, since early Christians generated these stories to express their Christology. The dialectical power which Strauss discovered (see above, note 162) was now put to use. If he could not reject a story because it was miraculous, he could do so because one of the Gospel versions contradicted another; then he argued that the remaining material was so permeated with Christian views, especially belief that the Old Testament expectations were fulfilled in Jesus, that this material too could not be regarded as solid history. Consistently, the Fourth Gospel was set aside as a deposit of early Christian theology.

The Critique of Schleiermacher in The Life of Jesus

In the first edition of *The Life of Jesus*, Strauss reveals

169. This was not written "just to console the reader," as Harris (p. 47) claims.

170. C. C. McCown observed that Strauss, however, did not mention Baur's *Symbolik und Mythologie* (*The Search for the Real Jesus* [New York: Scribner's, 1940], pp. 58–59).

171. Strauss's positive criteria approximate what today are called negative criteria. See Hodgson's introduction to *LJCE*, pp. xxvi–xxix.

an amazing breadth of reading in primary and secondary sources (see above, note 44). Among the latter are Schleiermacher's study of Luke[172] and *The Christian Faith.* However, not until the last chapter does the reader learn how deeply dissatisfied Strauss is with Schleiermacher. While he takes issue with him on exegetical or historical points from time to time throughout, the vast majority of references are favorable. Often Schleiermacher is the one cited in footnotes where the text speaks favorably of "more recent criticism."[173] But in the last chapter, where Strauss deals thematically with the dogmatic import of the life of Jesus, he devotes a separate section (par. 144) to him.[174] After a succinct digest of Schleiermacher's Christology he concentrates on two motifs, the person and the work of Christ.

Concerning the person of Christ, he grants that Schleiermacher's Christology is the greatest effort to make visual the union of the divine and the human in Christ, though without relying on the old "two natures" dogma. None-

---

172. *Über die Schriften des Lukas: ein kritischer Versuch* (Berlin, 1817), now in *Sämmtliche Werke* (31 vols. [Berlin: Georg Reimer, 1835–64]), 1, part 2.

173. Even when Strauss's *Life of Jesus* discusses themes important for Schleiermacher, such as Jesus' upbringing, temptation, miracle-working power, and resurrection, he does not criticize him. Paragraph 79, which deals with the authenticity of Jesus' discourses in John's Gospel, ignores Schleiermacher; only in connection with the mythological character of Luke 2 does Strauss criticize Schleiermacher for not seeing the whole chapter as myth (1:216–17). True, Strauss moves in a different direction at these points, and this implies a rejection of Schleiermacher. In the third part of his *Streitschriften* he defends himself against Rosenkranz's surmise that Strauss had followed Schleiermacher in details. Strauss replies that on most points he was repelled by Schleiermacher. But he mentions only Schleiermacher's concern to begin with Christian consciousness, his reliance on John, and his rationalist treatment of the transfiguration and resurrection. He does not concede that in many exegetical and critical questions he did in fact follow Schleiermacher (*Streitschriften*, 3:60).

174. In the fourth edition this appears as paragraph 148.

theless, the result is disappointing for both science and faith. Its scientific inadequacy is manifest in three ways. First of all, Schleiermacher's contention that in Christ the archetypal is simultaneously a historical individual cannot be maintained without an unhistorical miracle. True, Schleiermacher had concentrated on Jesus' God-consciousness, but this too is subject to the conditions of finitude and imperfection, and the ideal cannot be actualized archetypally without a miracle. Schleiermacher is said to grant this by saying that the emergence of Christ in history can be understood only as a creative divine act, but subsequently everything is natural. Strauss argues that this device cannot heal the rupture which has been made.[175] Secondly, Schleiermacher had distinguished the internal from the external aspect of Jesus and had restricted the conditionedness of Jesus to the external. But, in a historical person one cannot separate internal essence from external expression; what lies behind externalization of the internal is common human nature. If one therefore penetrates the external appearance one does not move toward his individual or peculiar dignity, but toward the conception of humanity in general. Thirdly, if one views Christ as a man, then his development must have been like that of all other men, not free from ambiguity or sin as Schleiermacher contended. Turning to what faith requires, Strauss says the resurrection cannot be treated as a matter of relative indifference, as Schleiermacher had it, because this belief was the foundation without which there would never have been a Christianity at all.

For Strauss, Schleiermacher is no more convincing regarding the work of Christ. Strauss insists that for Schleier-

---

175. Baur's influence is clear. Strauss had registered this objection during his Berlin days in a letter to Märklin (*AB*, no. 5). Alexander Schweizer noted that this reveals Strauss's misunderstanding of Schleiermacher, because for Schleiermacher divine activity is not a rupture of nature ("Das Leben Jesu von Strauss im Verhältnis zur Schleiermacher'schen Dignität des Religionsstifters," *Theologische Studien und Kritiken* 10 [1837]:502–06).

macher, the work of Christ is inferred from Christian consciousness. Schleiermacher's contention that sentient human nature could not generate a perfect archetype is wrong, says Strauss, because the same human nature conceives of the infinite.[176]   Indeed, the concepts of finite and infinite condition imply one another.   So why could not sinful humanity conceive of a sinless archetype?

In short, Strauss contends that Schleiermacher's Christ was not "a historical, but an ideal Christ."[177]   Though Schleiermacher was convinced his Christ was historical, the fact is that he never existed except as an idea.   Actually, had Schleiermacher known it, he could have agreed with Strauss, the latter implies, for "to effect what Schleiermacher makes him effect, no other Christ is necessary, and, according to the principles of Schleiermacher respecting the relation of God to the world, of the supernatural to the natural, no other Christ is possible, than an ideal one."   Thereby Schleiermacher is damned by his own intention to faithfully reformulate the real meaning of Christian orthodoxy, for which a historical Christ is both possible and necessary.[178]

After a brief resume of what Strauss takes to be Hegel's importance for the topic (not to be confused with Hegel's own view of the matter), he writes:

> This is the key to the whole of Christology, that, as subject of the predicate which the church assigns to Christ, we place, instead of an individual, an idea; but an idea which

176. Baur's inaugural lecture of 1827 had also made this point (see Hester, "Schleiermacher in Tübingen," pp. 182–83, n. 2).

177. Strauss consistently proceeds on the basis of an erroneous equation—that what Schleiermacher meant by Christ as the archetype (*Urbild*) was what Strauss meant by the ideal, the Idea; in other words, he imported idealist categories into Schleiermacher, and then criticized him for being inconsistent.   This mistake was seen almost immediately by Alexander Schweizer, "Das Leben Jesu von Strauss," p. 502. He owed the mistake to Baur.

178. *LJCE*, p. 773, retained from the first edition.

has an existence in reality, not in the mind only, like that
of Kant. In an individual, a God-man, the properties and
functions which the church ascribes to Christ contradict
themselves; in the idea of the race, they perfectly agree.
Humanity is the union of the two natures—God become
man, the infinite manifesting itself in the finite, and the
finite spirit remembering its infinitude.[179]

Strauss specifies what he means: humanity results from the
union of nature and spirit; it works miracles (subdues nature); and it is sinless because only individuals are blamable,
not the species. Then he states the concept in the representation, "By faith in this Christ, especially in his death and
resurrection, man is justified before God; that is, by kindling
within him the idea of humanity, the individual man participates in the divinely human life of the species."[180]

But how did the representation arise in the first place?
Jesus was the *occasion* for new consciousness, but there is
no necessary connection between him and that consciousness itself. Consequently, Strauss continues:

When the mind has thus gone beyond the sensible history,
and into the domain of the absolute, the former ceases to
be essential; it takes a subordinate place, above which the
spiritual truths suggested by the history stand self-
supported. . . . Our age demands to be led in Christology
to the idea in the fact, to the race in the individual: a
theology which . . . stops short at him [Christ] as an
individual is not properly a theology, but a homily.[181]

The Shift toward Schleiermacher in the Third Edition

In the third edition, Strauss moderated his critical judgments on the Fourth Gospel and made a greater place in his
Christology for the permanent significance of Jesus; both

179. Ibid., p. 780.
180. Ibid.
181. Ibid., p. 781.

shifts brought him closer to Schleiermacher, the only spokesman for traditional Christianity for whom he had a critical appreciation. While he worked on the third edition, his essay "Transient and Permanent Elements in Christianity" ("Vergängliches und Bleibendes im Christentum") signaled what was to come,[182] but we shall concentrate on the more developed conclusion of the third edition.[183]

In the penultimate section (par. 149 in the third edition, par. 151 in the fourth) important changes were made. He omitted the paragraph which denied an essential link between Christian salvation and Christ, and which denied the necessity of a Christology centered in Jesus even after we see the idea of the incarnation in humanity. Thereby he prepared the way for his new concluding section.[184]

Interestingly, to conceal his move toward Schleiermacher, Strauss implies that he is moving beyond his earlier views, for he begins by asserting, "Indeed, only when scientific Christology has passed beyond Jesus as a person will it be forced to turn back to a consideration of him again and again." Interesting also is the fact that he moves toward Schleiermacher, but does so behind Hegel's banner. He cites Hegel's dictum that "all actions, including world-historical actions, culminate with individuals as subjects

---

182. In *ZfB* (see above, note 58). In arguing that resurrection, atonement, miracles, virgin birth, and incarnation are superseded concepts, he anticipated his *Glaubenslehre*; in asserting that the solely valid category for Jesus is that of the religious genius, he put into popular form the view of the third edition.

183. This section is included in *LJCE*, pp. 798–802. Unless otherwise specified, all textual references are to this material.

184. Nonetheless, he retained the claim that when the mind goes beyond the historical phenomenon to its absolute idea, the former ceases to be essential. This leads Hodgson to say that Strauss now intended to refute his former view (see Hodgson's note on par. 151 [*LJCE*, pp. 797–98]). Yet the matter is not really clear; Strauss may have overlooked the tension between this retained assertion and what he now put forward.

giving actuality to the substantial."[185]   Christianity is no exception to the rule: "All new epochs and characteristic formations are attached to a prominent personality."   He claims he had never denied that Jesus was important for the new epoch of consciousness, but that he had insisted that this could not be demonstrated by philosophy, but only by history.[186]

To provide this historical demonstration, Strauss assesses the place of Jesus in history. "Jesus belongs to the category of highly gifted individuals who . . . are called to raise the development of spirit in humanity to higher levels"—that is, to advance the spirit's self-actualization in history, a Hegelian motif.   Such persons are called geniuses,[187] and so Christ stands among the "greats" from Homer to Mozart.   Strauss admits that "God reveals himself" in a founder of religion, and goes on to assert simply that "Christ, as the founder of the highest religion, transcends other religious founders."[188] Conceivably, in the future, Jesus also might be transcended, but this is not really likely.   There are areas of life in which we simply cannot imagine that anything surpassing could emerge; besides, one could no more establish this new super-

185. G. W. Hegel, *Rechtsphilosophie*, par. 348.

186. Strauss had asserted this in the *Streitschriften*, 3:73 (*LJCE*, p. xli).

187. In "Vergängliches und Bleibendes" he asserted that all of Christ which remains for us from the ruins of the past dogmas is the cult of genius. The category "redeemer" can be applied to the genius because he had a redemptive impact on his culture.   Thus Christ is accorded the place of first among equals (*ZfB*, pp. 101–09).

188. Strauss evidently was influenced by Alexander Schweizer's article "Das Leben Jesu von Strauss im Verhältnis zur Schleiermacher'schen Dignität des Religionsstifters" (See above, note 175), which Baur had sent him. In returning it he said that the conclusion of the third edition would refer to it.   Strauss's letter is quoted by by Ernst Barnikol in his article "Der Briefwechsel zwischen Strauss und Baur," p. 102, no. 10 (see note 67, above).   The new conclusion does, in fact, refer to Schweizer, among others (*LJCE*, p. 799).   Whether it was Schweizer who suggested the category "religious genius," or his friend Friedrich Vischer, is not clear. According to Sandberger (p. 136, n. 81), as early as 1830–31 Vischer had spoken of Jesus in this way.

iority than one can prove that Napoleon was a greater general than Alexander.

The historical argument next tries to show that "nothing higher can be imagined than the peculiar excellence of the religious personality and work of Jesus himself." Strauss now combines Schleiermacher's interest in Jesus' God-consciousness with Hegel's dialectic: "The antithesis of the human and the divine . . . was dissolved in the self-consciousness of Jesus." Like Schleiermacher, he appeals to John as well as to the Synoptics, claiming that, in both, the merging of Jesus' will with God's was "neither a mere feigning nor a transient surge of Jesus' feeling in single heightened movements; rather his entire life and all his sayings were permeated with this consciousness from the soul." He continues in a Hegelian vein:

> If religion is the awakening in the human spirit of the relationship between God and man, then the stages of the religious life mount from the dull lack of consciousness of this distinction, through an ever more highly developing estrangement and imperfect efforts at compensation in the religion of nature and of law, to a complete conquest of this schism in self-conscious spiritual unity. . . . If this unity existed in Christ, then in the religious aspect he is unsurpassable for all time.[189]

When Strauss continues, "The unity of God and man has not appeared in human self-consciousness with any greater creative power than in Jesus, having penetrated and transfigured his entire life uniformly and without perceptible darkness," he sounds like Schleiermacher speaking of Jesus' God-consciousness. Repeatedly he tries to show historically, as he had promised, that this unity with God functioned in Jesus as he claimed.

189. In "Vergängliches und Bleibendes" he made two additional claims: (1) even if someone should equal Jesus, he would be assisted by Jesus in his attainment; (2) man will never be without religion, and no true religion is possible without Jesus (*ZfB*, pp. 129, 131).

Just how far toward Schleiermacher does Strauss move in the conclusion to the third edition? Not very far, apart from his treatment of the question of miracles and the reliability of the Fourth Gospel. First, though he asserts that Jesus is unsurpassable, there is no hint of a Christian consciousness of dependence on Christ. Strauss's basic categories are not derived from Christian experience but from the role of the individual in the Spirit's movement in history, and the restoration of primal unity between God and man. There is no place for what was central to Schleiermacher—consciousness of redemption. Second, the uniformity and pervasiveness of the unity of God and man in Jesus has virtually no redemptive significance for man. For Schleiermacher, on the other hand, Jesus' perfect God-consciousness qualifies him to be the Redeemer; Christology and soteriology are two sides of the same coin. But Strauss, having no place for either sin or redemption in the traditional sense,[190] needs no redeemer either. Nor, in the third place, does Strauss speak of communion with Christ in the church, for his Jesus functions as a genius in culture. For Schleiermacher, the full humanness of Jesus is important as the prototype with whom one communes in the church. But for Strauss, the theological significance of Jesus' humanness remains somewhat negative—he was not supernatural. In short, Strauss's attempt to state a positive Christology also satisfies neither faith nor science—the latter, because his Christ also is historically unconvincing, seemingly often built to specifications;[191] the former, because it is not the

190. In "Vergängliches und Bleibendes" he argued that Jesus' real task was to share with all others what was peculiarly his; this self-imparting was Jesus' contribution to the advancement of the idea of the unity of God and man in the culture (*ZfB*, pp. 105–7, 118).

191. So also Hausrath (1:325) who observes that the Hegelian approach to history had accustomed Strauss to view history in terms of categories rather than in terms of facts, and to displace concrete persons with formulae.

faith of any religious community. At best this could be called a shotgun marriage between Schleiermacher's insistence on the permanent decisiveness of Christ and a modified Hegelian way of understanding it. Strauss annulled the arrangement shortly. In the next edition, he deleted this material and reverted to earlier critical judgments.

The Rejection of Schleiermacher

In the *Glaubenslehre* Strauss undertook to show how in the development of Western thought Christian dogma emerged, produced further problems, and came into irreconcilable conflict with the modern scientific mind (including philosophy).[192] Schleiermacher is the only theologian to merit a separate discussion (par. 65).

Strauss criticized Schleiermacher in that while his point of departure was the Christian self-consciousness, he relapsed into the old church doctrine by insisting that this self-consciousness must be derived from Christ. Strauss acknowledged Schleiermacher's achievement vis-à-vis rationalism in contending that the work of Christ cannot be separated from his person, and he also acknowledged the importance of Schleiermacher's surrender of the old orthodox formulas. But he had contempt for the readiness with which current theology abandoned the castle of orthodoxy for Schleiermacher's modern, elegant pavilion. "No wonder that the old rat's nest . . . was soon abandoned by all inhabitants, save a few old house cats" (unfortunately, he does not identify them!). But what a bargain that proved to be! No one noticed how thin the new walls were until the cracks appeared. Like Lessing, Strauss preferred orthodoxy be-

192. Hausrath (1:421) remarks that whereas Schleiermacher had grounded doctrine in Christian consciousness, Strauss sees dogmas as "the perfectly correct expression of imperfect thinking of an earlier time"; since modernity has displaced the ground on which Christian doctrine rests, the latter is now deprived of its content.

cause it was consistent though untenable;[193] mediating theology only appeared tenable.

Strauss claims to go the foundation, and denies Schleiermacher's claim that the pious consciousness cannot be self-generated but must be a response to Christ; Schleiermacher cannot deny that the new level of consciousness could come from the community. Consequently, one may not claim that the modern self must postulate a sinless and perfect Christ as the ultimate ground of pious consciousness. Against Schleiermacher's insistence that Christ must be regarded as the *Urbild*, not the *Vorbild* (the archetype, not the example), because conceivably mankind could surpass the example but not the archetype, Strauss argues: (1) if mankind is so sinful, then it could not determine whether the image of Christ is perfect or not; (2) denying the human origin of the archetype requires us to deny also man's ability to make abstractions in general;[194] (3) the example does come to serve as a prototype because it tends to become idealized. Strauss claims that by these arguments Schleiermacher's claim for the necessity of Christ has been destroyed and that his Christology is in shambles. But Strauss is not yet finished.

He goes on to find the Achilles' heel where Baur had found it—in the claim that the archetype became a perfectly historical individual and that in him every historical moment bore the archetypal in itself. Limiting the perfect actualizing of the archetype to religion, as Schleiermacher did, does not help, because religion does not actualize itself

193. G. E. Lessing (1729–81) had contempt for the accommodating theology which was emerging because "under the pretext of making us reasonable Christians we are turned into extremely unreasonable philosophers." Instead of adjusting Christian doctrines, he supported orthodoxy in order to make its downfall inevitable (Henry Chadwick, ed., *Lessing's Theological Writings* [Stanford: Stanford University Press, 1957], pp. 12–13).

194. This argument is but a paraphrase of his earlier point in the *Life of Jesus* (see above, p. xiii).

perfectly in an individual either. Furthermore, Strauss objects to Schleiermacher's contention that Christ developed in a completely natural and human way and yet was not affected inwardly by externals. On the one hand, only a barbaric or sophist metaphysics would contrast the perfect inner with the imperfect outer aspect of man;[195] on the other hand, if the origin of this Christ is an act of God, we cannot conceive of its improvement in time without conceding this also to humanity as a whole. If this option is closed, we are left with an absolute act of God—something Strauss cannot abide. Furthermore, while Schleiermacher's assertion that Jesus' God-consciousness was "a veritable being of God" in him at first comports with idealist philosophy, idealism could never concede that the perfect God-consciousness could be actualized in a single individual. Nor could Schleiermacher establish, exegetically or logically, that the historical Jesus was sinless and perfect. In short, Strauss claims that Schleiermacher's Christology is built on sand.[196]

Partly Toward Schleiermacher Again

When Strauss resumed his theological work after two decades, he was permanently alienated from theologians and hostile toward all efforts to harmonize the (reduced) core of Christian theology with modern science. Since Schleiermacher's work embodied precisely this effort, in *The Life of Jesus for the German People* Strauss criticized Schleiermacher for holding that the divine should be understood as Jesus' unalloyed God-consciousness which functioned in a natural, human way. This time he tested his argument against the New Testament itself. That the divine in Christ

195. In the *Life of Jesus* he had also registered this objection, but now his tone is acerbic.

196. The appreciative essay "Schleiermacher und Daub" (written two years before; see above, note 57) not only lacks these polemics, but says in its preface that contemporary theology must develop by correcting the Hegelian Daub with Schleiermacher, and vice versa.

appeared only according to the laws of the human and the natural never occurred to the Gospel writers, he claimed, for this is precisely what miracles deny because they assume a supernatural factor. Therefore Schleiermacher must either make the miracles "natural," as the rationalists had done, or eliminate them. The New Testament authors assume that only the divine in Christ determined his work, but we do not; that the divine in Christ could have expressed itself according to the laws of human nature is our assumption, not theirs. It is as wrong for them to force us to accept their assumption as it is for us to force them to accept ours. In the last analysis, the New Testament is docetic and we are ebionitic.

It is all the more remarkable, in light of these strictures, that the historical outline of Jesus' life in Book One nonetheless has a Schleiermacherian cast to it. Paragraphs 33 and 34, devoted to Jesus' religious consciousness, begin with Schleiermacher's point that "the peculiar self-consciousness of Jesus did not develop from the messianic predictions or from the conviction of being the Messiah, but the reverse: on the basis of his self-consciousness, he came to the view that no one else was meant by the messianic predictions." Even if this is a subjective judgment rather than a historical one, observes Strauss, it can be supported historically!

But since we cannot rely on Jesus' discourses in John to ascertain his self-consciousness[197]—and since also Matthew 11:27 has a Johannine ring to it[198]—where do we find it?

197. In addition to critical issues regarding the Fourth Gospel, Strauss raises a material issue about what the Johannine Jesus claims: "The saying, 'whoever sees me sees the Father' was never spoken by a man of true religiosity." ·

198. "All things have been delivered to me by my Father; and no one knows the Son except the Father, and no one knows the Father except the Son and anyone to whom the Son chooses to reveal him" (Matt. 11:27). Strauss's rejection of the genuineness of this saying has been sustained by most subsequent scholarship.

In the Sermon on the Mount! Especially important is Matthew 5:43–48, which is unquestionably authentic, he claims, because the church could not have coined such a generous saying. Here then we have a fundamental feature of Jesus' piety: he perceived and thought of the heavenly Father as "impartial goodness," something he could not have derived from the Old Testament, but only from within himself; in the impartial goodness of his own being he knew himself to be in harmony with God. This all-encompassing love which overcomes evil with good he transferred to God. Moreover, if all men are God's sons, then they are brothers; hence the golden rule contains the fundamental idea of humanity. From this attitude stems Jesus' inner happiness, in comparison with which all external joys and sufferings lost their meaning. Consequently Jesus was indifferent to anxiety for food or clothing, ready to turn the other cheek, and to forgive without limit. Thereby Jesus actualized in himself the prophetic idea of the covenant written on the heart (Jeremiah 31:31).

This pure, beautiful disposition can be called the Hellenic element in him. Still, what the Greeks could attain only through philosophy was in Jesus the natural disposition with which his training in the Scriptures equipped him. There is no trace in Jesus of severe spiritual struggles, such as occurred in Paul, Augustine, and Luther. "Jesus appears as a beautiful person from the start, who needed only to develop from within himself . . . but not to turn about and to begin another life," which (contrary to Schleiermacher) does not exclude isolated vacillations and the necessity of ongoing effort to overcome himself.[199] Moving toward Schleiermacher again, Strauss says, "The inner development of Jesus proceeded on the whole steadily, even if not with-

199. Schleiermacher had denied that Jesus ever had a "plan," for that would imply a weighing of alternatives and hence a measure of uncertainty. See Schleiermacher's *Life of Jesus*, pp. 123-35.

out powerful effort." This is the core meaning of the dogma of the sinlessness of Jesus. Moving away from Schleiermacher again, Strauss affirms that if someone were to arrive in whom the "religious genius" of modern times had become flesh, as in Jesus' case, such a person would not depend on Jesus but would work independently.

Strauss no longer classifies Jesus as a "religious genius" but as an "enthusiast" (*Schwärmer*) because of the apocalyptic element in the Synoptics, though he is uncertain about the genuineness of all the material (par. 39). Strauss softens his classification by pointing out that no great figure is without "a dose of enthusiasm." Moreover, the preacher of God's word, by which humanity would be judged, inevitably has a decisive role in the coming judgment. This is Strauss's way of dealing with the audacity of Jesus' words about the future. Strauss is not happy with his classification of Jesus, but he cannot avoid acknowledging the apocalyptic element.

What will come to be called Jesus' "messianic consciousness" plays a significant role in this portrait of Jesus; it differs from Jesus' God-consciousness as portrayed by Schleiermacher, even though the starting point is similar: "Only the foundations of his religious distinctiveness, the ideal feature (the orientation toward the inward, toward the separation of religion from the political on the one hand and from the ceremonial on the other)" were present in Jesus before he took up the messianic idea (par. 37). Later Jesus regarded himself as Messiah by relying on the religious and moral aspects of the messianic hope; then he applied the role of the Isaianic Servant to himself. Later, opposition induced him to add also the Servant's suffering role to his self-interpretation. For Schleiermacher what was decisive in Jesus sprang spontaneously from his inmost self and was not occasioned by external circumstances, including opposition. But at decisive points, Strauss has Jesus depend on external stimuli for his own development. Though Jesus was wrong about the coming of the Kingdom, this did not involve him in what Strauss regarded as blameworthy; that is, Strauss's Jesus is also, in Straussian terms, "sinless." Still, Strauss is no more able to account historically for the rise of this religious purity in the Jesus surrounded by misshapen Judaism than is Schleiermacher, even if acknowledging external factors does make Strauss's Jesus more credible. Because Strauss denies that Christian consciousness depends on Jesus, he is freer to let Jesus inherit his environment, whether as an enthusiast for a purified eschatology or as a poor exegete.[200]

In paragraph 5 Strauss criticizes Schleiermacher's attempt to expand the natural in order to encompass those miracle stories which he retained. But Strauss is more open to their historicity than we expect. In his earlier *Life of Jesus* he traced the miracle stories to early Christian views of Jesus as Messiah, of whom miracles were expected. Now he pushed them back into the lifetime of Jesus. After Jesus was taken to be a prophet, wondrous powers were ascribed to him, and once this happened, healing also occurred—Strauss does not say that Jesus healed people, but that people were occasionally healed because they expected to be. In short, whereas Schleiermacher traced the healings to the power of Jesus' inner life to affect the body, Strauss traces them to the expectation of the sick. When Jesus replied, "Your faith has saved you," he "could not have expressed himself more honestly, more circumspectly, more correctly, more precisely."

Strauss's Jesus is no longer a "religious genius," yet he

---

200. "That Jesus shared the . . . wrong mode of exegesis of his day and people . . . is as clear as that he did not know anything yet about the Copernican astronomy; but precisely in this we see his greatness, for he read the old Scripture with a new spirit. Thereby he was a prophet even if he had been an even worse exegete" (par. 41).

stands heroically as a solitary figure against both his Jewish heritage and his followers, who scarcely understood him (par. 43). Indeed, Paul's prominence shows that there was no disciple who could extend Jesus' own ideas appropriately into the new situation. No memory of Jesus checked Paul's fantasies. "The deification of Jesus was begun by Paul . . . and was completed by the author of the Fourth Gospel who was even more removed from him in time and place." For Schleiermacher, on the other hand, the Christology and faith of the early church is part of the event of Christ.[201]

This basic point—that we may regard the life and faith of the Christian church as a supplemental source of information about Jesus—is explicitly denied (without mentioning Schleiermacher) at the end of Part Two, where Strauss deals with the rise of the Christ-myth. Even in New Testament times, the church was influenced by factors other than the impact of Jesus; besides, had Jesus returned in A.D. 70 he might not have recognized himself in what was being said about Christ (par. 99). Strauss disclaims the view that the archetypal Christ would be present in us even if the historical Jesus had never lived.[202] Actually, the ideal Christ is an evolving ideal, to which Jesus contributed significantly. But Jesus' contribution was incomplete, for what he said about the family, business, art, and the state is too limited to be useful. Nor can we fill in the gaps on the basis of his principles. Rather, in these areas, the ideal must be enriched from other quarters.

Final Repudiation of Schleiermacher

In his last work, *The Old Faith and the New,* Strauss

201. See Schleiermacher's *Life of Jesus*, p. 18.

202. This may be an allusion to Kant (see Immanuel Kant, *Religion Within the Limits of Reason Alone*, trans. T. M. Greene and H. H. Hudson [New York: Harper & Row Torchbooks, 1960], p. 56).

said *no* to the question, Are we still Christians? After show-
ing that no theologian since the Enlightenment has actually
held the real, common, literal meaning of the Christian faith
as defined by the Apostles' Creed,[203] he again devoted several sections to Schleiermacher. That great theologian surrendered everything save the centrality of Christ, but even
here he replaced the theory of Christ's vicarious satisfaction
with the theory of satisfactory vicariousness. Schleiermacher's insistence that we cannot generate the ideal Christ
ourselves because what activates our religiosity must come
from outside us is really nothing other than a remnant of the
old doctrine of the Fall. True, Christianity is peculiar
among religions, in that here alone the founder is simultaneously its content; but for precisely this reason, Christianity's foundation crumbles when it is discovered that what
is constitutive of religion does not apply to Jesus—namely,
divinity. Moreover, the Johannine Jesus is not even truly
religious, for no truly religious man asserts his identity with
God.[204] Schleiermacher's Christology is merely rhetoric.

Given the tone of *The Old Faith and the New,* it is not
surprising that Strauss is farthest removed from Schleiermacher here.[205] At every point where Schleiermacher had
sought mutually fructifying relationships between Christianity and culture, Strauss sees only hostility and antipathy.
Indeed, Jesus himself is hostile to culture, though Strauss
excuses him for this on the basis of social and political circumstances in Palestine (pars. 24–25). Interestingly, what
he asserted at the end of *The Life of Jesus for the German
People*—that Jesus remains one of those figures who ad-

203. Hausrath (2:359) observes that Strauss does not follow his stated
agenda, for he treats a number of doctrines not mentioned in the creed at
all, e.g., the Trinity, the six days of creation, the Fall, devils, and witches.
204. He had said this in *LJGP* (see above, note 197).
205. Max Huber has claimed that Schleiermacher, as opponent, is the real
heart of *The Old Faith and the New* (*Jesus Christus als Erlöser*, p. 118).

vanced humanity toward perfection—he now denies because we do not know enough about Jesus to say such a thing. We are not even sure that he did not die disillusioned. Such a dimly discerned figure can be the object of scientific investigation but can be of no practical help for life (par. 29). "The Jesus of history . . . is only a problem, but a problem cannot be the content of faith nor the model of life." This conclusion had been implicit from Strauss's first *Life of Jesus* onward, even though he appears to have resisted it from time to time.

In the supplement to the fourth edition of *The Old Faith and the New*, he mentions another problem—Jesus' apocalypticism—and says that he has wrestled with this factor from the begining of his career and learned but slowly how to deal with it.[206] Only now is he able to draw the full consequence: an apocalyptic Jesus cannot be our model. He insists that "not for the sake of what he was but for the sake of what he was not" did he become the center of the Christian faith, namely, for the sake of a prediction that did not come to pass.[207] Nor does Jesus' authentic teaching make him significant for us, for those ideas are also found elsewhere (par. 31). Inevitably he concludes that if we want to be honest we must confess, "We are no longer Christians."

206. The *Glaubenslehre* ends with a discussion of eschatology and immortality, and concludes that what Schleiermacher had said in the *Speeches* about becoming one with the infinite in the midst of the finite, and being blessed in every moment, is everything that modern science knows to say about immortality. The last sentence is: "For the beyond [*das Jenseits*] is indeed the one in all things, but in the form of the future it is the last enemy which speculative criticism must fight and, when possible, overcome" (*GL*, 2:738–39). Strauss had already asserted this in his dissertation. Since he had adhered to a monist view all his life, it is strange that he had not really faced up theologically to the apocalyptic element in Jesus before—especially since his first *Life of Jesus* recognized repeatedly the eschatological element, as Hodgson points out.

207. Strauss implies that Christology developed as compensation for the failure of the hope of Christ's return.

In connection with the second question, Do we still have religion? he makes three references to Schleiermacher. The first is ad hominem: even Schleiermacher no longer prayed in the real sense. Rather, all his prayers were spoken out of habit from his younger years and out of respect for his congregation, with whom he did not want to share his critical belief that prayer does not affect God (par. 37). In the second reference, Strauss rejects Schleiermacher's view of God and the world (in the *Speeches*); he denies that the one is the ground of the many and asserts that the one is *in* the many, and vice versa—a panentheist position. There can be no *source* of the universal (par. 39). Here we see Strauss's lifelong adherence to monism and his unrelenting hostility toward every form of dualism and theism. In paragraph 66 this is made explicit. The third reference is to Schleiermacher's conception of religion as a feeling of absolute dependence, which Strauss affirms because he redefines it. Man does indeed have a feeling of dependency insofar as he prays to the sun or a stream on which he feels dependent and which he seeks to influence (par. 42). But to understand this feeling rightly, Strauss appeals to Feuerbach: the origin and nature of religion is wish. If men had no wishes they would have no gods. The pure feeling of dependence would suppress man and destroy him; he gains a measure of freedom by trying to control that upon which he is dependent. Thus, religion belongs to man's immaturity (par. 43).[208] In fact, "the religious domain in the human soul is like the area of the American Indians, which . . . is year by year ever more restricted by their white neighbors." Nonetheless, religion is not extinct; what remains is the sense of absolute dependence on the whole. Whether we call this God or the universal is unimportant, and in the face of this

208. In "Vergängliches und Bleibendes" Strauss averred that man will never be without religion, and that true religion without Jesus is impossible (*ZfB*, p. 131).

mystery Strauss would rather say too little than too much. "We demand for our universal the same piety which the old style pious person did for his God. Our feeling for the all reacts, when it is attacked, precisely in a religious way." Only on this basis will Strauss concede that he still has religion.[209] Throughout, Strauss reaps the harvest of his own relentless "either/or" and of his longstanding contempt for mediating theology. "If the old faith was absurd, then the modernized . . . is twofold and threefold absurd. The old church faith really contradicted only reason, but not itself; the new faith contradicts itself in all parts, so how could it then agree with reason?" (par. 87; see above, note 193).

The Christ of Faith and the Jesus of History

Tracing the fluctuations of Strauss's ongoing debate with Schleiermacher has provided the setting of the present volume. When Rütenik published Schleiermacher's lectures on the life of Jesus in 1864, Strauss seized the opportunity to deal thoroughly with Schleiermacher's Christology and, through it, to attack once more the prevailing Christology of the church.[210] In the foreword Strauss says that he can do this, because "only now, a generation after his death, has it more or less caught up with him." He himself sets the book in context: "The illusion . . . that Jesus could have been a man in the full sense and still as a single person stand above the whole humanity, is the claim which still blocks the harbor of Christian theology against the open sea of

209. It is not really the case that whereas Schleiermacher attempted to move the "cultured despisers of religion" toward a more favorable stance, Strauss tried to confirm their antipathy, as Adolf Hilgenfeld's review charged (*Zeitschrift für Wissenschaftliche Theologie* 16 (1873): 305). Strauss's antipathy is for diluted liberal Christianity, not for religion as he understood it.

210. In preparation he read widely in Schleiermacher, including four volumes of Schleiermacher's letters (Ziegler, 2:620).

rational science. To break this chain is the purpose of the present work, as it has always been of all my theological writings."

Strauss's critique falls into three parts. In Part One he criticizes the work of the editor Rütenik, then deals with Schleiermacher's theological presuppositions and his view of the Gospels. In Part Two he takes the reader through Schleiermacher's lectures and puts his finger on important problems; his own critique is woven into the discussion at certain points. In Part Three he sums up the issues as he sees them. The book is written so well that it is unnecessary to provide a précis of the argument here.

It may be useful, however, to take note of the conclusion toward which Strauss presses—that the New Testament view of the person of Christ cannot be harmonized with our concepts of human life and with the laws of nature. For the New Testament, Christ is supernatural, and for us he is natural, and even if a great deal of the supernatural can be subtracted from the Gospels, what remains cannot be made credible by expanding the natural, as Schleiermacher had tried to do. Inevitably, "Schleiermacher . . . is a supernaturalist in Christology; in criticism and exegesis a rationalist." This strange mixture is readily explainable. Schleiermacher *must* be a rationalist in exegesis in order to remain a supernaturalist in Christology: "In order not to lose the supernatural Christ as a historical personality he cannot surrender the Gospels as historical sources." From Schleiermacher's failure, we learn that theology must either cease viewing Jesus as a supernatural being or cease viewing the Gospels as historical sources in the strict sense. One cannot have it both ways. If Jesus is supernatural, the Gospels are not historical sources; if the Gospels are historical sources about a wholly human being, Jesus is no longer supernatural. Positively this means that we must regard Jesus as a man like any other and the Gospels as the oldest collection of myths which were attached to him. In short, the Jesus of history must be radically separated from the Christ of faith.

Schleiermacher's theology, Strauss says, was the last attempt to make us agree with church theology, and since he failed, this should no longer be attempted. The old Christian theology had integrity, but Schleiermacher's, and all mediating Christology, lacked it. "We may no longer . . . speak of a redeemer after we have given up the God-man who offered himself as a sacrifice for the sins of the world . . . a Christ who, without knowing himself to be the God-man in the strict sense, had called himself the light of the world would have been a braggart. Whoever calls him this without taking him to be that is a flatterer. . . ." Schleiermacher's passion to identify the ideal Christ with a particular person is an anachronism in Schleiermacher's own sophisticated modern theology. Moreover, this Christ lacks reality; "he is only a memory from a long-forgotten time, like the light of a distant star which still strikes the eye today although the body from which it shone has been out for years."

THE LEGACY OF STRAUSS'S CRITIQUE

Though *The Christ of Faith and the Jesus of History* is no landmark in the history of theology, it so well exposes fundamental issues in Christology that through it we can assess the theological work of Strauss as a whole and relate his issues to our own questions. Strauss's theological work illumines post-Enlightenment theology as a whole. However, we shall rely on three questions, each with several components: (1) Does Christianity have a future? (2) Does Christology have a future? and (3) Does the study of Jesus have a future? From Strauss's lifelong concerns these questions flow through *The Christ of Faith* into our own theological work, and so become his legacy to us.

Does Christianity Have a Future?

Strauss's increasingly negative answer is attributable only in part to his personal alienation from Christian theology. As he saw the issue, it was primarily a matter of intellectual honesty. As noted, from Hegel's distinction between representation and concept Strauss inferred that philosophy replaced religion. This conclusion was all the easier because Strauss viewed Christianity as a body of beliefs and dogmas. Once he had identified the ultimate truth of Christianity as the identity of God and man, he had located the idea in the image, and hence could abandon the latter for the former. This was reinforced by Hegel's view that in his own philosophy, Spirit was expressing itself in a new, definitive way which incorporated past truth while transcending it—that is, the era in which philosophy recognized the identity of God and man was now arriving. Christianity, on the other hand, was for Strauss a system of beliefs which represented God as distinct from the world, and whose eschatology epitomized this with the belief in judgment and salvation. Christian dogmas, taken as statements of knowledge of God and man, were now outmoded by modern scientific knowledge, including philosophy. Hence Christianity had no future because its knowledge of God and the world was superseded; the dualism inherent in its representational dogmas was now seen to be inadequate logically and transcended (*aufgehoben*) historically. From this perspective Strauss saw himself battling for the truth of the future.

From this angle of vision, Strauss assessed Schleiermacher and found him wanting at every point that mattered. However, it is at least doubtful whether he understood him. It was Schleiermacher's aim to assure Christianity of a future by distinguishing it from a system of beliefs. The essential independence of religious consciousness from metaphysics or from Kantian practical reason was the cornerstone of his theological construction. From his early study of Schleiermacher, Strauss apparently retained but one concept—the primary role of consciousness as the ground of theology. But whereas Strauss spoke of the consciousness of identity, Schleiermacher spoke of the consciousness of immediate dependence on God and of redemption by communion with Christ. Furthermore, for Schleiermacher, the essential independence of religious consciousness implied that philosophy/science and Christian faith could coexist in the same person since they were not of the same order; theological doctrines, being the explication of Christian consciousness, could not conflict with scientific knowledge of the world. Doctrines which did not explicate Christian consciousness could be surrendered without loss. What the future of Christianity depended on was the vitality of the Christian community in which consciousness of redemption was communicated; Strauss, on the other hand, had no place for the church, since it was obviated by the real truth of incarnation in humanity.

Following Baur, Strauss inevitably regarded Schleiermacher as a "mediating theologian," one who made minimal concessions to modernity while asking in exchange that the modern mind be less hostile. Schleiermacher did, of course, surrender (with relief) a number of doctrines, such as that of the virgin birth, just as he sought to make an opening for the miraculous by insisting that we cannot rule something out as being supernatural until we know the limits of the natural. Since Schleiermacher was, apart from Baur and his disciples, the only theologian Strauss took seriously, rejecting Schleiermacher involved rejecting all lesser mediating theologies as well. If Christianity had no future along *Schleiermacherstrasse*, it had none at all.

From this issue and its several implications four trends emerged: (1) the orthodox tacitly agreed with Strauss that Christianity is a body of knowledge of God and the world, but undertook a vigorous defense; (2) the mediating theologians sought by various devices to reconcile modern knowledge and Christian knowledge; (3) Protestant liberalism generally followed Schleiermacher and attempted to distinguish carefully theological from scientific knowledge, and to ground the former in religious experience; (4) others followed Strauss, who surrendered Christianity without regret in favor of modern science and philosophy. These alternatives had existed previously, of course, but Strauss sharpened the issues so well that the whole of Protestant theology was ruptured until the present.[211]

Orthodoxy in America was expressed in various forms of fundamentalism and through the "Princeton orthodoxy" of B. B. Warfield. Mediating theology has taken such diverse forms that it is difficult to find typical examples of it. Yet, like today's conservatives, it accepted moderate biblical criticism and the modernized world view which it sought to harmonize with classical theology.

More interesting are the liberals, who inherited Schleiermacher's concern for grounding theology in Christian experience. Their leader, Albrecht Ritschl,[212] began his career under Baur's tutelage, but soon moved away toward Reformation theology and emphasized the experience of justification and forgiveness of sins—categories which repulsed Strauss. Moreover, Ritschl and those influenced by him (for example, Adolf von Harnack and Wilhelm Herrmann in Germany, and Walter Rauschenbusch in America) renounced metaphysics and returned to a Kantian accent on the moral base of religion. In a way, this permitted them to be mediating theologians as well, for if religion had a

---

211. This may be traced in Elert, *Der Kampf um das Christentum.*

212. For a useful survey see David L. Mueller, *An Introduction to the Theology of Albrecht Ritschl* (Philadelphia: Westminster, 1969). See also Philip Hefner's excellent introduction in *Albrecht Ritschl: Three Essays* (Philadelphia: Fortress Press, 1972), pp. 1–50.

moral base, they were free to champion scientific biblical criticism and to see in the historical experience of Western culture evidence of the truth of Christianity. While this earned them the epithet "culture theologians" after Kierkegaard was rediscovered, they saw themselves as church theologians. Even today, liberal Protestant theology, for all its diversity and intramural polemic, remains heir to Schleiermacher's concern to ground the viability of Christianity for the modern world in some form of experience rather than in metaphysics or science.[213]

The role of Strauss with regard to the question of Christianity's future is manifest in the fact that his *Life of Jesus* was the last theological work to have excited the whole culture. Later, the orthodox defended a ghetto they did not recognize, and the mediators built bridges which stood on but one side of the stream because the secular world was no longer interested. Worst of all, because Christianity was being explicitly rejected, and sometimes religion as well, the Ritschlian liberals became theologians of a shrinking minority, and of a particular socioeconomic stratum at that. Insofar as the masses remained Christian, they remained conservative (if not fundamentalist) and pietistic, because they were touched by the evangelical movements. But it is Strauss's relation to an outright rejection of Christianity that merits further comment.

Strauss found himself defenseless against Feuerbach. Having affirmed the identity of God and man, he could only agree when Feuerbach replaced this "objective" identity with a "subjective" one, claiming that this identity is grounded not in the nature of the divine Spirit but in the needs of man, and that the word *God* refers to a projection of man—from which he becomes so alienated that he

213. Process theology is, of course, a protest against such efforts, contending that modern science cannot be isolated permanently from theology.

worships it and expects salvation from it. Nor did Strauss have anything to say to Marx, who argued that the moving force of history is not the divine Spirit but a very secular economic factor.

The renunciations of Christianity that came from the school of Hegel were but part of a much larger phenomenon. Nineteenth-century Germany saw significant intellectuals openly adopt paganism in place of Christianity. Schopenhauer turned to Indian religions; Wagner turned to Germanic gods; formative for the mind of the intelligentsia were the writings of Goethe, Schiller, and Hölderlin, whose works were permeated by a fascination for the gods of Greece.[214] As part of the reaction against the new empire there arose an "ideology of resentment," as Fritz Stern calls it,[215] marked also by explicit hostility toward Christianity. Particularly influential was the notorious Paul de Lagarde (1827–91), who began as a disciple of Hengstenberg but reversed himself, repudiated Christianity as being too Jewish, and called for a new Germanic religion purged of liberalism and Jewishness.[216] Nietzsche's contempt for Christianity is well known. At the beginning of the nineteenth century, Schleiermacher could still reach the "cultured despisers" of religion, and Hegel could still be believed when he called Christianity the "absolute religion"; but by the end of the century all this had changed. By the mid-twentieth century Christianity, for vast numbers, had become so thoroughly antiquated that calling for its repudiation would have seemed anachronistic. Nor was this a

214. This has been analyzed by E. M. Butler in *The Tyranny of Greece over Germany* (Boston: Beacon Press, 1958; originally published by Cambridge University Press in 1935).

215. Fritz Stern, *The Politics of Cultural Despair* (Garden City: Doubleday Anchorbooks, 1965; orginally published by the University of California Press in 1961), p. 12.

216. For a good biographical treatment see ibid., ch. 1.

phenomenon peculiar to Germany; the French Revolution had already buried Christianity before Strauss was born, and among the Anglo-Saxons, the demise of Christianity proceeded relentlessly even though, on the surface, churches and paraecclesiastical movements thrived. The drastic de-Christianization of Christendom is not really Strauss's legacy, for he neither inaugurated it nor gave it definitive shape. But it is the context in which his legacy must be seen; at a decisive juncture, he gave this snowball a significant push.

Does Christology Have a Future?

Strauss's answer was a clear *no* from the start. But, largely because of Strauss, christological questions have dominated Protestant theology ever since. From the web of issues and alternative proposals three considerations, each somewhat complex in itself, merit further comment.

Christology and Soteriology

The first consideration is that of the relationship of Christology to soteriology. To begin with, the conclusion of *The Christ of Faith* shows that Strauss is aware that the need for Christology disappears if redemption in Christ disappears. Schleiermacher would have agreed. For Schleiermacher, of course, this redemption was a given; the task of theology was not to show that it is necessary or possible, but to give an adequate account of it.[217] For Strauss, on the other hand, redemption is no longer a tenable

217. For Schleiermacher, the task of theology was "only to give guidance . . . for determining whether the expressions of any religious consciousness are Christian or not, and whether the Christian quality is strongly and clearly expressed in them. . . . We renounce all attempts to prove the truth or necessity of Christianity . . ." (*The Christian Faith*, trans. H. R. Mackintosh and J. S. Stewart [Edinburgh: T. & T. Clark, 1928; New York: Harper Torchbooks, 1963], par. 11, sec. 5). In short, "Christian doctrines are accounts of the Christian religious affections set forth in speech" (par. 15).

category because it requires particular divine action. Strauss was not an atheist, except in that he denied that God was extrinsic to the world. But an immanent God who actualizes himself in the whole of the world and mankind is no longer the God of redemption and judgment. What for Schleiermacher was a given, for Strauss was a problem.

Consciousness of redemption implies consciousness of sin, for sin and redemption, however understood, are always coordinated. While Schleiermacher's view of sin has been criticized as lacking the depth of traditional Christianity, it is nonetheless clear that he did try to recast the traditional doctrines, including original sin, in ways consistent with his emphasis on God-consciousness.[218] On the other hand, Strauss lacked not only a consciousness of sin but a sense of empathy with those who had it, to say nothing of solidarity with the downtrodden and exploited whose plight set Karl Marx into motion. Strauss's last book reveals what had been there all along—an identification with the intelligentsia and sophisticated landowners. Nor did his own bitter fate, or that of the revolution of 1848, lead him to reflect theologically on the nature of man; it was enough to blame stupidity and prejudice. Though he could speak of religion as the consciousness of unity between the infinite and the finite, human finitude apparently presented him with no deep moral problems which called for some form of redemption. Hegel's dialectic apparently succeeded sufficiently in overcoming antinomies that the theodicy problem disappeared. Strauss unavoidably had an optimistic view of man in the modern technological world. With no fundamental plight to which redemption was an alternative, it was meaningless to speak of a redeemer. Accordingly, Christology had no future in the world.

But still, there is this man Jesus. If a soteriological

218. See *The Christian Faith*, pars. 62–82.

understanding of Jesus is no longer relevant, how is he to be understood? Strauss did not get beyond classifying him as a religious genius. At the end, Strauss could no longer say that much, for Jesus was not interested in the things which concerned Strauss: the fine arts, politics of the new empire, technology, and science. It should not be overlooked, however, that Strauss neither returned to the deist view of Jesus as the teacher of timeless morality, nor followed Engels in seeing Jesus and Christianity as an aborted proletarian movement. He had too much historical consciousness for the former and was too bourgeois to pursue the latter. Nor did he slip into contempt for Jesus, as did Nietzsche. Jesus remained a figure who in his own time and place made a significant contribution to humanity. Still, such a Jesus can be neither the object of faith nor the ground of redemption. In short, the historical Jesus is one thing, the Christ of faith is another. If man does not need redemption, this separation of the Jesus of history from the Christ of faith, and the death of Christology that accompanies it, is not to be lamented but celebrated. Only then, Strauss thought, could Jesus be appreciated for what he actually was. But if man does need redemption, and if there continues to exist a community which contends that in Jesus it has come to know redemption, can there still be a Christology after Strauss has exposed how little of the historical Jesus we can know?

The Historical Jesus and the Christ of Faith

This brings us to the second consideration. Has Strauss separated properly the historical Jesus from the Christ of faith? If not, what are the alternatives? To answer these questions fully is to tell the story of Protestant theology since Strauss, a task as impossible as unnecessary here. However, a look at several alternatives may help us focus Strauss's legacy. These alternatives, on the one hand, all agree with Strauss that there is a fundamental distinction between the Jesus of history and the Christ of faith; on the other hand, they move toward Schleiermacher in the various ways in which they work with the distinction. Because Strauss sought to force a choice between Schleiermacher and himself, he would probably have been contemptuous of the whole development.

We begin with Martin Kähler,[219] who agreed with Strauss that the historically reconstructed Jesus was one thing and the Christ of faith another, and therefore refused to separate them. He agreed with Strauss[220] in contending that the Gospels do not permit us to write a biography of Jesus (p. 48), that they are not eyewitness reports but faith-impregnated accounts, that the "inner development of a sinless person is as inconceivable to us as life in the Sandwich Islands is to a Laplander" (p. 53), and that "Christian faith and the history of Jesus repel each other like oil and water" (p. 74). Nonetheless, from considerations such as these he draws quite the opposite conclusion from that drawn by Strauss—that the whole life of Jesus is a "blind alley" (p. 46).

Having seen the consequences of separating the Jesus of history from the Christ of faith, Kähler refuses to let that separation occur. For one thing, he rejects Strauss's view that the historically reconstructed Jesus is truly freed from Christology. The Jesus of biographers, he claims, is nothing other than theology smuggled into the church under the guise of objective history (p. 56). While not rejecting outright the historical study of Jesus, Kähler insists that the

219. Martin Kähler, *The So-Called Historical Jesus and the Historic Biblical Christ*, ed. and with an introduction by Carl E. Braaten (Philadelphia: Fortress Press, 1964); all page references are to this edition. See also D. L. Deegan, "Martin Kähler: Kerygma and Gospel History," *Scottish Journal of Theology* 16 (1963):50–67.

220. Strauss is "present" in Kähler's discussion far more than the few references to him (pp. 54, 55, 79) suggest.

object of inquiry is the Jesus Christ who cannot be contrasted with his effects (Christianity) but must be continuous with them. Hence "the real Christ is the Christ who is preached" (p. 66). Schleiermacher would have agreed that *"Christ himself is the originator of the biblical picture of the Christ"* (p. 87; Kähler's italics). Kähler could write like this because, even more than Schleiermacher, he was a theologian of Christendom, able to say that we do not need the historical Jesus inasmuch as the effective, biblical Christ has been implanted within us since childhood (pp. 79, 85), and through him we know redemption and forgiveness of sins. Even though Kähler had appropriated Strauss's critical views of the Gospels, Strauss would have regarded Kähler's choice of the biblical (that is, the mythical) Christ as a relapse. But he would have been pleased to know that for the time being, at any rate, Kähler was a voice in the wilderness.

The strategy of Protestant liberalism was more complex. It not only accepted the separation of the Christ of faith from the Jesus of history, but opted for the latter; then it made this Jesus the Christ of faith. The Ritschlians were opposed to virtually everything Strauss had fought for, except the freedom of historical critical inquiry and the separation of Jesus from the Christ of orthodox Christology. It is not known to me whether Strauss's reading in connection with his return to theology included Ritschl, whose important work appeared after Strauss's death. But clearly Strauss would have regarded Ritschlianism the way Herod regarded Jesus: "John, whom I beheaded, has been raised." Instead of philosophical concepts replacing religious images and representations, the representations returned, Reformation theology included—and in conjunction with the Jesus of history!

It is useful to note the characteristic emphases of Ritschlian theology. (1) However diverse internally, it presented a united front against metaphysics. "The idea of God does not belong to metaphysics," Ritschl claimed.[221] The history of Christianity was not the story of the fate of the idea of the union of God and man, but the story of how the church was or was not true to the idea of justification by faith. Thus Christianity became once more a matter of faith, of personal religion, and doctrines were grounded, not in speculative philosophy, but in the experiences of faith and forgiveness—a reformulation of Schleiermacher's ideas. (2) With the return to the Bible as the witness to revelation, and to Luther as its soundest expositor, went a concentration on sin and guilt; accordingly there was a renewed interest in the meaning of Jesus' death. (3) The Ritschlians, being committed to the reconstruction of the past "as it really was" rather than as the manifestation of the absolute, were committed to the recovery of the historical Jesus as well.[222] Indeed, he was central to their theology. They could not reject the christological categories found in the New Testament (for example, the Son of God) but recast them in terms of Jesus' own religious faith and vocation. Because Jesus committed himself to God's kingdom, and because as our representative he relates us to God by the power of his life-commitment, we may say that he is the Son of God. Jesus has the value of God for us, and so may be said to be divine. The Jesus of history, they were convinced, could be known clearly enough to be able to affirm such things.[223]

With the collapse of Protestant liberalism after World

221. "Theology and Metaphysics" in Hefner, *Albrecht Ritschl: Three Essays*, p. 157.

222. See D. L. Deegan, "Albrecht Ritschl on the Historical Jesus," *Scottish Journal of Theology* 15 (1962): 133–50.

223. See Adolf von Harnack, *What Is Christianity?* (New York: Harper & Row Torchbooks, 1957), and Wilhelm Herrmann, *The Communion of the Christian with God*, ed. and with an introduction by Robert Voelkel, Lives of Jesus Series (Philadelphia: Fortress Press, 1971). These works are landmarks in the Ritschlian understanding of Jesus. For an alternative approach see Alfred Loisy, *The Gospel and the Church*, ed. Bernard Scott, Lives of Jesus Series (Philadelphia: Fortress Press, 1976).

War I, a third alternative emerged—the theology of the Word of God associated with Barth and appropriated by Bultmann. In Bultmann's theology, the separation of the Jesus of history from the Christ of faith was central, as it was for Strauss, but Bultmann combined this with Kähler's emphasis on the preached Christ.

No one has pressed harder the separation of the Christ of faith and the Jesus of history than Bultmann. For Bultmann as for Strauss, this was a critical necessity inherent in modern historiography. He too saw the New Testament portrait of Jesus as mythicized by the early Christian kerygma,[224] just as he agreed with Strauss that the modern world view made it impossible for us to believe literally what the New Testament says about him. But whereas Strauss argued that the myth must be abandoned, Bultmann sought to restate its existential meaning, to "demythologize" the kerygma.[225] A demythologized gospel could summon the hearer to a decision for or against the faith. This demythologized gospel was not an account of the historical Jesus recovered by substracting the myth. In fact, presenting the historical Jesus in preaching would threaten the gospel itself, because recovering such a Jesus was the work of man. But the work of man cannot be the object of faith.[226] In other words, Bultmann insisted on the necessity of separating the Christ of faith from the Jesus of history for theological

224. For an analysis see Günther Backhaus, *Kerygma und Mythos bei David Friedrich Strauss und Rudolf Bultmann.*

225. Rudolf Bultmann, "New Testament and Mythology," *Kerygma and Myth*, ed. H. W. Bartsch, trans. R. H. Fuller (London: S.P.C.K., 1957), pp. 1–44; see also Bultmann, *Jesus Christ and Mythology* (New York: Scribner's, 1958).

226. Bultmann regularly viewed the effort to get behind early Christian preaching to Jesus himself as an attempt to legitimate one's faith, that is, to base it on something other than the Word. Hence he could argue that rejecting the historical Jesus as the content of faith was simply being faithful to justification by faith, since the historical Jesus was recovered by human effort—i.e., was a form of "works."

reasons. Only if they were separate could it become evident that the Jesus of history is not the content of preaching or the object of faith; only the preached Christ, the Christ present in the Word of God, could be that.

Bultmann's rejection of liberalism brings with it a repudiation of Schleiermacher as well, including the latter's identification of the Jesus of history with the Christ of faith. But does it also include a rejection of the experience of redemption as the subject matter of theology? Despite Bultmann's tacit assertion that it does, the matter is not too clear. True, Bultmann is not at all interested in tracing pious feeling to its source in Jesus' God-consciousness or his inner life (as was Herrmann; see above, note 223), but he does make faith's reflection on itself central, and decrees that God may be spoken of legitimately only in faith. A careful analysis will show, I believe, that there is far more Schleiermacher in Bultmann than one might suppose. Be that as it may, the radical disjuncture of the Jesus of history from the Christ of faith for which Strauss argued is carried out by Bultmann precisely because he opts for the Christ of faith. Schleiermacher might not have been pleased, but he would have understood. Strauss would not have been pleased and would not have understood.

But this radical separation of the Jesus of history from the Christ of the Word and of faith raised the question of whether the latter has any basis in the former at all. In affirming that it has, another alternative was developed—the "new quest" of the historical Jesus.[227] This combines Bultmann's emphasis on the Word with Schleiermacher's emphasis on Jesus' inner life, restated as Jesus' own faith. Thus Gerhard Ebeling and Ernst Fuchs argue that the Jesus who was recovered from the critical analysis of the sources was not left alongside the kerygma nor behind it as a mere

227. The standard survey remains that by James M. Robinson, *A New Quest of the Historical Jesus* (Naperville: Allenson, 1959).

fact.[228]   Rather, the understanding of man's existence before God which is built into the genuine materials could be shown, they argue, to be repeated in the church's kerygma (in what Strauss called "myth"). Thus Jesus becomes the criterion of the kerygma.   Furthermore, Fuchs emphasizes Jesus' desire to share his own faith; for Ebeling, Jesus is not the object of faith but the witness to faith, whose own testimony engenders faith in others.   Schleiermacher and Herrmann would agree with both claims, even though it is a post-Bultmannian Jesus, greatly "reduced" by criticism, that is in view.

Since Strauss, there has been no letup in the critical effort to ascertain as precisely as possible the authentic Jesus tradition (the genuinely historical Jesus) by separating this from the Gospels as they stand (the Christ of the early Christian faith).   But ever since Strauss the dominant question has been: Once this separation is made, what is one to do with the results?   Strauss succeeded fully in bequeathing this question to his successors.   But he failed totally in thinking that his separation spelled the end of Christology and of faith directed toward a particular human being who could be understood in wholly human terms. Despite Kähler and Bultmann, Christian faith and theology were repeatedly able to find in the historical Jesus one through whom redemption, in some form, was experienced. And so the historical Jesus becomes the Christ of faith again.[229]   Each time this happens, the influence of Schleiermacher appears.   The whole story is an account of the swing of the pendulum toward the one or the other.   Set-

228. See Gerhard Ebeling, *Theology and Proclamation*, trans. John Riches (Philadelphia: Fortress Press, 1966) and the essays by Ernst Fuchs, *Studies of the Historical Jesus*, trans. Andrew Scobie (Naperville: Allenson, 1964).
229. See Leander E. Keck, *A Future for the Historical Jesus* (Nashville: Abingdon, 1971).

ting that pendulum in motion is the heart of Strauss's legacy.

The Incarnation

There is yet a third aspect of the future of Christology which Strauss considered—the incarnation. Strauss's denial that an incarnation in a single person is possible has not been accepted. The most impressive recent attempt to make the incarnation central to Christology is that of Paul Tillich.[230] Nonetheless Tillich finds it necessary to qualify the category by insisting that it is not transmutation but the appearance in time of an eternal relationship, and that what appears is not a divine being but the New Being.[231] Curiously, he does not find it necessary to mention Strauss, though he rejects Strauss's main objection—that the absolute or ideal Christ could not incarnate itself in an individual. To the contrary, Tillich asserts, "If there were no personal life in which existential estrangement had been overcome, the New Being [what Strauss would have called the ideal Christ] would have remained a quest and an expectation and would not be a reality in time and space. Only if the existence is conquered in *one* point—a personal life representing existence as a whole—is it conquered in principle. . . ."[232] Strauss is rejected but not answered. It is curious that these two figures, both of whom had drunk deeply of the idealist wine, should speak in opposite ways

230. Paul Tillich, *Systematic Theology*, 3 vols., vol. 2, *Existence and the Christ* (Chicago: University of Chicago Press, 1951–63); all references are to this volume. See also D. Moody Smith, "The Historical Jesus in Paul Tillich's Christology," *Journal of Religion* 46 (1966): 131–47.

231. Tillich also speaks of the New Being as essential man, Essential God-Manhood, Eternal God-Manhood, or "the eternal relation of God to man."

232. Tillich, p. 198. He also writes that the New Being had to appear in a personal life, "for the particularities of being are completely actual in personal life alone" (p. 120).

about the incarnation, and that in doing so, Tillich should not find it necessary to speak to Strauss directly.

Since Tillich's Christology is admittedly Schleiermacherian,[233] it is not surprising that he deals tacitly with other contentions advanced by Strauss. For one thing, whereas Strauss denied that finite and sinful man is incapable of conceiving the ideal Christ, Tillich says that a picture of the New Being imagined by those who were not Jesus' disciples would have expressed only "their untransformed existence in their quest for a New Being," not the New Being itself (p. 115). Moreover, Tillich recognized the soteriological ground of Christology and tacitly denies that the early church could have mythicized Jesus the way Strauss said it did. Tillich implies that the Gospel picture of Jesus results from transformation by the New Being in Jesus. The power of the New Being meets us in the biblical picture, and whoever this New Being heals knows that Jesus was its bearer.[234] "Faith itself is the immediate . . . evidence of the New Being within and under the conditions of existence" (p. 114).

Throughout the diverse New Testament, Tillich sees the power of the New Being shine through as the "undisrupted unity of the center of his being with God; second, as the serenity and majesty of him who preserves this unity against all attacks coming from estranged existence; and third, as the self-surrendering love which represents and actualizes the divine love in taking the existential self-destruction upon himself" (p. 138). Had Strauss objected that this represents the arbitrary assumption that the ideal Christ is identical with Jesus, he would have failed to read Tillich with

233. Tillich, p. 150. He sees that "the ontological element" differentiates his Christology from Schleiermacher's.
234. Therefore Tillich, following his teacher Martin Kähler, insists that the historically reconstructed Jesus recovered from the Gospels is irrelevant (pp. 101–07).

due care. Tillich, in the first place, admits that historical inquiry cannot show that Jesus was the bearer of the New Being, nor can faith (p. 107). Moreover, he does not say that Jesus *was* the New Being, or that the New Being *became* Jesus, but that the New Being appeared in him; it is Jesus as the Christ who manifests the New Being, and his being the Christ depends on his being accepted as the Christ. As if to get past Strauss, Tillich agrees that the ideal is not identified with a particular human being but only becomes actual in him and through him. We may surmise that Strauss would not have been satisfied.

Does the Study of Jesus Have a Future?

Strauss could not foresee the avalanche of books and articles about the historical Jesus, to say nothing of the blizzard of polemics among those who produced them. Even today, a clear-cut *yes* is still not in hand, despite undeniable advances in historical knowledge and in methodological sophistication. Indeed, these very advances have made the question acute.

Before factoring this question into three component parts, it is well to remind ourselves of the advances Strauss himself achieved. First, he forced into bankruptcy three competitors: the supernaturalist defense of the historical accuracy of the Gospels, the rationalist attempt to rescue their history by tracing the miracle stories to the misunderstanding of observers, and Reimarus's view that Gospel stories were designed to conceal the facts from the public. For Strauss, the difference between the reports and the facts is not due to deception but to the spontaneous creativity of faith. The miracle stories are not to be rewritten and corrected into accounts of natural events but must be seen for what they were intended to be. Thanks to Strauss, a return to supernaturalism, naturalism, or radical reconstruction based on deceit is untenable. Secondly, Strauss showed how the miracle stories are to be understood, though he was not as far from Schleiermacher as he thought. Today we also assume that the exorcisms and healings were psychosomatic events which we do not yet fully understand, just as the so-called nature miracles are seen as stories generated for the sake of their religious meanings. Thirdly, Strauss's contention that the postresurrection appearances of Jesus were visions grounded in an intensified psychic condition has come to be widely accepted, even though many would refuse to say that resurrection is "humbug" (as he once called it) and would insist that "something" outside the disciples triggered those visions. And finally, though Strauss himself was not wholly free from the rationalism he derided, he nonetheless saw clearly the difference between exegesis of the text and historical reconstruction. He showed that it is better to be fair to a text one cannot believe than to misinterpret it so that one can. This enabled him to see more clearly than many of his successors the character of the Fourth Gospel.

Through these advances, Strauss forged the question of whether the study of Jesus can go beyond him to recover a historically credible Jesus. The discussion of whether the study of Jesus has a future requires us to deal with three factors which he did not treat satisfactorily: criteria for genuineness, the relationship of Jesus and the church, and the inner coherence of the Jesus materials.

Criteria for Genuineness

We still lack criteria for detecting the full range of genuine Jesus material in the Gospels. In fact, there has been a steady erosion of criteria which has gone largely undetected. Strauss himself, of course, was not interested in criteria for genuineness; what interested him was criteria for the unhistorical, which he called myth. What remained after this mythic material was substracted was of minor interest. Procedurally, however, we still follow Strauss—we substract the material which is not historically accurate and "Jesus" is what remains. Baur, who criticized Strauss for not analyzing the Gospels before analyzing the materials in them, understood the Gospels in terms of particular points of view of the Evangelists and the circles they represented, that is, he related them to party struggles and intramural polemics. Roughly speaking, form criticism stood closer to Strauss, redaction criticism to Baur. For the task of Gospel criticism, Baur and redaction criticism can only be regarded as advances; for historical reconstruction, however, form and redaction criticism work together like upper and lower millstones. Between them they have ground down the criteria for historical knowledge of Jesus to the degree that such knowledge is exceedingly difficult to find.

Several factors combined to produce this situation. First, Strauss's positive criteria for identifying myth have become negative criteria for locating what is genuinely historical—that is, those materials are considered to be genuinely from Jesus which differ from both Judaism and Christianity. Only by substracting from the Gospels the material which looks suspiciously Christian or carried along from Judaism could one arrive at indubitably genuine material. All historical study of Jesus has used the negative criterion with respect to Jesus and Christianity; after Colani discovered that Mark 13 is a little Jewish apocalypse,[235] the same criterion was applied to Jesus and Judaism as well. Secondly, the effort to test the Jesus traditions against both Judaism and Christianity required growing expertise as the possibili-

235. Timothée Colani, *Jésus et les croyances messianiques de son temps* (Strasbourg, 1864). Colani argued that Mark 13:5–31 was a Jewish apocalypse, and that Jesus himself must be distinguished sharply from apocalyptic thought. For a history of this theory see G. R. Beasley-Murray, *Jesus and the Future* (New York: St. Martin's Press, 1956). Beasley-Murray's attempt to reclaim this material as part of the genuine Jesus tradition has not succeeded.

ties grew geometrically. We have come to see that the first revolt in 66–70 C.E. produced far-reaching changes within Judaism, and that prior to this Judaism was a much more diverse phenomenon than it was in the second century when the early rabbinic texts were written. Similarly the "history of religions school" taught us to see that early Christianity was a much more diverse movement and that its relations with Judaism and Hellenism were far more complex than we had surmised. For the study of Jesus, this means that the possibilities of consigning the various elements of the Jesus traditions to stages in the development of Christianity or to groups within it are expanded drastically. What does not fit Jerusalem Christianity can now be attributed to later Hellenistic-Jewish or Hellenistic-gentile Christianity. Inevitably, the richer the possibilities for attributing items in the tradition to stages and groups, the more that which remains attributable to Jesus seems to shrink. Thirdly, Strauss and the form critics read the Gospels as deposits of the traditions as they circulated in the churches. But redaction criticism made it more difficult to get back to Jesus, for the greater the hand given the Evangelists in writing the Gospels, the more difficult it is to get at the tradition they used. When redaction criticism is pushed to its limits, it is as hard to get at the pre-Marcan tradition, for example, as it was for an earlier generation of form critics to get behind the oral tradition to Jesus. In short, now we have a double screen to penetrate. Moreover, redaction criticism also has called into question what the negative criteria left intact. What once was regarded as solid, historical evidence because it is not the sort of thing the church would have created, is now traceable to the interests of the particular Evangelist. For example, if an earlier generation could regard Mark's unflattering portrait of Peter as evidence of solid tradition in view of Peter's role in the church, Weeden can now declare it to result from the Evangelist's effort to discredit a type of Christianity.[236]

This is a somewhat surprising outcome of a century of intense work since Strauss. Even by the end of his work, things looked more promising, for the rise of the two-source theory demolished Baur's view that the Gospels were second-century products, and showed that Mark was written no more than forty years after Jesus' death. And for those who saw at its base the eyewitness tradition of Peter, Mark provided as good a historical source as one could wish. Studies in Aramaic showed that much of the Gospel material had been translated, and hence was not created by the second-century Greek church. Harnack spoke for the consensus when he contended that although allowances for secondary material and for editing must be made, on the whole we have a quite reliable base for the study of Jesus.[237] But then Wrede shook the foundations by arguing that Mark is a theological document, not a historical account.[238] Since form and redaction criticism, the list of indubitably genuine materials recognized by all students has become rather small because widely accepted criteria for identifying them are still wanting. Repeatedly, scholars rely on subjective, aesthetic criteria instead—such as the striking quality of a parable, or its radicality. But the more we know about various groups in Judaism or Christianity, the more difficult it is to specify what is radical enough to be traceable only to Jesus. And so we stand where Strauss left us—knowing what we are looking for, but not knowing how to recognize it if we should find it.

236. Theodore J. Weeden, *Mark—Traditions in Conflict* (Philadelphia: Fortress Press, 1971), ch. 2.

237. Harnack, *What Is Christianity?*, lecture 2.

238. Wilhelm Wrede, *The Messianic Secret,* trans. J. C. G. Greig (Cambridge & London: James Clarke, 1971; German edition 1901).

The Relationship of Jesus and the Church

Secondly, the historical study of Jesus will move beyond Strauss only if it can relate Jesus to the church more credibly than he did. But Strauss is not the only one to have fallen off his horse at this hurdle. The danger lies in the race itself, of course. That is, it was agreed that one must distinguish Jesus himself from the church's Gospels; inevitably the distinction became a contrast. But at what point does this become counterproductive for the historian? What degree of commensurability must one assume (or require) between Jesus and early Christianity if we are to have a credible historical view of the whole? Scholars face analogous problems in recovering Epicurus or Socrates. But would one recover Epicurus or Socrates from the works of their followers by driving as many wedges between them as possible? What one misses in so much recent literature on Jesus is any sense of continuity between what he was and was about and what Christianity became in his name. This is what Loisy saw (see above, note 223). To reconstruct a Jesus who is at variance in all essential points with Christianity, and contrasted with Judaism as well, is to reconstruct a historical situation which is at least as hard to believe as the Gospel miracle stories—and this time it is we ourselves who are expected to walk on water.

Strauss saw, more clearly than Schleiermacher, that a truly historical Jesus must be related in a historically convincing way to Judaism as well as to the church; otherwise one can understand neither. If Jesus had no essential links to Judaism or Christianity, what prevents us from returning to Bruno Bauer and Arthur Drews, who argued that there never was a Jesus in the first place?[239] But if one

239. Bruno Bauer's Gospel criticism became ever more radical until in 1850–51 he concluded that Jesus never lived. For a survey of his work see Schweitzer, *The Quest of the Historical Jesus*, ch. 11, and Brazill, pp. 177–208. Later Arthur Drews repeated the argument in *Die Christusmythe*

cannot rid oneself of the suspicion that had there been no Jesus there would have been no Christianity, then surely one can expect some historical continuity as well as discontinuity. Unless this dimension of the study of the Jesus traditions receives its due, redaction criticism may take us back to Bruno Bauer after all.

Inner Coherence of the Jesus Materials

The third factor involved in the future of the study of Jesus concerns the internal coherence of the Jesus materials which have survived our various analyses. This factor is more subtle and more important than the common cant that every generation and every scholar has constructed Jesus in its own image. The question is whether the genuine Jesus materials cohere, or whether they are a pile of disparate evidence which defies understanding as a whole. For example, if the Kingdom is the core of Jesus' message, then either we must illumine all the parts from this core, or we must infer that Jesus' mission lacked inner coherence or that we are unable to know what it was. Nor can we speak of basic shifts in Jesus' outlook, for doing so requires us to have all the evidence in correct chronological sequence, and this is now seen to be impossible.

In the last analysis, the coherence of the genuine Jesus materials is more important than his originality. It is the Christian fear of Judaism that has led to the placing of such an inordinate premium on originality and uniqueness. The historian is of course interested in uniqueness as well as similarity. But those who are interested in Jesus for religious reasons care less about his originality than about whether Jesus makes sense and whether his work coheres.

(Jena: Eugen Diederichs, 1910). In this country, William Benjamin Smith represented similar views. See *The Birth of the Gospel*, ed. Addison Gulick (New York: Philosophical Library, 1957; MS completed 1927). A flood of literature replied, e.g., Maurice Goguel, *Jesus the Nazarene—Myth or History?* (New York: Appleton, 1926).

The historical study of Jesus will move beyond Strauss only if it is able to make sense of the authentic material—all of it.

What Strauss bequeaths to us in the present volume is the challenge to think historically about theological texts (the Gospels) and to think theologically about the process, and the results, of critical historical analysis of them. This is why reading *The Christ of Faith and the Jesus of History* is such a rewarding and educating experience. If reading it sharpens our perceptions and elicits from us deeper insight into the theological tasks today, then not only will both Schleiermacher and Strauss become our contemporaries as we go to work, but the entire Lives of Jesus Series will fulfill its vocation as well.

SELECT BIBLIOGRAPHY

Letters of David Friedrich Strauss

Barnikol, Ernst, ed. "Der Briefwechsel zwischen Strauss und Baur." *Zeitschrift für Kirchengeschichte 73* (1962): 72–125.

Maier, Heinrich, ed. *Briefe von David Friedrich Strauss an L. Georgii.* Tübingen: J. C. B. Mohr, 1912.

Rapp, Adolf, ed. *Briefwechsel zwischen Strauss und Vischer.* 2 vols. Veröffentlichung der deutschen Schillergesellschaft 18. Stuttgart: Ernst Klett, 1952–53.

Zeller, Eduard, ed. *Ausgewählte Briefe von David Friedrich Strauss.* Bonn: Emil Strauss, 1895.

Collected Works

Zeller, Eduard, ed. *Gesammelte Schriften von David Friedrich Strauss.* 12 vols. Bonn: Emil Strauss, 1876–78. (Not complete; the *Leben Jesu* and the *Glaubenslehre* are not included.)

Original Editions of Strauss's Works

Das Leben Jesu, kritisch bearbeitet. 2 vols. Tübingen: Osiander. 1st ed. 1835–36 (reprinted Darmstadt: Wissenschaftliche Buchgesellschaft, 1969); 2d ed. 1837; 3d ed. 1838; 4th ed. 1840.

Streitschriften zur Verteidigung meiner Schrift über das Leben Jesu und zur Charakteristik der gegenwärtige Theologie. 3 parts. Tübingen: Osiander, 1837.

"Über Vergängliches und Bleibendes im Christentum." *Zwei friedliche Blätter*. Altona, 1839. (Originally published in *Freihafen*, 1839).

Charakteristiken und Kritiken. Leipzig: Otto Wigand, 1839. (Includes book reviews and "Schleiermacher und Daub in ihrer Bedeutung für die Theologie.")

Die christliche Glaubenslehre in ihrer geschichtlichen Entwicklung und im Kampfe mit der modernen Wissenschaft. 2 vols. Stuttgart and Tübingen, 1840–41. (Reprinted in 1973 by Wissenschaftliche Buchgesellschaft in Darmstadt.)

Der Romantiker auf dem Thron der Cäsaren, oder: Julian der Abtrünnige. Mannheim, 1847.

Christian Märklin. Ein Charakterbild aus der Gegenwart. Mannheim, 1851.

Ulrich von Hutten. 2 vols. Leipzig: Brockhaus, 1858.

Gespräche von Ulrich von Hutten, übersetzt und erläutert. Leipzig, 1860.

Hermann Samuel Reimarus und seine Schutzschrift für die vernünftigen Verehrer Gottes. Leipzig, 1861.

"Schleiermacher und die Auferstehung Jesu." *Zeitschrift für wissenschaftliche Theologie* 6 (1863): 386–400.

Das Leben Jesu, für das deutsche Volk bearbeitet. 2 vols. Leipzig: Brockhaus, 1864.

Der Christus des Glaubens und der Jesus der Geschichte. Eine Kritik des Schleiermacherschen Lebens Jesu. Berlin: Franz Duncker, 1865. Reprinted as edited by Hans-Jürgen Geischer as vol. 14 of Texte zur Kirchen- und Theologiegeschichte. Gütersloh: Gerd Mohn, 1971.

Die Halben und die Ganzen. Eine Streitschrift gegen die HH. DD. Schenkel und Hengstenberg. Berlin: Franz Duncker, 1865.

Voltaire. Sechs Vorträge. Leipzig: Hirzel, 1870.

Der alte und der neue Glaube. Ein Bekenntnis. Leipzig: Hirzel, 1872.

English Translations

Soliloquies on the Christian Religion. London, 1845. (Translation of "Über Vergängliches und Bleibendes in Christentum.")

The Life of Jesus Critically Examined. Translated by George Eliot. 1st ed. 3 vols. London: Chapman Brothers, 1846. 2d ed. 1 vol. London: Swan Sonnenschein, and New York: Macmillan, 1892. Reissued, 1898. (Reprinted with introduction and notes by Peter C. Hodgson. Lives of Jesus Series. Philadelphia: Fortress Press, 1972.)

A New Life of Jesus. 2 vols. London: Williams and Norgate, 1865. (Authorized translation of *Das Leben Jesu für das deutsche Volk bearbeitet.*)

The Old Faith and the New. Translated from 6th ed. by Mathilde Blind. London: Asher & Co., 1874.

Ulrich von Hutten: His Life and Times. Translated and abridged from 2d ed. by Mrs. G. Sturge. London: Daldy, Isbiter & Co., 1874.

Secondary Sources

Backhaus, Günther. *Kerygma und Mythos bei David Friedrich Strauss und Rudolf Bultmann.* Hamburg-Bergstedt: Herbert Reich Evangelischer Verlag, 1956.

Barth, Karl. *David Friedrich Strauss als Theologe.* Theologische Studien 6. Zollikon: Evangelische Buchhandlung, 1939.

―――. *Protestant Thought: From Rousseau to Ritschl.* Translated by Brian Cozens. New York: Simon & Schuster, 1959. Pp. 362–89.

Benz, Ernst. "David Friedrich Strauss." *Zeitschrift für Religions- und Geistesgeschichte* 27 (1975): 57–74.

Brazill, William J. *The Young Hegelians.* New Haven: Yale University Press, 1970. Pp. 95–132.

Elert, Werner. *Der Kampf um das Christentum.* Munich: O. Beck, 1925.

Fischer, Kuno. *Über David Friedrich Strauss. Gesammelte Schriften.* Philosophische Schriften von Kuno Fischer 5. Edited by Hugo Falkenheim. Heidelberg: Carl Winter, 1908. (Essays and reviews of Strauss's work from *Hutten* onward.)

Geisser, Hans. "David Friedrich Strauss als verhinderter (Züricher) Dogmatiker." *Zeitschrift für Theologie und Kirche* 69 (1972): 214–58.

Gunther, Ernst. "Bemerkungen zur Christologie von David Friedrich Strauss." *Zeitschrift für Theologie und Kirche* 18 (1908): 202–11.

Harris, Horton. *David Friedrich Strauss and His Theology.* Monograph Supplements to *The Scottish Journal of Theology.* Cambridge: Cambridge University Press, 1973.

Hartlich, Christian, and Sachs, Walter. *Der Ursprung des Mythosbegriffes in der modernen Bibelwissenschaft.* Tübingen: J. C. B. Mohr, 1952.

Harvey, Van A. "D. F. Strauss's *Life of Jesus* Revisited." *Church History* 30 (1961): 191–211.

Hausrath, Adolf. *David Friedrich Strauss und die Theologie seiner Zeit.* 2 vols. Heidelberg: Basserman, 1876–78.

Hein, Arnold. "Die Christologie von David Friedrich Strauss." *Zeitschrift für Theologie und Kirche* 16 (1906): 321–46.

Hester, Carl E. III. "Schleiermacher in Tübingen: A Study in Reaction." Ph.D. dissertation, Columbia University, 1970.

Hillerbrand, Hans J. *A Fellowship of Discontent.* New York: Harper & Row, 1967. Ch. 5.

Hirsch, Emanuel. *Geschichte der neueren evangelischen Theologie.* 5 vols. Gütersloh: C. Bertelsmann, 1949–54. Vol. 5, pp. 492–518.

Hodgson, Peter C., ed. *The Life of Jesus Critically Examined.* Translated by George Eliot. Lives of Jesus Series. Philadelphia: Fortress Press, 1972. (See editor's introduction, pp. xv–l, and annotations, pp. 785–802.)

———. *The Formation of Historical Theology: A Study of Ferdinand Christian Baur.* Makers of Modern Theology. New York: Harper & Row, 1966.

Kohut, Adolf. *David Friedrich Strauss als Denker und Erzieher.* Leipzig: Alfred Kröner Verlag, 1908.

Massey, Marilyn Chapin. "David Friedrich Strauss's Christological Thought: The Influence of Friedrich Schleiermacher." Ph.D. dissertation, University of Chicago, 1973.

Müller, Gotthold. *Identität und Immanenz. Zur Genese der Theologie von David Friedrich Strauss.* Basler Studien zur historischen und systematischen Theologie 10. Zürich: *EVZ-Verlag*, 1968.

Sandberger, Jörg F. *David Friedrich Strauss als Theologischer Hegelianer.* Studien zur Theologie und Geistesgeschichte des neunzehnten Jahrhunderts 5. Göttingen: Vandenhoeck & Ruprecht, 1972.

Schweitzer, Albert. *The Quest of the Historical Jesus.* Translated by W. Montgomery. London: A. & C. Black, 1910.

Welch, Claude. *Protestant Thought in the Nineteenth Century.* New Haven: Yale University Press, 1972.

Wolf, Ernst. "Die Verlegenheit der Theologie. David Friedrich Strauss und die Bibelkritik." *Libertas Christiana* (F. Delekat Festschrift). Edited by W. Matthias and Ernst Wolf. Beiträge zur Evangelische Theologie 26. Munich: Kaiser, 1957. Pp. 219–39.

Zeller, Eduard. *David Friedrich Strauss in seinem Leben und Schriften.* Bonn: Emil Strauss, 1874.

Ziegler, Theobald. *David Friedrich Strauss.* Strassburg: Karl Trübner, 1908.

FURTHER READING

Useful bibliographies of primary and secondary sources may be found in the books by Harris, Hodgson, Müller, Rapp, and Sandberger. More of Strauss's letters and documents are contained in the works of Harris, Hausrath, Sandberger, and Ziegler.

THE CHRIST OF FAITH
AND THE
JESUS OF HISTORY

A Critique of Schleiermacher's *Life of Jesus*

FOREWORD

In my new revision of *The Life of Jesus* I sharply opposed Schleiermacher's views in various matters.[1] I did this on the basis of notes of his lectures on the life of Jesus, which I had before me in earlier days and had excerpted. Meanwhile, these lectures have appeared in print in the form in which Schleiermacher gave them in one of the last years of his life.[2] It is virtually certain that those to whom my judgments were offensive will say that it is easy to do battle with unprinted notebooks, since one can bypass what one does not know how to refute, but that dealing with printed lectures would have been more difficult for me. It is not known to me whether such expressions were used openly, but I accept the summons before I receive it because it is, moreover, a necessity for me to come to terms with Schleiermacher's work, and because I may hope that on this occasion I can at the same time make even clearer several points in my own book on the same subject.

1. [Strauss refers to his *Life of Jesus for the German People*, in many ways a new work; it is surprising that Strauss calls it a "revision," for a revision is precisely what he had decided *not* to produce. See above, p. xli; for Strauss's criticism of Schleiermacher in this book see above, pp. lxi–lxiv.]

2. [*Das Leben Jesu*, ed. K. A. Rütenik. Friedrich Schleiermacher, *Werke* 1, part 6 (Berlin: Georg Reimer, 1864) (hereafter cited as *Werke*). English edition, *The Life of Jesus*, trans. S. MacLean Gilmour, ed. Jack C. Verheyden. Lives of Jesus Series (Philadelphia: Fortress Press, 1975). All page references to Schleiermacher's *Life of Jesus* are to this English edition.]

German theology still stands—or actually just now stands —at Schleiermacher. He was ahead of his time, as are all significant intellects; only now, a generation after his death, has theology more or less caught up with him. Caught up with him, that is, the way the masses can catch up with a great individual; the blunted meaning of the outlines of his views are repeated crudely. Today it is with Schleiermacher's theology exactly as it was sixty years ago with Kantian philosophy. While true scholarship had already moved forward with Fichte and Schelling to deepen and develop the principle established by Kant, Kantian philosophizing had spread abroad, had entered general consciousness, and had become the average wisdom of the era. In exactly the same way, all those theologians who have not stiffened in dull-minded reaction or have not moved forward to the standpoint of free science—hence the vast majority of the theological world (perhaps with all sorts of exceptions)—still occupy a standpoint which one can only designate as Schleiermacher's. Nowadays one hears even ecclesiastical authorities speak from this perspective—certainly the surest proof that it has been superseded.

Schleiermacher's *The Christian Faith* has really but a single dogma, that concerning the person of Christ. If one takes this away there indeed still remain, in the doctrines of God and of the world, and throughout the elucidation of church doctrines as well, highly worthwhile philosophical discussions. But the really positive element of the work lies only in what it advances about the person of Christ. Schleiermacher's Christology is a last attempt to make the churchly Christ acceptable to the modern world. That Christ was a man in the full sense of the word, as today's mentality desires, and at the same time, as traditional piety wishes, can be a divine redeemer, the object of our faith and of our cultus for all times—that view, even though everyone makes his own idea of that true humanity and this true divinity, has through Schleiermacher become a prejudice of the time.

Whether this presupposition is tenable must show itself when the Gospel reports about Jesus are systematically subjected to examination. The critical investigation of the life of Jesus is the test of the dogma of the person of Christ.[3] It is well known that this dogma in its churchly form has not survived the test well. I have maintained the same concerning the dogma in Schleiermacher's form; here I subsequently deliver the proof in detail. Schleiermacher's Christ is as little a real man as is the Christ of the church. By means of a truly critical treatment of the Gospels one reaches Schleiermacher's Christ as little as he does the church's Christ. The illusion, which is supported primarily by Schleiermacher's explanations, that Jesus could have been a man in the full sense and still as a single person stand above the whole of humanity, is the chain which still blocks the harbor of Christian theology against the open sea of rational science. To break this chain is the purpose of the present work, as it has always been of all my theological writings.[4]

Berlin, January 1865

3. [See above, pp. lxvi, lxxi–lxxvi.]
4. [This issue had dominated Strauss's long debate wtih Schleiermacher; see above, pp. lv–lxxxii. For some reason Strauss writes as if he still hopes to liberate Christian theology from its outmoded dogmatic tradition.]

PART ONE
INTRODUCTION

CHAPTER ONE

SCHLEIERMACHER'S LECTURES ON THE LIFE OF JESUS

Among the lectures given by Schleiermacher, those on the life of Jesus became especially famous already in his lifetime because they were a novelty in the sphere of academic presentations. That nevertheless after his death, while the rest of his more important lectures were published in succession by his students, these remained unprinted for fully thirty years, must occasion astonishment. Their present editor explains it as due to the fact that in Schleiermacher's papers little was found on the life of Jesus in written form, and that it was therefore doubtful whether with such inadequate material one could present a work worthy of Schleiermacher's name. However, also in this form the material from other lectures was inadequate and could not have been used without supplements from the notebooks of the hearers. However, among such notebooks there were available very suitable and detailed ones precisely for the life of Jesus, as the editor himself attests. One could hardly avoid seeking another basis for such reticence. Then, if one recalls the case of the letters about *Lucinde*,[5] the surmise emerges that also here something may have been at work which the piety of the disciples wanted to hide rather than to disclose.

Now I can indeed say, without having to fear the accusation of glory-seeking and virtually without contradiction: if in the year following Schleiermacher's death my *Life of Jesus* had not appeared, his would not have been kept in hiding so long. Until the present time, it would have been received by the theological world like a savior. But for the wounds which the former work inflicted on the hitherto prevailing theology, Schleiermacher's book had neither healing herb nor bandage; indeed, it showed its author to be largely coresponsible for the malaise which, let in one drop at a time by Schleiermacher, has now, mocking his rules of caution, poured in. He had wanted to occupy a middle position between faith and science; but with regard to that work of mine, only an either/or decision was in order, and the previous mediation, which naturally was not wanting, still had to be formed and grounded with respect to the new book. Now it has taken shape and has taken over vir-

5. [Strauss refers to an intriguing aspect of Schleiermacher's life. In 1797 Schleiermacher became a good friend of Friedrich Schlegel, a leading member of the Berlin circle of Romantics; for a few months they even shared an apartment. Schlegel published a work called *Lucinde* in which he sought to articulate the Romantics' view of marriage, according to which each self completes itself in a genuine harmony by uniting itself with another. The book was considered a failure; Schleiermacher, unfortunately, defended it in *Vertraute Briefe über Friedrich Schlegels Lucinde* (*Werke*, 3:1.) Strauss implies that this work, which Schleiermacher's disciples would have preferred to hide, could now be included in the collected works because the master was long dead. He sees a parallel in the delay in publishing Schleiermacher's *Life of Jesus*.

During the same period in which Schleiermacher was defending *Lucinde,* he was courting the unhappily married wife of a Berlin pastor, Eleonore Grunow, whom he urged to obtain a divorce. She declined; later Schleiermacher, who had changed his view of marriage, conceded that she had made the right decision. For details see Martin Redeker, *Schleiermacher: Life and Thought,* trans. John Wallhausser (Philadelphia: Fortress Press, 1973), pp. 64–72.]

tually completely the churchly and theological domain. Now it probably will no longer hurt to bring the work of the famous predecessor out of its long obscurity. One could hope to draw advantage from its strong parts, and from its weak parts one could hope to enliven his awareness of how wondrously far we have come since the author's death in regard to the establishment and defense of the faith and of one's own position.

SCHLEIERMACHER'S LECTURES IN GENERAL

Consequently, now that Schleiermacher's *Life of Jesus* lies before us in print, all theological parties can first of all gather around it in honest joy. The appearance of a work of Schleiermacher will invariably be an enrichment of literature; whatever has come from a mind such as his cannot do other than have an illuminating and enlivening effect on minds far and wide. And of works of this sort our theological literature truly has no excess. Where for the most part the living are like the dead, it is in order for the dead to rise and bear witness.[6] Thus year after year we see new treasures offered from the still unexhausted resources of Baur's literary remains,[7] compared with which the products

6. [The recent German edition omits the rest of Chapter One. (David Friedrich Strauss, *Der Christus des Glaubens und der Jesus der Geschichte,* ed. Hans-Jürgen Geischer, Texte zur Kirchen- und Theologiegeschichte 14 [Gütersloh: Gerd Mohn, 1971, hereafter cited as Geischer]). Geischer was useful in providing numerous bibliographic details for Strauss's footnotes.]

7. Most recently, the lectures on New Testament theology have appeared (Leipzig, 1864), in a book which makes available in the most convenient form the results of many years of laborious investigations, and therefore is especially able to make intelligible the true essence and the historical development of early Christianity. [These lectures, as well as other major works, were published by F. C. Baur's son, F. F. Baur, and were republished in 1973 by the Wissenschaftliche Buchgesellschaft in Darmstadt (*Vorlesungen über neutestamentliche Theologie,* ed. W. G. Kümmel). For an overview of F. C. Baur's career, with special attention to his relation to Strauss, see Hodgson, *Formation,* ch. 1 and pp. 73–84.]

of most living theologians pale like lead beside gold. In the same way, also these lectures of Schleiermacher show us again that, in comparison with the achievement of his disciples, the great theologian indeed left them his mantle but not his spirit.[8]

To be sure, lectures such as Baur's could not long remain unprinted because they were already virtually ready for publication; moreover, the absence of the material, about which the editors of Schleiermacher's lectures had so much to complain, did not exist at all. Indeed, one will say, that works to the advantage of the editors and readers; but the hearers had to pay for it, since Baur did not lecture extemporaneously, as did Schleiermacher, but read from his notebook. Certainly there is an advantage in an extemporaneous lecture, but I believe that it is now widely overestimated. This capacity was lacking in our teacher Baur, it is true, as at the time he entered academic life it was something unheard of at the state university in Württemberg. But I do not believe that his lectures therefore aroused our attention the less, or took our thinking less in hand, or moved our imaginative power the less, or left our dispositions colder. Here, too, everything finally depends on the personality of the teacher. The man of spirit and character will also know how to enliven the lecture tied to the notebook, just as he will compose his notebook itself while visualizing the presence of his hearers, whereas the chatterbox without a written foundation will only chatter the more baselessly, and

8. [Strauss alludes to a poem about Schleiermacher which he wrote in 1844:

> In his last moments
> He saw the disciples approach:
> "Leave us your mantle, and
> Your spirit, as did the prophets."
> But he, seeing their faith,
> Gave but half the request:
> The cleric's mantle he left behind,
> But took the spirit with him.
> (*Poetisches Gedenkbuch* in *GS*, 12:26).]

10

the muddled head will only the more aimlessly lead himself and his hearers in circles.

Schleiermacher, as is known, lectured extemporaneously, with at most the aid of quite summary outlines, as he did also in his sermons which, after thinking them through several times in advance, he used to produce freely in the pulpit. The number of his hearers in church and lecture hall, the deep and effective stimulation which they experienced from him, and the inextinguishable memories which they preserve of his lectures are so many proofs of the fact that in this art he achieved something extraordinary. But one had to get used to his style. After completing my university studies and coming to Berlin from Tübingen,[9] I myself still had not had the experience of hearing an extemporaneous lecture. In lieu of this, however, through exact knowledge of Schleiermacher's writings and through philosophical studies I was better prepared for his lectures than his average hearer. Even so it was not easy for me to be comfortable with his style, and actually, after a half year's experiment, he satisfied me more in the pulpit than at the podium. The general disadvantages which more or less adhere to every free discourse, and which one could call the stylistic weaknesses in the broader sense, were common to his pulpit and podium presentations and were more than compensated for by the vitality of his oral presentation. The special weakness of his lectures lay in precisely that point which was also their strength, namely, the fact that they employed exclusively the dialectical method.

In itself, what can be more instructive for the hearer than when the teacher presents nothing in the form of a dead report but everything as a problem whose solution they now seek together, when the teacher transmits his ideas not as completed ones but allows them to emerge and grow, become intricate, and be solved in his presence? In scien-

9. [See above, pp. xxiii–xxv.]

tific writings, does one not praise the genetic approach above all? But between this and the former manner of delivery there is still an essential difference. The genetic presentation proceeds from a thought-complex which already exists, and presents this not the way it really happened in its process of development, a process which never avoids all kinds of accidents and irregularities—but rather the way it *should* have developed; the genetic presentation is, as is every artistic or scientific one, an ideal one. Schleiermacher was an unsurpassed master of the genetic presentation in those writings which he himself published, and on this peculiarity rests that incomparable, stimulating, and instructive quality which we know in them. But when he spoke from the podium he had, to be sure, the general results in hand already and had repeatedly been through the course of thought by which he had reached them. But now, the thought-sequences which he had spun out in his study, and which in quiet literary activity he would have worked out in all ideal regularity, were to be delivered afresh in rapid oral improvisation. It was quite natural, then, that accident played its role here, that the finely spun threads occasionally became tangled, and that what was tangled was torn off, so that the whole presentation in no way bore the marks of order and regularity, but occasionally even bore those of thoughtlessness or confusion. In regard to preaching, Schleiermacher himself once counseled that the speaker with a more quiet temperament may enter the pulpit without having worked out precisely the details and grasped them in his mind, but that he with a more animated temperament should rather from the start bind himself to the previously written word in order to achieve that calm and moderation which facilitates clear understanding for the hearer.[10] By

10. *Predigten*, Sammlung 1, Nachschrift zu der Zueignung. [(Berlin: Verlag der Realschulbuchhandlung, 1816, 3d ed.) Schleiermacher had added this postscript to the second edition.]

nature Schleiermacher decidedly stood on the side of highest animation and quicksilver mobility; in the pulpit this was counterbalanced by the note of seriousness which of course brings a certain solemnity with it. At the podium all this disappeared, and there he surrendered to a restlessness in taking up and abandoning problems, in seizing something now from this side and now from that—which could have made the hearer dizzy if the animated, constantly striking, and vivid speech of the teacher at hand had not led him and helpfully carried him along over the gaps in the presentation.

EDITING LECTURES

But now think of the task of keeping up in writing with such a presentation. It is like photographing a dancer in full motion. It is not only a matter of the difficulties which the rapid delivery make for transcription; even assuming the most accomplished stenographer and literal notation, the situation remains the same. Schleiermacher knew very well why, in the preparation of his sermons for publication, he had to thoroughly rework the transcripts which were given to him. At least one revision is always needed for lectures which are to be published mainly from notes. Indeed, this is a delicate undertaking and requires a facile hand and a person acquainted with the man as well as with the content of the lectures. As is well known, Hegel's lectures were also published by his students. Here, too, the difficulties were not small; the sparse notations by the philosopher himself, delivered extemporaneously by him at the podium, required supplementation throughout from the notes of the hearers. Even though nothing was less a problem for Hegel than rapid speech and animation—to the contrary, his failure was a heaviness and hesitating awkwardness—the editor, if he wanted to do justice to his task, still had no less to do. The task of an editor of lectures can be none other than that of offering a text which in reading at least approximately gives the instruction and satisfaction which the oral presentation gave in hearing. This does not mean that the lecture must become a book which loses its original character as an oral presentation; rather, those defects of that presentation which were bearable only because of the living presence of the teacher must be overcome by the editor insofar as they hamper understanding and profit in reading. Therefore, besides having to make improvements in the defective notes, he will also help the speaker himself to overcome what is awkward in expression, and to expand elements of thought which were not entirely developed. He will be concerned with slowing down the man who speaks too rapidly and skips about, in order to untangle the threads of his thought where they are confused, tie them together where they are fragmented, and make firm points discernible in the hastening flow of the investigation. As far as Hegel's lectures are concerned, according to common judgment only one of the editors fulfilled this task, and he was the one who went to work with the most freedom: Hotho, the editor of Hegel's *Esthetics*.[11] He helped the teacher in every way, not only in regard to his "Moses-tongue"[12] but also in regard to his laborious thinking and, in isolated cases, his defective knowledge; but he did it with such penetration into the meaning of the master and with such tact that one must say throughout: indeed this, and not something else, is what Hegel intended, even if he may not have said it quite this way. And in all this Hotho still knew how to preserve the essential features of Hegel's manner of expression.

11. [*Vorlesungen über die Aesthetik*, ed. H. G. Hotho. G. W. F. Hegel, *Werke* (Berlin: Duncker und Humbolt, 1835–38), vol. 10, part 3.]

12. [Strauss refers to Exodus 4:10, according to which Moses tried to decline God's summons to return to Egypt because he did not speak fluently.]

RÜTENIK AS EDITOR OF
SCHLEIERMACHER'S LECTURES

When in the course of the previous year I learned that Schleiermacher's lectures on the life of Jesus were being prepared for publication by Mr. Rütenik, I was immediately uneasy. Many years ago, Mr. Rütenik wrote a little book in which Christian doctrine in its Schleiermacherian form was worked up catechetically.[13] What a comfort to me was the existence of this book thirty-four years ago when, after the completion of my time at the university, I was dispatched from my study of Schleiermacher's *The Christian Faith* and Hegel's *Phenomenology* to the countryside as *Vikar*, responsible among other things for imparting religious instruction to the village youth. The chasm which I had to leap across was great, but I expected Mr. Rütenik to help me across. I thought he would show me how Schleiermacher's doctrine was to be made intelligible to the public, how the gold bars of his view of religion must be alloyed and minted for retail trade. But Mr. Rütenik did not show that to me. His catechetical handbook bore the most cumbersome weaponry of Schleiermacherian systematics; it clattered with formulae from which my peasant children would have fled. I could not use the little book at all and had to improvise for myself as best I could. I had exactly the same experience a few years later with a Hegelian. In Tübingen I wanted to lecture on logic in Hegel's sense, which at the time was accessible neither through the lectures of the philosopher, which have been published since, nor through critical discussions which were equal to the subject matter. But his student Hinrichs had written

13. *Der christliche Glaube, nach dem lutherischen Katechismus in katechetischen Vorträgen zusammenhängend dargestellt von C. A. Rütenik,* 1829.

Outlines of Logic.[14] How eagerly I now reached for this writing, in the hope that it would assist me in my effort to make the difficult work of the master more accessible to common understanding. But Hinrichs's little book helped me with the students no more than Rütenik's had done previously with the peasant children. Where the master had marched out armored in steel, the writings of the student seemed to me to be only hollow tin armor, without a body under it. These two similar experiences with students of opposing masters have given me a general prejudice against such disciples. One should think that they must understand the master best, but experience shows the contrary. Just as a new system of thought as a rule appears first in dry, abstruse form and uses strictly artificial language, partly to impress its peculiar content upon others and partly to bring itself to full consciousness, so students who attach themselves to the master in the beginning period easily retain a certain formalism and seldom achieve the capacity to move out of it to a more concrete development of the system. This is widely recognized with respect to the Old Hegelians;[15] but I saw in Mr. Rütenik that in this sense it was not wanting among the Old Schleiermacherians. And his preface to Schleiermacher's *Life of Jesus*, which was written a year ago, shows that in this respect he has made no progress since his little catechism book, and that even today the teaching of the master remains wrapped in the tightest bandages which prevent any vital movement.[16] A

14. [Apparently an allusion to Herrmann F. W. Hinrichs (1794–1861), *Grundlinien der Philosophie der Logik.* Halle: Friedrich Ruff, 1826.]

15. [Another term for the right-wing Hegelians, such as Georg Gabler, Carl Michelet, and the theologian and philosopher Philipp Marheineke. They interpreted Hegel to mean that philosophy and theology were consonant with one another. The Young Hegelians, or left-wing Hegelians, to which Strauss generally belonged, inferred that philosophy had superseded religion.]

16. [Strauss speaks of "Lazarus-bandages," referring to John 11:44, according to which Lazarus came out of the tomb, "his hands and feet bound with bandages, and his face wrapped with a cloth."]

free and liberating handling of the lecture material before him, for which Hotho as editor of Hegel's *Esthetics* is to be praised, accordingly was not to be expected from Mr. Rütenik.

RÜTENIK'S EDITING OF SCHLEIERMACHER'S *LIFE OF JESUS*

Mr. Rütenik speaks of notes from "at least" five semesters; thus it appears that Schleiermacher lectured this many times on the life of Jesus (it is appropriate that the editor report this accurately). If Rütenik refused to integrate the notebooks from all these years, considering it an unreasonable and ultimately fruitless task, then he is not wrong, since in light of Schleiermacher's manner of producing the lecture completely extemporaneously every time he repeated it, the transformation not only of particulars but also of the conception as a whole was so significant that all of it cannot be brought together in a single text. That at the same time the editor kept to the last revision as not only the basic one but also the most mature is quite appropriate. If, however, in doing this he had wanted to do full justice to his task, he should have indicated in footnotes all significant deviations from earlier years; or, if they were longer passages, he should have included them in appendices, partly to make evident individual shifts in Schleiermacher's views and judgments, and partly so that where in the last year's lectures a subject was mentioned only briefly which earlier had been handled in detail, the detailed passage would not be lost. That he intends to offer these appendices in a special supplementary volume makes the matter even more inconvenient; yet he intends to add other material in this supplementary volume which really belongs in the present one, and indeed which ought to constitute the present book.

In order to present the lecture text of the summer of 1832 Mr. Rütenik uses, beside the brief notes which Schleiermacher made for himself for the individual sessions (they are missing for the last twelve of the seventy-one sessions)—if I understand correctly—five student notebooks, among which, as he complains, one was more detailed but none complete and verbally accurate. And yet such a notebook was available, in the possession of Mr. Lancizolle, and Mr. Rütenik finds it very "reassuring" to be able "to make, hopefully, productive use of it shortly for the planned supplementary volume." To the contrary, we find it very unreassuring that productive use was not made of it for the book presently before us, and that the text of Schleiermacher's lectures was not produced from a single accurate notebook instead of from five more or less imprecise and incomplete ones. In thirty years one would certainly have had enough time to come upon the trail of the best notebook, and the "tirelessly searching friend" must have been situated in extremely unfavorable circumstances if he stumbled upon the notebook of a Pomeranian pastor while that belonging to one of the best-known personalities in Berlin escaped him.

Thus the editor puts first the brief sketch which Schleiermacher wrote for each lecture, and thereafter compiles the text from his five notebooks as well as possible, and now and again he shares a variant or a conjecture in a footnote. That he does not permit himself somehow to improve Schleiermacher's own presentation one must deem proper to the extent that he is really not the man to do it. But if he had only assisted the note-takers more, and at least improved upon their clear failures in understanding or notation! He may have done it often without our knowing it; but much too often he also neglected it.[17]

17. [At this point, Strauss suggests numerous improvements of the Schleiermacher text. These sentences have been omitted here.]

CHAPTER TWO

SCHLEIERMACHER'S ATTITUDE TOWARD THE TASK

HIS DOGMATIC PRESUPPOSITIONS

Whoever undertakes to write the life of a person finds, as a rule, a widespread conception of this person which he himself also more or less shares at first. But then, if he concerns himself further with the sources from which knowledge of his hero's life is to be gained, it is almost certain that this common conception is corrected in many points; perhaps even the overall judgment about the person undergoes a transformation. In view of this correction, the biographer's previous judgment—and that of the masses —from then on appears as a prejudice, and he must either be very much taken by this previous judgment or be guided by very impure purposes if he wants nevertheless to adhere to his prejudice despite the correction which came from the sources.

In the common conception of Christendom, Jesus is taken to be the God-man, a being—in spite of his human appearance—different from all other men, one in whose entire life powers are thought to have been at work as in the case of no other human life. Now if someone with this conception decides to work on the life of Jesus, and to this end concerns himself with the sources, then the case will be exactly the same as we have just ascertained in general—that insofar as this conception finds no support in the sources, he should have to surrender it as prejudice. Or possibly it could even be found also in the sources, but then the sources would show themselves as transmitting not the pure facts but only a later conception. In this case, he likewise would have to set aside this conception in the sources and search them calmly for the original facts.

How does Schleiermacher stand with respect to this requirement which we have made, as of any other biographer, also of the biographer of Jesus? Schleiermacher himself asks in his introduction (p. 20) whether in a presentation of Jesus' life one may proceed directly from faith. He denies this not only on the basis of faith in the Scripture and its inspiration through the Holy Spirit, but also on the basis of faith in Christ itself. If we wanted to presuppose this faith, he judges, we could not fulfill the task in a purely historical way, and the presentation which we would have created would have value only for those who are united with us in faith in Christ. "Rather we must," he explains (p. 21), "go to work in the fulfillment of our task just as in the fulfillment of every similar task concerning a person who in no way is the content of faith for us."[18] Now that sounds as if Schleiermacher, in the treatment of the life of Jesus, occupied a standpoint of pure, presuppositionless science.[19]

But, he then asks further, may we really occupy this standpoint? May we be indifferent as to whether the result

18. [At this point Geischer (p. 15, n. 6) notes that frequently Strauss does not quote precisely, but combines phrases and changes the grammar without distorting the sense.]

19. [Strauss assumes that adhering to Christian assumptions is prejudice, while abandoning them for scientific inquiry is freedom from presuppositions. In the preface to the first edition of his *Life of Jesus* he wrote, "If theologians regard this absence of presupposition from his [Strauss's] work as un-Christian, he regards the believing presuppositions of theirs as unscientific" (*LJCE*, p. lii).]

of our investigations confirms our faith or dissolves it? "If we intend to assert the scientific viewpoint," he answers (p. 23), "then we may not shrink from the investigation; but if we intend to remain theologians, then the scientific orientation and the Christian faith must be compatible." The latter, as we may anticipate from a later passage (p. 264), may not be assumed in advance to be already settled, but we must repeatedly make the answer to the question depend on whether or not it is confirmed in the investigation. Where it is confirmed, then all is well, and we remain theologians; where it is not, "a choice must be made" between unscientific faith and unbelieving science.

Still, this dependence turns out, on closer study, to be only apparent. For Schleiermacher it was decided at the very outset that science and Christian faith cannot and may not contradict each other. "My philosophy," he wrote in the year 1819 to Jacobi, "and my dogmatic are firmly committed not to contradict each other; but for just this reason neither will ever be complete, and as long as I can recall, they have mutually affected one another and gradually approached each other."[20] There are few statements from Schleiermacher which permit one to see so clearly the basis for his character. The science in him is tuned to faith, that is, it seeks to trace back its propositions to a less definite comprehension with which it hopes to agree.[21] And in the same way, faith is tuned to science in that faith induces science to give faith's formulae a breadth which promises

20. *Aus Schleiermachers Leben in Briefen* [4 vols. (Berlin, 1858)], 2:343.
21. [Strauss writes as a left-wing Hegelian; that is, science (including philosophy) represents for him an advance over faith because science deals in concepts (*Begriffe*), whereas faith and religion deal in images and representations (*Vorstellungen*). On this basis, Strauss argues that in accommodating itself to faith, science loses precision; in accommodating itself to science, piety gains a measure of security. This is clearly a tendentious reading of Schleiermacher. For a recent discussion of the matter see Redeker, *Schleiermacher: Life and Thought*, pp. 100–24.]

shelter for its pious concerns. As soon as it is established
that a schism between faith and science absolutely may not
erupt, then one can be certain that with such a brilliant man
as Schleiermacher no expedients will be lacking for conceal-
ing this rupture even from his own consciousness.

The Christian faith as it has come to prevail in the
church, says Schleiermacher (p. 25), distinguishes Christ
from all other men, while it nevertheless regards him at the
same time as a true and actual man. This proposition of
the union of the divine and the human in Christ has always
been endangered on two opposing sides: on the one side by
the scientific, and, insofar as Christ is to be an example for
us, also by the practical necessity of conceiving of him as
fully human; on the other side, by the concern of faith to
presuppose in him the divine in the full sense. The one-
sided emphasis on the former necessity leads to Nazorean or
ebionitic views of Christ, and overemphasis on the latter to
docetic views of Christ—two extremes which we must
avoid equally.[22] Among the latter, one understood originally
only the foolish notions of certain Gnostics who took the
body of Christ to be only an apparent one. But Schleiermacher uses the expression in the broader sense for every
view of Christ which does not permit the human in him to
come into its full right alongside the divine in him, and to this
extent Schleiermacher places also the church doctrine of the
two natures in Christ on this side, since also in this doctrine there can be no talk of a truly human life of Christ.
On the other hand, there is nevertheless still a difference
between the view of the old Nazoreans, who as Jews be-

22. [In *The Christian Faith* (trans. H. R. Mackintosh and J. S. Stewart
[Edinburgh, T. & T. Clark, 1928; New York, Harper Torchbooks, 1963],
par. 22) Schleiermacher discusses four "natural heresies" which mark the
limits within which Christian theology must operate: Docetism and
Ebionism endanger the humanity and divinity of Christ, respectively, and
Pelagianism and Manicheeism endanger the view of man and his salvation.
He also links Pelagianism with Ebionism, Manicheeism with Docetism.]

lieved in revelation and in miracles and granted them also to Jesus as the greatest prophet but refused only to grant that he was a supernatural being, and that of today's Neologists,[23] who do not believe in the divine in Christ because they reject the notion that any individual being of the human species distinguishes himself from all other individual beings of the same species in any way other than through a diverse mixture of common human powers and capacities, or that "in the area of nature something above nature could take place" (p. 25). Of these two opposing views, the latter—the ebionitic-neoteric, which denies the miraculous—will facilitate the presentation of the life of Jesus, "because throughout it keeps to the same course as all ordinary persons." On the other hand, it dissolves the specific dignity of Christ, and "then there remains no reasonable basis for making him somehow the content of faith, a central point of the world" (pp. 30, 82). The docetic view, on the other hand, "does not injure faith, since faith in redemption rests on the presupposition of the divine in Christ; but the task of forming a real view of the life, of the human existence and work of Christ, cannot be carried out on this basis," and to the extent that he cannot be an example, either if he was not a man in the full sense, even faith is concerned to repel such a concept (p. 31).

"But now," Schleiermacher here admits, "if I should say which appears easier for me," on the natural basis of the neoteric view "still to reach the point of ascribing to Christ a specific dignity or, proceeding from the basis of that creedal

23. [The Neologists were eighteenth-century German theologians (e.g., J. S. Semler, J. A. Ernesti, J. J. Spalding, J. D. Michaelis) who laid the foundations for modern biblical scholarship and, by identifying the essentials of Christianity, began the long tradition of trying to formulate its "essence" in terms of leading ideas. Interestingly, Emanuel Hirsch regarded Schleiermacher as Semler's real heir (*Geschichte der neueren evangelischen Theologie*, 5 *vols.* [Gütersloh: C. Bertelsmann Verlag, 1952], 4:88–89. Chs. 36–38 are devoted to the Neologists).]

formula of a duality of natures, to reach a human view of the life of Christ, I would rather undertake the former than the latter" (p. 85). A divine nature will always degrade the human, with which it is to constitute a single person, to a mere appearance; on the other hand, human nature is quite capable of containing the existence of the divine within it, if only this divine is not conceived as a nature with its own knowledge, will, and so forth, alongside the human.

Here Schleiermacher makes a supporting digression in the area of another dogma, the doctrine of the church (pp. 29, 96–100). "For the Christian church the Holy Spirit is identical with what, for an individual life, constituted the divine in Christ," and yet we find that the purely human and historical conception of what occurs in the church is not endangered by the presupposed divine factor operative in it. But why can one assume a divine element only here in the church, without dissolving the continuity of the human? For this reason: "Because in this the divine is thought of not in the form of an actual distinct consciousness but only as what lies at the base of the common consciousness, only as the energizing power at the inmost center," in contrast with which we "understand everything which externalizes itself as purely human." If we think of the divine in Christ according to this analogy, then we no longer think of it in personal terms, no longer as a divine being united with the human, but only as an effective impulse working on it, that is, as a heightening of its natural powers, especially of its God-consciousness, which we assume in Christ to be something absolute, powerful, and exclusively determinative of all aspects of life. As is known, Schleiermacher also called this "constant potency of the God-consciousness" a "veritable existence of God in him,"[24] but the very fact that he

24. *The Christian Faith*, par. 94.

24

calls it a real existence shows that he rather senses that it is an unreal one.   One need only note how he further explains this existence of God in Christ.   Properly, he says, there is an existence of God in a single entity only together with all other individual entities, that is, in the world.   An existence of God in a single entity alone could be predicated only to the extent that, by living receptivity made possible by general reciprocity, that single entity represented the world. But this is the case neither in an unconscious being nor in a conscious but unintelligent one, but only in a rational individual being, and indeed in his God-consciousness; but it is present in him only where it appears pure and absolutely powerful, and this in turn was the case only in Christ.   This is nothing else than Spinoza's *"aeterna Dei sapientia, quae esse in omnibus rebus, et maxime in mente humana, et omnium maxime in Christo Jesus manifestavit"* ("eternal wisdom of God, which has manifested itself in all things, more especially in the human mind, and most of all in Christ Jesus").[25]   The escalation itself shows that here we are dealing with only relative entities and with something quite different from that which the church concept treats.

Now if, in the renunciation of a personal divine element in Christ, faith allows itself to be "tuned" to science, the latter still cannot somehow avoid making a concession to faith.   In this case, science should be on guard lest it is cheated, the way secular authorities commonly are cheated in compacts with religious authorities.   It has been indicated already in what this concession by science to faith consists, namely, in the acknowledgement that in Christ, in a way quite different from all other men, the God-consciousness is to have been the absolute, determinative factor in every moment of his life.   The sentient consciousness throughout

25. Epistle 21. [Geischer lists it as no. 73. Quoted from Spinoza's letter to Henry Oldenburg in A. Wolf, *The Corrspondence of Spinoza* (London: Allen and Unwin, 1928), no. 73, p. 344.]

ruled without opposition, yet without impairing his complete humanity. If from this point we look back to the parallel which Schleiermacher used to prepare the way to his concept of the divine in Christ, then it becomes evident that subsequently it was given up again: the bridge—hardly used—is broken again. The divine in Christ is to relate to his individual human life the way the Holy Spirit as the divine element is related to the Christian communal life in the church. Still, there is a difference—in Christianity, as in every single Christian, that which emerges as actual decision and deed is always imperfect, infected with sin; in Christ, to the contrary, "that which appears as human was indeed also single, definite as well as limited, but in its human form was to be explained purely on the basis of the divine in him," and was perfect and sinless (p. 98). This means that the relation of the divine and the human in Christ is to be thought of like the same relation in the church, yet totally differently; in common life we would think ourselves victims of a hoax if someone talked us into something in this way. Previously, we mentioned the impersonal conception of the divine as the basis for the fact that, with respect to the church, the acknowledgement of the divine factor operative in it comports with the human and historical conception of what occurs in it; now here we see that this is but one reason why only the one but not the other factor is applicable to Christ. The other reason is equally important, namely, that through the operation of this divine factor the imperfection and impurity of the human which unfolds in the church is not dissolved.

Apart from the comparison by which Schleiermacher leads us to this conception of the divine in Christ, there is still another motif: that in Christ the God-consciousness, that is, the religious and ethical mainspring, was the sole determinant, and that in him there never was even the slightest struggle between inclination and duty. Rather, duty was always expressed as inclination, and pleasure and displeasure only as quiet consciousness, as indicators of a state, but never as provocation to change it.[26] This whole strict concept of sinlessness, not only as the possibility of not sinning but as the impossibility of sinning, is something which utterly dissolves the asserted similarity of Christ's human nature with that of the rest of mankind. The same thing is true of the other formulation, which Schleiermacher ascribes to the church doctrine of the two natures in Christ, that in him the archetypal was completely historical, and at the same time every historical moment was completely archetypal.[27] Even if Schleiermacher were able to limit this archetypicality to the religious area, in order to preclude the surmise that on the basis of this ascribed archetypicality Christ would have to have attained the highest also in all knowledge and ability which otherwise is developed in human society,[28] then also in the smallest circle which he is able to mark off the relation between archetype and reality would remain the same: in not a single appearance are they congruent; the single actuality—even if in the most varied grades of approximation—still never coincides with the archetype, and even the maximum still is no absolute. Baur rightly protests against this presentation: "What can be said only of the God-consciousness in general, insofar as it belongs to the perfection of human nature, is what Schleiermacher transfers directly to Christ and assumes existed in him as absolute reality—something which can be thought of as a limitless potential only in humanity as a whole. His Christ is the ideal man, or the idea of humanity viewed in

---

26. *The Christian Faith*, par. 98, sec. 1.

27. *The Christian Faith*, par. 93. [The Mackintosh-Stewart translation unfortunately uses "ideal" instead of "archetypal." This perpetuates the confusion.]

28. [Schleiermacher does, in fact, restrict Christ's archetypicality to the religious dimension of his life; see *The Christian Faith*, par. 93.]

its concrete appearance, in a particular individual, who offers idealizing fantasy the natural point of departure."[29] How correct this conception of the Schleiermacherian Christology is comes to light in such general expressions of Schleiermacher as, "To the specific difference of Christ belongs the fact that as a single individual he encompasses the spiritual life entirely within himself; the whole Kingdom of God, that is, the actual power of God in human nature, was in him originally and developed from him" (pp. 289–90). It is even more apparent in such simple comments as that Christ, to be able to be the example for all men equally, must have "related himself in an equal way to all original differences of individuals,"[30] and consequently must have had, to a certain extent, a universal nature.

Accordingly, if, in order to compensate for his renunciation of a personal divine element in Christ, science for Schleiermacher had to be determined by faith to the extent that it acknowledges a person so essentially differentiated from all other men—and indeed, acknowledges Christ as the one who ruptures the general rule of the relation of idea and reality, of species and individual—one can only be amazed at how science was able to present faith with the demand for that renunciation in the first place.[31] If science

29. F. C. Baur, *Kirchengeschichte des neunzehnten Jahrhunderts*, ed. Eduard Zeller (Tübingen: L. F. Fues, 1862), pp. 200, 202. [Introduced by Heinz Liebing, it was republished as vol. 4 of *Ausgewählte Werke* (Stuttgart-Bad Cannstatt, 1970). Strauss juxtaposes sentences taken from these pages as if they followed one another (see above, note 18). In 1827 Baur had levelled this same criticism of Schleiermacher in his inaugural lecture in Tübingen; Strauss, having learned it from his teacher, repeated it again and again. See above, pp. lii–liv.]

30. *The Christian Faith*, par. 93.

31. [The sentence, and the argument, are highly compressed. Still working with the view that Schleiermacher tuned science to faith and faith to science, Strauss argues that faith gave up a divine nature in Christ in order to be "scientific," while science had to concede that Christ was unique. But if science conceded that Christ was unique, why should it demand that faith cease speaking of a divine element?]

28

once and for all had accepted the divine in Christ in the sense of the church's faith, then everything which it still must acknowledge in him would have followed naturally as a simple consequence: his sinlessness and absolute perfection. On the other hand, now that that foundation has been removed, these properties which are nevertheless to remain in Christ are without foundation. A sinless, archetypal Christ is not one whit less unthinkable than a supernaturally begotten Christ with a divine and a human nature. On the contrary, since he appears on the basis of a world view which otherwise excludes miracles or uncaused effects, a further contradiction clings to him from which the church's Christology, which presupposes belief in miracles, is free.

If one confronts Schleiermacher with the contradiction of constructing, within an otherwise rational world view, a Christ completely unintelligible on its own grounds, then, as everyone knows, he answers, "If science must admit the possibility that even today matter could conglomerate and begin to rotate in limitless space, then it must also concede that there is an appearance in the realm of spiritual life which likewise we can only explain as a new creation, as the pure beginning of a higher spiritual life-development."[32] In the letter to Jacobi he is somewhat more to the point: he reassures himself with the fact that he "will understand the second Adam (Christ) as easily as the first, or Adam's original [nature], which of course he must also accept without understanding."[33] In *The Christian Faith* this view is

---

32. The second *Sendschreiben an Dr. Lücke* concerning *The Christian Faith*. ["Über seine Glaubenslehre an Herrn Dr. Lücke, Zwei Sendschreiben," *Theologische Studien und Kritiken* 2 (1829):255–84, 481–532. *Werke* 1, part 2. Republished by Hermann Mulert, *Schleiermachers Sendschreiben über seine Glaubenslehre an Lücke* (Giessen: Töpelmann, 1908). The passage to which Strauss refers is on pp. 40–41 of Mulert's edition.]

33. *Aus Schleiermachers Leben in Briefen*, 2:343.

traced back to the statement that in general "the beginning of life is never to be understood."[34]   However, if we are prepared to grant this of actual beginnings—such as the origin of the heavenly spheres, the emergence of the organic from the inorganic, and the beginning of the human race— we must deny that in the development of humanity there is another such actual starting point.   After there once existed a human organism, whatever emerged further within the human race was a development either more sudden or gradual, and in any case natural; and this development did not involve the appearance somewhere of an absolutely new thing any more than it did the appearance of an absolutely higher or perfect one.   Even Christianity cannot be shown to be either the one or the other; through it men have not become essentially other than they were previously, and an absolute control by the God-consciousness over the sensual can no more be shown in Christianity than anywhere else. Even if the religious and moral advance which characterizes Christendom with respect to the old religions must certainly be acknowledged, still, in the first place, already within the ancient world, alongside all decay—which was not absent from Christians either—progress is not to be denied; in the second place, the progress produced by Christianity is explained by the collaboration of completely natural causes; to account for this we need not assume an author in whom there must have existed as absolute that which, in the society he founded, everywhere becomes actuality only in a very relative way.   Since it is widely recognized that Schleiermacher constructs his concept of Christ only by means of a conclusion traced back from the effect to the cause, he has

---

34. *The Christian Faith*, par. 93, sec. 3.   See also the sermon "Dass der Erlöser als Sohn Gottes geboren ist," *Schleiermachers Predigten*, Sammlung 5, *Festpredigten* 1 (1826):92. [*Werke* 2, part 2.]

no right to posit more in the latter than he can demonstrate in the former.[35]

While the question of how an archetypal man could ever have become actual is to remain unanswered to the same extent as the question about every actual beginning of life generally, according to Schleiermacher's assurance it is enough to say that "it would perfectly meet the requirement of a perfect historicity of this perfect archetypal reality if from that time forward he had developed in the same way as all others."[36] We can admit this but must ask, What then happens to the archetypicality? One can predict what will happen to it: if the archetype really develops the way everyone else does, then the archetypicality is doomed; but if in the course of development this should remain constant, it could not develop as in all others.[37] According to Schleiermacher, how then did this archetypal Christ develop in a purely human way? In such a way, we take it, "that from birth onward, all his powers developed naturally, and from zero-point at appearance unfolded to completion in the natural order for the human race." No more than other children did he "at the outset have a clearly defined self," or speak even in the cradle; even the God-consciousness in him existed at the beginning only germinally; and only gradually, namely, with the gradual development of sentient awareness, unfolded precisely to its full extent. But at

---

35. [Emanuel Hirsch has flatly denied this assertion (*Schleiermachers Christusglauben* [Gütersloh: Gerd Mohn, 1968], p. 49), as has Redeker (*Schleiermacher: Life and Thought*, p. 131). Schleiermacher does trace consciousness of redemption to the Redeemer, but his Christology is more complex and subtle than Strauss allows. Strauss had made the same point in his *Glaubenslehre*; see above, pp. lxix–lxx.]

36. *The Christian Faith*, par. 93, sec. 3.

37. [Here we see clearly how Strauss equates (wrongly) Schleiermacher's archetype with idealism's absolute. Actually, an archetype which did not develop would cease to be archetypically human.]

every point of his development it had strength enough to suppress the sentient awareness; this superiority was never in the least bit in doubt. In all periods of his life Christ was not only free of sin but also free from all struggle and vacillation. "The formation of his personality from initial childhood to the completion of his maturity we must think of as a steady transition from the situation of purest innocence to one of a pure spiritual power, which, though it matured gradually, is distinguished from virtue by the fact that it had to proceed through neither error nor sin, nor even through inclination to one of these."[38] If from here we look back to Schleiermacher's explanation that an archetypal Christ is to have developed as did all men, then to the contrary we know that not a single person developed this way, that vacillation and struggle, errors and mistakes, are spared no one, and that therefore his Christ, if his development is to have been free of all of this, did not at all develop as other men do.[39] Hence he remains in his development as in his being an unreal mental construct, a lifeless ideal drawn according to a stencil. When Schleiermacher explains how in Christ indeed "all powers, the lower ones to be ruled as well as the controlling higher ones, unfolded only gradually and progressively, so that the latter could master the former only to the extent that they had developed; yet the mastering itself was perfect in every moment,"[40] then this clearly operates by a very simple mathematical formula: $3:2=6:4=12:8$, and so on. But by means of mathematical formulae no human development is to be constructed.

38. *The Christian Faith*, par. 93, sec. 4; see also *The Life of Jesus*, p. 99, and the sermon on Hebrews 4:15 in *Predigten*, 3: 427 ff. [*Werke* 2, part 3.]

39. [Strauss is misleading here. Schleiermacher's point is that Christ the archetype did develop as all men also develop, not that the development itself was similar.]

40. *The Christian Faith*, par. 93, sec. 4.

Now Schleiermacher ostensibly does not want to presuppose this conception of Christ, in which he believes he has preserved the kernel of the churchly one, when he undertakes the enterprise of producing a Life of Jesus, but wants to make it depend step by step on whether by means of true scientific exegesis he finds it in the sources. Indeed, if he does not find it, then the contradiction between science and faith would exist, which from the start Schleiermacher was determined not to permit to emerge; he could still, of course, be a man of science, but no longer of believing science, that is, no theologian, which of course he wants to remain. As is well known, to those who found his philosophical mode of thought incommensurate with his activity as a clergyman he asked whether they took him to be "so impoverished that he could have found no existence apart from a profession which actually (on the presupposition of his opponents) in the highest degree must be contrary to him?"[41] Surely this refutation applies to only those who saw the contradiction in Schleiermacher as a conscious one, and who viewed his refusal to admit it as hypocrisy. But the contradiction lay so deep in the being of this remarkable man that for just this reason it never entered his consciousness.

At any rate, what first strikes one about Schleiermacher's temperament is this uncommon discernment which penetrates all recesses of things and concepts, coupled with a hardly less exceptional capacity to see the most disparate things together and to combine them—hence his excellent scientific gifts. Whoever found himself especially attracted or rebuffed by these qualities could easily overlook—or view as less essential—another element which lay equally deep in Schleiermacher's temperament. This was the ardent religious feeling [*Gefühl*] which indeed grew to a robustness,

41. In the first *Sendschreiben* on *The Christian Faith*, at the beginning. [See above, note 32.]

which it would not have attained otherwise, through his education in the *Brüdergemeinde*. But Schleiermacher would hardly have endured so long in this community and would hardly have maintained a lifelong partiality to it,[42] had not his pious feeling been balanced by the equal force of his critical understanding. He wrote to Jacobi, in response to the latter's complaint that he was a pagan in his mind but a Christian in his disposition, "This is my statement in opposition: with my mind I am a philosopher, and with the feeling [*Gefühl*] I am completely a devout man, and indeed as such a Christian."[43] We must acknowledge this as the full truth spoken out of the awareness of his innermost temperament. But in this duality Schleiermacher saw no contradiction; rather for him there was "an immediate awareness that they were only the two foci of his own ellipse" and that in the "oscillation" or "vacillation" between them he had "the whole fulfillment of his early life." This too is a statement as true as it is profound. Actually, the most ardent devout feeling must be harmonizable with the most analytic mind; the only question is that of how the balance is to be achieved.

Here then commences that reciprocal "tuning," in which everything depends on the middle line which defines the limits of one force against the other. We have seen already what we will see again at all points of our examination, that with Schleiermacher this line gives piety the advantage and science the disadvantage. Basically, this is found already in his admission to Jacobi, when he calls himself according to his mind only generally a philosopher, but according to feeling not only a devout man in general but specifically a Christian. Pious feeling in him therefore opposes a philosophiz-

42. [For a discussion of Schleiermacher and the Moravian *Brüdergemeinde* see Redeker, *Schleiermacher: Life and Thought*, pp. 9–12.]
43. *Aus Schleiermachers Leben in Briefen*, 2:342. See also the additional material here.

ing mind not only with a certain degree of strength, but also in very definite conceptualities[44] which he was not disposed to have melted away by the mind. Rather, the mind was able to modify and smooth out only the superficiality of pious feeling. All the more Schleiermacher thereafter believed he could adhere to its content—in fact, not only the emotional content but also the essence of its conceptual content—as truth which had been justified by the mind. Among these pious concepts which he wanted the mind to taste but not to devour belongs first of all that concerning the personal redeemer; in this concept also one can see an aftereffect of his education in the *Brüdergemeinde,* whose religious poetry is built especially on this personal love-relation.[45]

If, then, this Christ was a necessity for Schleiermacher as a pious man, and if he believed that as a theologian he could hold fast to him scientifically at the same time, then his dealing with the gospel story must be oriented to ascertaining just this picture of Christ; what went beyond this effort decisively was rejected in order to avoid entanglements with science, and what reflected the picture's features or appeared to do so was kept. Moreover, every emergent suspicion that even these features might have been imposed only later on a still more natural image of this man were zealously repelled. Statements that this or that "is not harmonizable with our presupposition about Christ," or that "he could be what he is in our faith only if . . . ," and so on (pp. 11, 14, 111, et al.)—these and similar phrases are repeated endlessly as reasons why this or that passage is to be interpreted in a certain way, or why this relation or this action of Jesus

44. [Strauss manifests his view of Christianity as a system of concepts, and thereby misses what Schleiermacher meant by saying he was a Christian with his feeling.]

45. [Strauss alludes to poetry and hymnody which repeatedly speaks of the believer's love for the Savior.]

is to be understood in this way. Now one could say that every biographer finds himself in the situation of having to illumine as best he can dark or dubious parts of the life of his hero on the basis of the general conception of his character or his relationships; the same thing is to be allowed him who is occupied with the life of Jesus. However, the difference is that the ordinary biographer, if he is competent, will have derived that overall conception only from his critically tested sources;[46] on the other hand, the theologian, and especially Schleiermacher, derives his conception of Christ, which accompanies him as he works through the Gospels, from the church's faith, even if intelligently trimmed. Thereby he makes the same mistake as the biographer who, in tension with the results from his sources, still in main matters maintains the common prejudice about his hero. This is to be seen as well in a seemingly insignificant connection: though Schleiermacher designates his lecture course as one on the life of Jesus, as it progresses he uses the name "Christ" virtually throughout. But this is a title of office and status which includes the entire church conception of that person, and whoever uses it preferentially thereby betrays his standpoint as more dogmatic than historical. The human historical name is Jesus, and that one customarily speaks of the life of Jesus, not of the life of Christ, instinctively expresses the presumed standpoint which this discipline is to occupy.

Schleiermacher's treatment of the life of Jesus, insofar as it promised at the outset to commence without dogmatic presuppositions, cannot keep its word; to be sure, it liberated itself from some of the fetters of church prejudice, but by no means did it liberate itself from all. And if previous theologians were like the companions of Ulysses who

46. [Despite his own biographical writing, it is strange that Strauss should not have seen that a biographer's overall view of his hero is not derived only from his sources but also from his own sense of what is important.]

stopped their ears against the Sirens of criticism, then Schleiermacher indeed kept his ears open, but had himself tied with cables to the mast of the Christian faith in order to sail past the dangerous island unharmed. His conduct is only half-free, therefore also only half-scientific. The truly scientific conduct is to engage in criticism unfettered and with open ears, in which case it will turn out that the entire legend of the Sirens was but the whisperings of the old sorceress Circe.

CHAPTER THREE

SCHLEIERMACHER'S VIEW OF
THE SOURCES OF THE LIFE OF JESUS

In the lectures on the life of Jesus Schleiermacher does not deal further with the sources of the gospel story, since in this regard he can refer his hearers to his lectures on the introduction to the New Testament.[47] He suggests only (p. 37) that the investigation of the origins of and relations among our four Gospels actually would first have to be completed before the task of presenting the life of Jesus could be accomplished; yet that investigation is so difficult and far-reaching, and at the same time so pressing, that it is impossible to wait for its completion.[48]

47. In the second *Sendschreiben*; see also *Einleitung ins neue Testament*, pp. 315 ff. [*Werke*, 1, vol. 8.]

48. [By 1832 the basic "solution" to the problem of the Gospels had not yet been proposed (in 1835, Lachmann proposed that Matthew and Luke used Mark; Q was not "discovered" until Holtzmann's work in 1863). Schleiermacher, like virtually everyone else at the time (including Strauss), worked with Griesbach's view that Mark was the last of the Synoptics, and depended upon both Luke and Matthew (the oldest). This view is currently being championed by William R. Farmer, whose book *The Synoptic Problem* (New York: Macmillan, 1964) also provides a thorough history of research from the eighteenth century onward. For a recent response to the attempt to rehabilitate the Griesbach hypothesis see Charles H. Talbert and Edgar V. McKnight, "Can the Griesbach Hypothesis be Falsified?" *Journal of Biblical Literature* 91 (1972):338–68. Schleiermacher had in mind also the relation of the Synoptics to John. Today there is a general consensus that while John did not know the Synoptics in their present form, he did know some of the traditions which they used.]

With regard to the relation of these writings to the task at hand, we have, according to Schleiermacher, "in our four Gospels, strictly speaking, only two different sources: the Gospel of John is one, and the other three together are the other." As a whole the latter, which have a considerable amount of their content in common, are merely aggregates of individual narratives;[49] the former, which coincides only rarely with the others, is a connected narrative composed according to a single plan. If, then, as was assumed in the church since ancient times, both the Gospel of John and, of the others, at least the Gospel of Matthew are to have been authored by immediate disciples of Christ, it is difficult "to explain the fact that one arranges an aggregate of individual narratives in which there occurs so little of that which the other tells, and conversely, that the other offers a more coherent Gospel in which there occur so few of the particulars which the former has collected" (p. 40). Still, it is not merely that the one lacks so much of what the other includes, and vice versa, or indeed, that it lacks the sort of thing concerning which, for every purpose which may underlie it, "one must say, 'He surely would have had to include that,'" but also with regard to the place and time of Jesus' life, completely different conceptions are evident on both sides. "According to the Synoptic Gospels it appears as if Christ had his actual residence in Galilee, and particularly in Capernaum; but in the Gospel of John nothing of this is to be noted, and instead a special reason is always given for Christ leaving Jerusalem and its environs and going to Galilee" (p. 42). In the same way, John speaks of the several Passovers which occurred during the time of Jesus' public life; yet according to the others, which mention but

49. [Actually, Schleiermacher suggested a somewhat more complex reconstruction. In the various Christian communities, locally known traditions about Jesus came together in cycles or complexes, then found their way into the Synoptics (*Einleitung ins neue Testament* [Berlin: Georg Reimer, 1845], pp. 235–236; *Werke* 1, vol. 8).]

a single Passover, one could believe that the public activity of Christ did not last for more than a year.

Schleiermacher had sharper insight than most theologians into the total difference between the first three Gospels and the Fourth; he recognized that here it is an *either/or* matter, that one cannot take the Gospel of John *and* the Gospel of Matthew as apostolic writings, but that one can take at most either the one or the other. Particularly, he did not recognize this any less sharply than Bretschneider, but, as is known, in the dilemma he decided for precisely the opposite alternative. "Who will not rejoice," he says with reference to Bretschneider's *Probabilia*, "that the otherwise scattered hints of the character of our Gospel of John have now emerged in the efficient form of a critical hypothesis? This," he then breaks off superficially, "indeed could have no other outcome."[50] Certainly it could have no other outcome in the course of things in the twenties, whose romantic sympathies were throughout on the side of John, and hence against Bretschneider; but all the more a later, more sober generation knew how to prize the achievement of this scholar. In this matter Schleiermacher paid a heavy toll to the times and to the educated circles to which he attached himself. Between him and Bretschneider, as far as intellec-

50. In the second *Sendschreiben*; see also his *Einleitung*, pp. 315 ff. [The reference is to Karl G. Bretschneider, *Probabilia de evangelii et epistolarum Ioannis apostoli indole et origine* (Leipzig, 1820). Bretschneider (1776–1848) denied the apostolic authorship of John, but then modified his views. In *The Life of Jesus Critically Examined* Strauss had followed Bretschneider's radical views and thereby inaugurated the practice of setting John aside (except for occasional details) for life of Jesus research. In 1847 F. C. Baur published his investigation of the Gospels, *Kritische Untersuchungen über die kanonischen Evangelien* (Tübingen: L. F. Fues), in which he argued for a late second-century date for John. Strauss regarded Baur's work on John as a vindication of his own views, but was embittered because Baur distanced himself from Strauss. See above, p. xxxiv; see also *Formation*, pp. 73–84.]

tual power is concerned, there is no possible comparison; the dogmatics, especially, of the two men are related somewhat like Fichte's *Wissenschaftslehre* and Krug's *Fundamentalphilosophie*.[51] But in criticism of the Fourth Gospel, Bretschneider is the strong man of science, and Schleiermacher the man of a frail religious-aesthetic partiality. While the former labored for the future, the latter spoke only for the moment. In fact, every word which Schleiermacher utters about the Johannine question shows his embarrassment. Contrary to his custom, he becomes superficial whenever he must deal with the Gospel critically. "The Gospel of John," he says, "presents itself everywhere as one which originates from an immediate eyewitness, in contrast with which the others' compilation from single elements is subject to comparable doubt, and all three without exception are to be seen as coming to us secondhand. This is not the case with the Johannine Gospel; it clearly has the character of originating from a single person who narrates what he himself experienced" (pp. 171, 159). One sees that for Schleiermacher the unified character of the Fourth Gospel has already decided the question of its having originated with an eyewitness. "The Gospel of John," he says at another time (p. 433), "is a report of an eyewitness and is of a piece." But even if the certainly mosaic-like compilation of the first three Gospels is a proof of their later origin, still the unified systematic arrangement of the Fourth is no more a proof that its author was an eyewitness and a disciple of Jesus than the same quality of Sallustius's *Jurgurtha* proves that the author flourished under Metellus

51. [J. G. Fichte, *Wissenschaftslehre* (1804) [vol. 2 of *Nachgelassene Werke* (Bonn, 1834–35); republished with introduction and commentary by W. Janke as *J. G. Fichte, Wissenschaftslehre 1804* (Frankfort: Vittorio Klostermann, 1966)]; W. T. Krug, *Fundamentalphilosophie* (Leipzig: Leopold Voss, 3d rev. ed. 1827).]

or Marius, or that he must have stood before the platform of Mammius.[52]

Schleiermacher himself has the feeling that in this matter things are not as they should be. "I cannot deny," he once admits, "that it will appear to many as a kind of partiality that I always present John as the correct, authentic foundation and the other Gospels as those which are to be used only with a very critical circumspection" (p. 223). Immediately, however, only the latter (the critical caution in the use of the Synoptics) but in no sense the former (the prevailing preference for John) is justified by him. In connection with various miracle stories, which cannot be made conceivable by any artifice of a natural explanation,[53] Schleiermacher suggests that finally one can find help only "through a hypothesis concerning their character," that is, "concerning the genesis of the narratives"; but it is possible to attain this only "if we have a completely certain theory about the origin of the first three Gospels" (pp. 220–24). One can see that something of the mythical view begins to dawn, for to explain a miracle story on the basis of the gene-

---

52. [Strauss refers to Gaius Sallustius Crispus (86–35 B.C.), a political ally of Caesar; after Caesar's assassination he retired to write history. Strauss refers to Sallustius's second historical work, *The War with Jugurtha.* Even more than the previous *The War with Cataline,* this work rearranges historical events in order to produce a better, more vivid story. The events of which he wrote occurred in the previous century, and the figures he mentioned lived two generations before Sallustius. Strauss's point is that the integrated, vivid, and lifelike quality of a story is no evidence for its being the account of an eyewitness—a point which was unfortunately lost on much subsequent Gospel criticism.]

53. [The allusion is to the rationalist treatment of miracles; the historicity of the event is preserved by rewriting the story. Thus, for instance, a miraculous feeding of the crowd did occur, but what really happened was that the example of the boy who shared his loaves and fish induced others to share what they had. Strauss is critical of Schleiermacher's inability to free himself from this rationalist approach, yet he too used it. See Hodgson's introduction, *LJCE,* pp. xxv–vi.]

sis of the narrative is to perceive it to be mythic.[54] But why is this the case only in the origin of the first three Gospels? Because "if also in the case of the Gospel of John we found it necessary to see the narrative as derived second- or third-hand and to have been modified in manifold ways, nothing reliable would be left for us" (p. 223). For this reason Schleiermacher reminds us so often, almost anxiously, that "we are by no means in a position to draw conclusions about this subject," that this "must remain for the future to decide," and that we "can only set it aside as a task, but one which is not necessary to have solved" (pp. 221, 224, 225). Manifestly, this situation is not safe for him; he surmises that if one ever got to the bottom of the Synoptics critically, one would have to do so also for John, and then "nothing reliable would be left for us!"[55]

54. [Strauss alludes to his understanding of myth, which he developed in his first *Life of Jesus*. For Strauss, a narrative was either a historically accurate account or a myth (or had mythical elements in it which prevented one from accepting it as a historical account). Paragraphs 15 and 16 of *LJCE* define "evangelical *mythus*" and explain the criteria by which one can distinguish myth (the unhistorical element) from history in the Gospels. Hodgson compares Strauss's method with the recent clarification of the "negative criterion"; see his introduction, pp. xxvi–xxix.]

55. [The relation between this paragraph and subsequent Gospel criticism in terms of life of Jesus research is that of prophecy and fulfillment, even though the sequence—Synoptics, John—has been reversed. That is, after the thoroughly theological character of John was perceived, the theological character of the Synoptics began also to emerge at the beginning of the twentieth century, especially since Wilhelm Wrede's *The Messianic Secret* of 1901, which was translated from the German only recently by J. C. C. Greig (Cambridge and London: Jas. Clarke & Co., 1971).

The attempt to reconstruct the life of Jesus rested on the historical reliability of Mark. But Wrede's insistence that Mark is governed throughout by theological concerns (which Strauss would have called myth), coupled with Schmidt's demonstration that Mark stitched together individual traditions and thereby created the outline of Jesus' life, meant that now indeed "nothing reliable" was left except in the individual pericopes, and these had to be tested for their historical accuracy as well—which form criticism proceeded to do (Karl Ludwig Schmidt, *Der Rahmen der Geschichte Jesu* [Berlin: Trowitzsch & Sohn, 1919; reprinted by the Wis-

For this reason, when at one point the bases for suspicion of the genuineness and trustworthiness of the Johannine Gospel are expressed, Schleiermacher puts them in a form in which they are easy to refute. Dealing with the origin of the discourses of Jesus in John, he is led to speak of "the view which has arisen in German theology" that John here "mixed in a good deal of his own ideas" (pp. 261–62). But then he presents this view in such a way as to imply that his opponents really regarded the apostle John as the author of the Gospel; they only believed that, on the basis of John's previous mystical orientation, which also combined with his

senschaftliche Buchgesellschaft in Darmstadt in 1969]). T. W. Manson resisted because he saw the issue clearly: "It is a case of Mark's order or none at all" (*The Teaching of Jesus* [London: Cambridge University Press, 1931], p. 26). Just as Schleiermacher argued for the eyewitness tradition for John, to make reliance on John tenable, so Manson argued for the Petrine base of Mark ("The Foundation of the Synoptic Tradition: The Gospel of Mark" [1944], now in *Studies in the Gospels and Epistles*, ed. Matthew Black [Philadelphia: Westminster Press, 1962]).

Today none of the Gospels can be shown to be traceable to an apostle. This was seen long ago by Martin Kähler (*The So-Called Historical Jesus and the Historic Biblical Christ*, trans. and ed. Carl Braaten [Philadelphia: Fortress Press, 1964], p. 48). The attempt to confirm the historical reliability of the Gospels by establishing their eyewitness base was a curious one all along. This effort reflected the need to overcome the legacy of Lessing and Baur. The former had argued that the reliability of an account diminishes with the distance in time from the event, and the latter had dated the Gospels as second-century writings. Therefore an early date for the Gospels, coupled with an eyewitness origin, appeared to provide solid history. But Strauss had already implied the flaw in this reasoning by arguing that what eyewitnesses told of Jesus was shaped not only by *his* impact on them but also by the impact of *their* Old Testament and Jewish Messianic expectations. After the resurrection faith arose, eyewitnesses to the pre-Easter Jesus did not narrate the stories of his life in a merely "factual" way. Consequently, eyewitness tradition is not necessarily historically accurate. To overcome this dilemma, the so-called Scandinavian School argued that much of the teaching tradition actually comes from the lifetime of Jesus because he taught the disciples to memorize his words. See, for example, Harald Riesenfeld, "The Gospel Tradition and its Beginnings," *The Gospels Reconsidered* (Oxford: Blackwell, 1960), pp. 131–53.]

enthusiasm for Christ, he made of Christ's sayings something they had not been originally. A view presented in such a way is easy for Schleiermacher to refute by the question, How did that mystical orientation find its way into the disciple of the pragmatic Baptist, how did the presumably Alexandrian speculation reach the unlearned fisherman of Galilee, and furthermore, how had it done so at a time when such Egyptian wisdom had as yet found little acceptance in Palestine? But was it permissible to present doubts about the Johannine discourses of Christ in a form which at that time had long been surpassed by criticism, and to act as if the "robust critical hypothesis" (that of the *Probabilia*) were not available, which, far from being satisfied with a mixture of subjective conceptions on the part of the apostle, rather viewed the Gospel as the work of an unknown Alexandrian of the second century?[56] In order to cling firmly to the Johannine Gospel as apostolic and trustworthy, despite such reasons for suspicion, Schleiermacher manifestly makes a highly unsatisfactory attempt to derive the discussion of the Logos in the introduction not from the Logos doctrine of Philo, but rather from what Jesus now and again said about his word or his words. He thinks he

56. [It is necessary to distinguish current treatment of this issue from that of both Schleiermacher and Strauss. The question concerns the possible juxtaposition of genuine and nongenuine materials in Jesus' discourses in John. Schleiermacher denied that Alexandrian materials and ideas are mixed with genuine words of Jesus because it is impossible to think that John, the Galilean fisherman, knew about such ideas. Hence he could not have mixed them into the Gospel. Strauss rejects this consideration because John's Gospel was written in Alexandria late in the second century. Today, redaction criticism has superannuated such arguments over the date and provenance of the Gospels. The traditionalists appealed to the old material in the text to argue an early date for the whole, while the others used the late material to argue that everything in the text is late. Actually the argument is wrong because both are right; the Gospels (all of them) contain early and late material side by side. Redaction criticism helps us to distinguish one from the other, and to see that old material is used in a much later text.]

can explain the profound difference between the Johannine discourses of Christ and the Synoptic ones by the fact that the first three Gospels emerged from collected oral traditions whose original source was the oral narratives of the apostles and others who accompanied Jesus. These probably were careful lest they transmitted the sort of thing which could be readily misunderstood and distorted at third or fourth hand. Conversely, John is said to have been the only one of the immediate disciples of Christ who wrote down his memories, and "he could then share such discourses and sayings which would have been risky to transmit in the oral tradition because they could be distorted easily" (pp. 260, 262). Now that is certainly not a "robust critical hypothesis," but an expedient of desperation of the poorest sort, whose refutation would have to have been the easiest matter in the world for Schleiermacher, were it not his own despair that the refutation was to remedy.

It is well known that from ancient times onward the church regarded the Synoptic Gospels to have been written first, whether in the sequence in which they stand in the canon, or even in the order of Matthew, Luke, Mark; only after these three, for spiritual as well as for material supplementation, was the Johannine Gospel written.[57] For Schleiermacher, the first three Gospels were not written by the apostles or disciples of apostles but were secondary compilations, but he accepted the Fourth as the work of an apostle. So he could not assume that this apostle, however old he may have grown, wrote his Gospel only after the

57. [Until recently, Strauss's statement could have stood unchallenged. But the more clearly the tradition-history of John comes into view, the more evident it becomes that the Johannine tradition existed alongside the Synoptic stream, and that at certain points they affected one another. Nor can one show that John was intended to be a supplement to the Synoptics. For a recent survey of the issues see Raymond E. Brown's commentary on John in the Anchor Bible Series, 2 vols. (Garden City: Doubleday, 1966), 1:xxiv–li. Brown sees five stages in the development of John's Gospel.]

emergence of those later collections; rather he took the Johannine Gospel to be the older and the Synoptics the later writings. "At the time," he says, "when John wrote his Gospel, the contents of the other Gospels existed only as scattered pieces which were collected only later" (p. 393).[58] How much more historical truth lies in the tradition, how much more historical rhythm in the church's decision concerning the sequence of the Gospels, than in such arbitrary assertions from an incomplete and one-sided criticism which simply stands the obvious fact of the matter on its head.[59] But now, let us take up the life story of Jesus, beginning with the first period—the life of Jesus before his public appearance.

58. [Erwin R. Goodenough argued that John is older than the Synoptics ("John a Primitive Gospel," *Journal of Biblical Literature* 64 [1945]: 145–82).]

59. In any case, nevertheless, Schleiermacher's preference for the gifted and congenial John is more readily intelligible than the recently emerged preference for the insipid and colorless Mark, whose tertiary character Schleiermacher, on his part, perceived in an unprejudiced way (cf. my *Leben Jesu für das deutsche Volk bearbeitet*, p. 128). Our young and old "Mark-lions" [an allusion to the traditional way of symbolizing this Gospel] may roar as loudly as they like. So long as every one of their apparent reasons for the priority of their Gospel can be opposed by six real ones, and indeed are partly opposed by the advocates' own admissions that Mark was later reworked, and so on, this whole orientation remains for me passing humbug—like "futurist music" or the agitation against smallpox vaccination. And I seriously believe that it is this same kind of mind which, according to the situation, will be subject to the one humbug or the other. Especially as far as Mr. Holtzmann's crude attacks on me are concerned, they only show that when the highest degree of passionate irritation is expressed, one can easily compare the professor whose first publication has been ignored with the lioness who has been robbed of her cubs. The long separation from theology of which Mr. Holtzmann accuses me I owe, among other things, to the fact that from such a perspective the critical molehills, which he and those like him have constructed, could not appear like mountains to me. [Evidently Strauss refers to the attack by H. J. Holtzmann (see below, note 151). Here Strauss shows himself at his worst, manifesting his petulance, prejudice against Wagner's music, and inability to deal seriously with a challenge to his (and Baur's) critical dogmas.]

PART TWO
SCHLEIERMACHER'S
LIFE OF JESUS

CHAPTER FOUR

THE FIRST PERIOD: THE LIFE OF JESUS BEFORE HIS PUBLIC APPEARANCE

In this section, manifestly, a rather liberal position is made possible for Schleiermacher on two sides—on the critical side, by the fact that his single actual historical authority, John, is silent about this whole period; on the dogmatic side, by the fact that he regards the heart of this prehistory, the supernatural procreation of Jesus, to be something which is not important for Christian faith (p. 58).[60] Still, on the other hand, Schleiermacher's freedom is restricted again by prejudice. Even if he no longer regards the first three Gospels equally as works of the apostles or of apostles' associates, still the churchly view follows him in that he assumes the closest possible relationship between their reports and the facts; in particular, he lacks a conception of the intervention of an independent, productive, legend-creating activity. Even where he acknowledges fiction, something factual is still supposed to be its foundation, and where the text contains something unacceptable he often prefers to do away with it through a twisting and a

60. *The Christian Faith*, par. 97, sec. 2.

far-fetched interpretation, in the manner of the rationalist exegesis, rather than by an open admission that the entire text has no claim to historical validity.

THE INFANCY STORY

Schleiermacher approaches the infancy story of Jesus, as we see it in the First and Third Gospels, with the natural question, which was also particularly adapted to convince those who are still caught in the old conception of biblical history, "Where, then, can these reports of the birth of Christ, and what goes with it, originate?" (p. 45). Jesus' own conversations with his disciples, insofar as the Evangelists report them, do not give the impression that such matters were discussed. His mother, Mary, to be sure, was with the disciples after his resurrection, and especially with John, and she could have told such stories; but why did precisely John not include anything about it in his Gospel? What about Jesus' brothers?—although it is well known that it is problematic whether they were real siblings of Jesus, children of Joseph from a previous marriage, or even mere nieces and nephews of Mary. Simeon and Anna, no less than the shepherds of Bethlehem, doubtless were long dead when the material of our Gospels was collected; therefore these stories must come from somewhere else "and not from such an immediate source" (p. 47).

Besides, at least part of the questionable stories has a form which is not that of a historical source at all. "One part of the report of Luke has a poetic quality, in which are found definitely poetic passages written according to the contemporary mode of Hebrew poetry, in a psalm style; is someone to have composed these hymns in such a way that one can accept them as an accurate report?" (p. 49). In addition, "in Luke the whole presentation, apart from the lyric pieces, has a dramatic quality in which Zechariah and Elizabeth counterbalance Joseph and Mary" (p. 49), and then there are the corresponding appearances of the angels and the similar doubts of Zechariah on the one hand and Mary on the other, though they are treated differently. These are indications of "an artistic composition"; still, according to Schleiermacher, from this it does not follow that everything was invented, but only that the original historical reports were worked over from a particular point of view (pp. 49, 52).

In contrast with this poetic form of the first narratives in Luke, those of Matthew have a seemingly more historical one. But at the same time something else is evident, namely, that both Evangelists offer differing arrative sequences which must come from different source, and one must ask whether they are harmonizeable. Manifestly, Matthew presupposes that Jesus' parents lived in Bethlehem before his birth, and Luke presupposes that they lived in Nazareth. Both cannot be correct at the same time; but if one asks which is supposed to be true, he becomes embarrassed, for one can conclude equally that Bethlehem was the original residence of Jesus' parents because the ancestors of the Messiah came from Bethlehem, and that Nazareth was their home because later Mary and her children resided there (pp. 53, 54).[61] Likewise, the two genealogies in the two Gospels do not agree; either one or both of them may be incorrect. Still, Schleiermacher thinks they nonetheless support Jesus' Davidic descent (p. 54).

With regard to the annunciation of Jesus' birth, there is a divergence between Matthew and Luke which, according to Schleiermacher, cannot be explained as the one having merely ignored what the other reports; rather, here he recognizes an actual contradiction. "Had Mary received such information" (in advance, according to Luke), "it would be contrary to the nature of her relationship to

61. See Schleiermacher on Luke, pp. 45, 49. [*Über die Schriften des Lukas. Ein kritischer Versuch* (Berlin, 1817). *Werke* 1, part 2.]

Joseph had she told him nothing about it; but if she had, his suspicion (according to Matthew) would be inexplicable, since in the other narrative he appears as believing in such an epiphany" (p. 57).[62]

While Schleiermacher was merely indifferent about the reports discussed thus far, in the narratives of the fatherless conception of Jesus there appears an element which, as unnecessary offense, is definitely alien to him, and which he therefore seeks to make historically untenable with much more diligence than the foregoing passages. He rightly points out, as he had done already in *The Christian Faith*,[63] that in regard to the conception of Jesus an escalation of views is manifest in the New Testament. In the Gospels there are people who speak of Joseph as the real father of Jesus without the Evangelists adding a correction. Mark and John are completely silent about the matter, which is reported only by Matthew and Luke. It is evident, then, that even "the assertion of the supernatural conception of Christ was valued differently" (p. 57). But now in his zeal to withdraw the exegetical basis from this dogma, Schleiermacher goes still farther and seeks to show a variation also between the reports of Matthew and Luke. In the latter's narrative, the assertion of the virgin birth is "not presented with utter clarity"; by itself the passage would "permit [indeed!] also another interpretation in which it remains possible that Christ was conceived with the assistance of Joseph" (p. 59). But how, since Mary protests to the angel that she does not know a man (Luke 1:34)? Yes, counters Schleiermacher, that is what she says, but one should "not take it so literally, since she was engaged to Joseph; consequently she knew about a man through whom

---

62. So already in his book on Luke [see foregoing note], pp. 42 ff., 49.
63. Par. 97, sec. 2.

she could conceive" (p. 57).[64]   But the angel announces
rather that the Holy Spirit will come over her and the power
of the Most High will overshadow her (1:35).   That,
Schleiermacher thinks, "refers more to the fact that the son
who was to be born is the Messiah than to the fact that he
will begin life without the assistance of a man" (p. 57).
Only in Matthew is the latter assertion definitely made, for
in Joseph's distrust lies the fact that "he knew that he was
not the cause of the origin of this life."   Still, according to
Matthew, in a dream he receives the assurance that "no
other man was the cause of it" either, "and it goes with
this," says Schleiermacher, "that it was determined by other
means, that the dream was affected by divine means; but
that is not found in the story, and therefore it does not make
the matter certain" (p. 59).   But is it not found in the story
if it expressly says that it was the angel of the Lord who
appeared to Joseph in the dream (Matt. 1:20)?   And if the
assurance contained in the dream does not guarantee that no
other man is the father of the child, while he himself is
not—of which Joseph was certain when awake—then the
whole origin of Jesus nevertheless turns into the "sinful"—
something which Schleiermacher wants to avoid (pp. 56,
58).

This is the first and at the same time quite glaring test
case of how Schleiermacher and his exegesis never completely outgrew the conceptual mode of rationalism and the
halfway measures of its natural explanation of miracles.[65]

There follow the narratives of the "three wise men" (as

64. [Evidently Schleiermacher forgot that here "to know" means "to
have sexual relations," as in Gen. 4:1—"Now Adam knew his wife Eve,
and she conceived . . ."]

65. [Strauss sees that Schleiermacher adduced various considerations which
cumulatively weakened the historical evidence for the virgin birth, and so
made it easier to set it aside.   Strauss did not see that, in his own way, he
frequently had done precisely the same thing in *The Life of Jesus.*]

Schleiermacher, amazingly, virtually always calls them), the massacre of the innocents, and the flight into Egypt on the one hand and the circumcision and presentation in the temple on the other. How these narrative sequences are to be related to one another is a problem. Here Schleiermacher judges that "the three wise men are difficult [historically] to reconstruct": if one thinks of them as non-Jews, one does not know how it occurred to them to interpret the star with reference to a Jewish king; if they were proselytes, one does not understand why they went to Herod and not to the scribes (p. 62). But since, on the other hand, "a very definite tendency is to be found in this story to set up, right at the beginning, an acknowledgement of Jesus as Messiah outside the proper national Jewish area, it looks very much as if the narrative could have arisen only as an expression of this idea, interpolated into the beginning of the life of Christ" (p. 71).[66] It is evident that here Schleiermacher very definitely formulates the mythical explanation; yet even here, at the outermost edge of the gospel story which is unimportant for him, he carries it out only partially. For however suspicious the silence of Josephus also in respect to the bloodbath in Bethlehem appears to him, he still thinks there must be "a fact at the bottom" because it cannot be inferred exegetically out of the Matthean quotation from the prophet about the lamenting Rachel (p. 66). That the murder of children, which was ordered by the tyrant for the purpose of destroying the last redeemer, is but the reflection of the one which was once arranged by another tyrant and almost put an end to the first redeemer, does not occur to him.[67] It is equally unlikely that one could have invented

66. See Schleiermacher's *Über die Schriften des Lukas*, p. 47.
67. See my *Leben Jesu für das deutsche Volk bearbeitet*, p. 376–78. [Strauss saw the parallel between the story of Pharaoh's slaughter of the Hebrew babies in Exodus 1:15–22 and the story in Matthew. He had dealt extensively with this story in *LJCE*, par. 36.]

the flight to Egypt for the sake of the passage in Hosea (Matt. 2:15), and since also Celsus discusses it (but manifestly only on the basis of Matthew and similar Christian reports),[68] such a fact surely must have been well known; indeed, Schleiermacher does not hesitate to credit this feature in Matthew's narrative complex—which one could almost say is its most fictitious—with "the most external attestation" (p. 69).

In Luke's narrative of the presentation in the temple Schleiermacher indeed also finds a tendency like that in the story of the Magi—namely, that "already at the beginning of Jesus' life the messianic promises were interpreted with reference to him and the messianic hopes were directed toward him" (p. 65). But here, since Simeon could have regarded almost anything natural as a sign of the fulfillment of his hopes, the marvellous appears so lacking that Schleiermacher can confer "the highest internal attestation" on this narrative (p. 68), ignoring the parallel with the story of the Magi, which he had designated as unhistorical, indeed as apocryphal. At the same time we find the rightful observation that "according to the tendency one ought to expect to find the story of the wise men in the Hellenistic Gospel (Luke) because it expresses the acknowledgment of Jesus outside Judea, and the presentation in the temple in the Judaizing Gospel (Matthew); but we do not know how it could happen that the one came into the possession of the one narration, and the other into the other" (p. 68).

In looking back on both narrative sequences in Matthew and Luke, Schleiermacher declares that it is impossible for

68. [Celsus wrote an anti-Christian work, *The True Word*, around 175–80 A.D. About seventy years later Origen wrote his refutation, *Contra Celsum*. Strauss protests that Schleiermacher cannot rely on Celsus to argue for the historicity of the story because Celsus did not have access to non-Christian tradition but relied on Matthew. The standard text and commentary of Origen's reply, which quotes Celsus, is Henry Chadwick's *Origen: Contra Celsum* (Cambridge: University Press, 1965²).]

"both series" in their present combination "to be correct at the same time, and everything which has been attempted to bring them into complete agreement has been done so artificially that it cannot stand up to historical criticism" (p. 71).[69] But individual pieces from the one series can be coordinated with individual pieces from the other quite well. For example, the flight to Egypt, which Matthew links with the visit of the Magi, could readily "have come from the story in Luke because one could have feared that Herod would come to know something about such a scene in the temple" (p. 69).

THE BOY JESUS IN THE TEMPLE

Until now the dispensability of the individual Gospel stories for his theology made it easy for Schleiermacher to render unbiased judgments on their historical worth, a process in which he was hampered now and again only by the habit of rationalist criticism and exegesis. But the situation changes in the case of Luke's story of the visit of the twelve-year-old Jesus to the temple at Jerusalem. Understandably, the fact that the lad designates God as his Father must have a special significance for one who has set himself the task of presenting the God-consciousness in Jesus as being peculiar and equally as having come into being by way of purely human development. Hence all doubts must suddenly cease here. Schleiermacher says:

> Luke's story has for me to a great extent the character of something authentic; there is nothing in it which is under suspicion of being told for the sake of a theological trend; it is the naive expression of a scene which is highly probable under the circumstances. Because of this great naturalness we can acknowledge no doubts about the authenticity of this story, and we can view it quite differently from those

69. *Über die Schriften des Lukas*, p. 45.

earlier stories, where in part, a definite theological trend is perceptible, as well as, in part, a definite form which shows something artificial and fabricated. [p. 76]

Indeed, this visible poetic form, which is peculiar only to the first chapter of Luke, is absent also from the story of the Magi, which Schleiermacher nonetheless did not acknowledge as historical; on the other hand, the miraculous or the exceptional is by no means wanting from our story in the features about the twelve-year-old's questioning and the consciousness of being God's son which dawned so early in him. But the tendential element here is expressed as discernably in this motif as in any other story. In the first place, the remarkable intention in Luke's entire prehistory to illumine the legal piety of Jesus' parents is found both here in the comment (2:42) that they had gone to Jerusalem "according to the custom of the festival," and previously (2:22) where it was said that they fulfilled the purification customs "according to the law of Moses." Then comes the parallel of the development of the messianic lad and that of other prophetic children, in the comment borrowed from the story of Samson (2:52) that Jesus grew in wisdom, stature and in favor with God and man; the same point was made previously in the story of the presentation in the temple (2:40)—that the boy grew and became strong in the Spirit and the grace of God was upon him. Further, the disparity between that which developed in the wonder child and the understanding of his parents is seen in the comment (2:50) that they did not understand the word which he spoke to them; similarly, in the presentation in the temple (2:33) they marvelled about what was said about the child.

But the distinctive tendency here, and that which distinguishes the story about the twelve-year-old Jesus from others, is one which is customary, in both the good and bad senses, in all hero-stories. Namely, it is that just as the nettle stings prematurely, so the rose is fragrant already in the green bud. To a certain extent it is actually the case that the exceptional talent, the decisive vocation, often bursts forth early in surprising manifestations. But even more commonly, in poetry and folk-legends, such precocity is anticipated spontaneously. Since I have already collected elsewhere the relevant illustrations from the legends of Moses, Samuel, and Cyrus,[70] perhaps I may mention one such legendary creation which I myself, obviously in the worst sense, have become. It is well known that to the masses (of all classes), whoever denies the divinity of Christ is as good as an atheist. When I first asked for this accusation by my work on the life of Jesus I was in my twenty-seventh year. But was the nettle to have waited that long to sting? I was still a lad in a Württemberg monastery school and about seventeen years old when, with several of my companions, I was interrogated as a witness in a matter concerning an examination. Then the young nettle is said to have refused the required oath by saying that he could not give the oath because he did not believe in God. This is what the examining official, who is still alive and working in another position, says about that event; from his mouth a credulous man, whose written report about it lies before me, heard it on two different occasions. Certainly it is a well-attested story, and there is still not a true word in it; doubtless the narrator himself has long since come to believe it, and yet it is a lie. Even today, if a legal oath were required of me solely in the name of God, I would give it without question, on the certainly established presupposition that it could not concern the more precise determination of the conception of God in this case; but then, in my seventeenth year, no religious doubts whatever had yet awakened within me, and I remained for years, as is known

70. *Das Leben Jesu für das deutsche Volk bearbeitet*, p. 387–88. [*The Life of Jesus Critically Examined* does not have these parallels.]

to my peers, an orthodox Christian. Nevertheless, if that storyteller should accidentally have been the pastor who confirmed me, then certainly even in my fourteenth year I would have to have given him a similar answer, since the seventeenth year is much too late for the initial sting of such a nettle.

From this illustration at least this much becomes apparent: such a story, even if it is told by someone who claims to have been there and actually was there as well, still can easily be told by him as happening in a way it never did. Concerning the story of the twelve-year-old Jesus, Schleiermacher has maintained already in his book on Luke that "manifestly, it could be traced back only to Mary."[71] Nonetheless, he himself finds it necessary to ask whether, in Jesus' remark that he must be in his Father's house, we have his own words used at that time, or whether Mary merely took the expression from his later usage of it. And if Schleiermacher, ignoring his having traced the story to Mary,[72] nonetheless finds the latter possible and is able to grant the former only a greater degree of probability, how much less assurance do we have, in light of the total uncertainty about the origin of the story and in light of its interwovenness with a series of unhistorical pieces, that anything historical at all lies at its base?

THE DEVELOPMENT OF
JESUS' GOD-CONSCIOUSNESS

On this occasion Schleiermacher raises the question concerning the peculiarity of Jesus' God-consciousness and how we must conceive of its origin. When the Gospel reports

71. *Über die Schriften des Lukas*, p. 39.

72. [There is no reason to think that Schleiermacher forgot that he had traced the story to Mary. Schleiermacher simply asks whether in telling the story she repeated the words Jesus had used as a boy or used his words from his adult life.]

of Jesus' sayings about himself are viewed as a whole, he says that "this is certainly to be concluded—that he was conscious of a special unique relation to God; and just as we assume that to be a fact in his human consciousness, so we must also ask, How did he arrive at this consciousness?" For if we assume that this has always been in him in an original way, from the beginning of his life, "then immediately we are caught in the midst of Docetism" (p. 79ff.) But must we not assume this? Or rather, must not at least Schleiermacher assume it, if he takes the Fourth Gospel to be the work of the apostle John and says in particular, "What this man gives us as discourses of Christ really were discourses of Christ, and we have no reason to believe that John added anything of his own" (p. 262)? In these Johannine discourses, however, are found precisely the well-known sayings of Jesus about his pre-existence which appear to make superfluous every question about how the consciousness of his unique relation to God may have arisen humanly in him; for according to these he would have brought it with him, complete, from heaven. If this is Docetism for Schleiermacher, and if he does not want to get caught in it, then one must be curious about how, without giving up John's Gospel, he is to extricate himself from it. That the consciousness of a pre-existence, the constantly present memory of a life with God before the foundation of the world, must have disturbed the human consciousness in Jesus, is a settled matter for Schleiermacher (pp. 96, 268, 272). But if Jesus had had such a consciousness, he says, he must also have shared something of its contents and given his disciples a conception of it, of what circumstances his pre-earthly existence enjoyed; and these men, in turn, would not have kept it to themselves, because with it they could have generated more faith than with the preaching of his resurrection. But nowhere do they mention a word of this (p. 270). Certainly, if Jesus really had remembered a prehuman state it would be amazing if he had never said anything about it to his disciples; but the silence is quite natural if we see the Evangelist as the author of Christ's discourses, for to him only this was dogmatically certain—that there must have *been* such a pre-existence. But of *how* one is to think further about this, he had no more a conception than we do.

One sees that Schleiermacher does not know at all how to think his way into the problem. He speaks about Christ and what he must have done and not done, while we still stand wholly at the Evangelist and the question of whether his Christ is a real being at all.[73] In deciding this, precisely those sayings are of highest importance, but Schleiermacher does not trouble himself with them. He explains tersely, "The exegetical basis for the assumption of a pre-existence is very weak" (p. 94). "One doubtless," he says, "interpreted individual sayings of Christ in this direction; but doubtless nothing is easier" (what is not easy for a dialectician like Schleiermacher?) "than to show how these explanations are something very arbitrary, and that, for example, Jesus' saying that he had a glory with the Father before the foundation of the world (John 17:3) can be explained differently as well" (p. 96). Specifically, it is said to mean only that from the beginning God wanted the world to be such as should go through sin to redemption, and that therefore also Jesus was determined from the start, not actually but ideally, as included in the divine decree (p. 269). I can only repeat here what I said elsewhere:

If a Gospel commences with these sentences: "In the beginning was the Word, and the Word was with God and was

73. [Recently, Ernst Käsemann has reasserted Strauss's view that the Johannine Christ is really "a god striding across the earth," and that John approaches a "naive Docetism" (*The Testament of Jesus*, trans. Gerhard Krodel [Philadelphia: Fortress Press, 1968], ch. 2).]

God," through this Word the world was created and subsequently it became flesh in Jesus, and now this Jesus
appears, and affirms that he was before Abraham and speaks
of his glory which he had had with God before the world
was, then here we hear clearly the eternal Creator-Word
speaking and remembering his personal existence before the
incarnation, and we shall dismiss every other explanation of
his words as an artificial and an untrue one.[74]

With this interpretation Schleiermacher occupies the
standpoint of the worst Socinian-rationalist exegesis,[75] even
though it is imitated by numerous schools, and even by
those who do not dogmatically occupy its standpoint.[76]
This is also quite natural; if one does not want to give up
the Fourth Gospel, and at the same time does not accept its
fundamental doctrine, one must distort it. But it borders
on the incredible—if on this standpoint anything would be
incredible—that the Gospel of pre-existence itself, whose
Christ is there as if shot from a pistol, to the contrary is said
to attest to a gradual human development. When Jesus
says that he does nothing of himself, but that the Father

---

74. *Das Leben Jesu für das deutsche Volk bearbeitet*, p. 49. [Strauss's
point still stands.]

75. ["Socinianism" refers generally to a religious movement associated
with the Italian Faustus Socinus (1539–1609), whose lifework was in
Poland. The Socinians were anti-Trinitarian Christians who held that
although Jesus was supernaturally begotten, his atoning work resulted from
his teaching and moral example. After considerable success in Poland,
they were suppressed and banished in 1638. Their writings were known
to Hugo Grotius, Milton, Newton, and Locke, and influenced English
Unitarians. For an excellent survey see H. R. Guggisberg, "Sozinianer,"
Die Religion in Geschichte und Gegenwart, 6 vols. (Tübingen: J. C. B.
Mohr [Paul Siebeck] 1962[3]), 5:207–10, where basic literature is cited.]

76. Thus, what [W.] Beyschlag (in his lecture "What Can the Evangelical Church Gain from the Most Recent Treatments of the Life of
Jesus?" p. 41ff.) thinks he can use to go beyond Schleiermacher's conception of the pre-existence of Jesus consists of nothing but empty words,
in which one seeks in vain for a real idea. [This lecture has not been
accessible to me; Geischer lists it as published in Berlin in 1864.]

shows him everything and will show him yet even greater works than these (John 5:20), then Schleiermacher interprets it this way: by this "Christ describes his consciousness as one which has entered completely into human form, understood as human development" (pp. 101, 266). Indeed, the works of which the Johannine Jesus speaks here, and to which he ascribes an escalation, are nothing human at all, but the supernatural working of the Logos, who has just healed the lame man and one half-dead, but who is about to advance to the point of raising the really dead. Immediately in the twenty-first verse the resurrection of the dead is mentioned as that in which this greater element is to consist; and if previously the marvelling of the Jews about this was pointed to, then it becomes evident that by this greater thing one is to understand, apart from the future general resurrection of the dead, the impending example of the raising of Lazarus.[77]   Evidence for the gradual development of Jesus' God-consciousness can be found in this passage only by him who tears the passage out of its context; similarly, for the present mentality the Fourth Gospel can gain acknowledgement of its genuineness only at the cost of seeing its inmost essence denied.

Now in order to gain a conception of how the consciousness of a completely special relation to God has developed in Jesus, Schleiermacher refers to the fact that the bent toward the God-consciousness in human nature is to be observed generally, but that in regard to its actual development in individual persons a great difference is to be seen, ranging from a minimum to a maximum. The maximum he describes as "when the consciousness of a relation to God is an element of every consciousness, that is, when it is a

77. [While Strauss is on target with regard to the general character of John's Jesus, it is doubtful that 5:21 is intended to refer to the raising of Lazarus in ch. 11. It is, rather, a general statement concerning the Logos/Jesus as a giver of true, eternal life.]

concomitant 'given' in every natural consciousness which attains a certain clarity and completeness." The minimum is when "the individual always needs an external impulse in order to develop this consciousness in his inner life, or if he even struggles against the development of it" (p. 93). We must think of Jesus in this respect to be on the side of the maximum, the greatest vitality of God-consciousness; and Schleiermacher thinks he could have become aware of this already in his twelfth year if he had compared himself with others. Nonetheless, that would not have been anything specific—not yet a basis for expressing his relation to God in a way that others did not (p. 94). With this belongs his sinlessness, of which he also became aware by comparison with others. Thereby was given his specific difference from all other men, which he related to the divine in him, and which thereby gave his relation to God that distinctive expression (p. 95). On the one hand, to demonstrate the sinlessness of Jesus, Schleiermacher uses the argument that if we want to assume even a minimum of sin in him, then "he must of necessity cease to be a special object of faith" (p. 99); we will not let this circular argument stand. If, on the other hand, he insists that "herein is nothing which would stand in contradiction to the essence of a purely human development" (p. 100), then to some extent we have already spoken of this, and it will soon become evident what has been arranged with this allegedly purely human development.

JESUS' EDUCATION

Regarding the question of Jesus' education, Schleiermacher begins by speaking first of all of the three Jewish sects. With passion he seeks to set aside the influence of the Essenes on Jesus (pp. 102, 106, 115, 117, 120)—an influence like the more easily rebuffed Egyptian priestly wisdom as the source of Jesus' presumed miracle-working power; this idea found its expression in the exaggerations and romances of Bahrdt, Venturini, and others, which were still fresh at the time.[78] Likewise, according to Schleiermacher, Jesus took no part in the complicated rabbinic schools, divided into those of the Pharisees and Sadducees,[79] but kept solely to the popular means of education, which for Jews lay in the synagogue institutions and in the sacred Scriptures of his people. Thereby the possibility is not to be excluded that in certain difficult cases Jesus sought counsel from educated compatriots; this is why Schleiermacher surmises an extended stay in Tiberias, the headquarters of the Galilean scribes, during the interval between Jesus' twelfth and thirtieth years (pp. 107–21).

In Schleiermacher's discussions one finds many correct historical and sensitive psychological observations, which are governed throughout, however, by a dogmatic presupposition, and which thereby are made illusory in their result. As has been already noted, there is no general objection against Jesus' learning and going to school, only "that in this way he made himself a disciple of one other man, like Paul was of Gamliel, is improbable, for out of this there would have arisen a personal devotion which," says Schleiermacher, "I cannot believe that Christ would have allowed in himself" (p. 121). Likewise, that he had learned from Pharisees and Sadducees is "in and of itself not impossible, that is, it is not incompatible with our presupposition about

78. [Karl F. Bahrdt and Karl H. G. Venturini had sought to explain Jesus' knowledge and healing power with the hypothesis that he had learned these arts in Egypt and was a secret Essene. Scarcely anyone has taken these ideas seriously. For details see Albert Schweitzer, *The Quest of the Historical Jesus*, pp. 38–47. Recently a biography has been produced by Sten Gunnar Flygt, *The Notorious Dr. Bahrdt* (Nashville: Vanderbilt University Press, 1963), in which chapter 24 deals with his reconstruction of Jesus.]

79. [It is wrong to say that rabbinic schools were divided into Pharisees and Sadducees, because only the former were associated with rabbinic traditions; the Sadducees were their opponents.]

Christ; yet he could have done so only in such a way that he did not appropriate the onesidedness and the errors which he heard there," that is, that he did not share them for a while and then later emancipate himself from them, but right from the start "did not appropriate them at all" (pp. 107, 113). Here we see that what is impossible is whatever is incompatible with our dogmatic presuppositions about Christ, and that includes every personal devotion to a human teacher and every even momentary error, so far as a personal devotion is a relationship of dependence and error is never without sin. Here the theoretical side emerges with respect to the sinlessness of Jesus. The normal way of knowing proceeds, as Schleiermacher very nicely explains, from ignorance through undecidedness to certainty, which then, if everything goes properly, must be identical with truth; error arises through the fact that something strange intrudes and provokes a conclusion before truth is reached— that intruder can be either indolence, for which further investigation is inconvenient, or interest in an untrue result, which will always involve an impure motive. According to Schleiermacher we must think of Jesus quite differently: "not only his moral development was progress without struggle, but also his intellectual development was a progress without error" (pp. 108, 110).[80]

The difficulties in which such a conception of Jesus ensnares itself do not escape Schleiermacher, and he himself seeks to illumine them in order, as he hopes, to resolve them the more thoroughly. For example, he says that the movement of the earth around the sun was not known at that time. "What then did Christ think when he spoke of sunrise (Matt. 13:6)? If we would want to say, 'Christ alone knew at the time that this light does not come from the movement of the sun,' then *eo ipso* the whole true humanity

80. See *The Christian Faith*, par. 98, sec. 1.

of Christ would be dissolved, for (because what is true of one object must be true of all) then he would have borne in himself all human insight of future times, an actual omniscience would be posited in him," and "we would land in Docetism" (p. 111). Therefore in this matter Jesus shared the conception of the time. But since this conception was a false one, did Jesus err? Schleiermacher says, "He made use of expressions as he found them in life, but without such certainty that he would have wanted to defend their truth" (p. 112). Therefore he not only used the expressions but also shared the conceptions, only without forming for himself a definite judgment about their correctness or erroneousness. According to Schleiermacher he could omit that because they were conceptions which did not lie in the domain where imparting the truth belonged to his calling. Think of a contemporary of Jesus who surmised the erroneousness of the current conceptions of the movements of the planets: "If such a man had come to Christ and had asked him, 'Do you really know that the sun goes around the earth?'" says Schleiermacher, "then Christ would have said, 'That was not the content of my investigation; that is the adoption of such expressions whose contents in turn are conceptions which do not belong to the proper context of life at all" (have no practical meaning?) "but are always used only for the sake of other conceptions" (p. 112). Here Schleiermacher, or his stenographer, attributes a very unclear speech to Jesus, but one which contains clearly enough what Schleiermacher wants to avoid as docetic: that for himself Jesus knew quite well how poorly based those conceptions are. The middle ground between error and falsehood, which objectively is not to be the truth but subjectively is not to be error, does not exist. Just as we do not blame the greatest men of the past, whom we view in a purely human way, because new discoveries were foreign to them—for example, Socrates or Aristotle—because they had no intimation of the Copernican system, so it is certain that the presupposition of an absolute freedom from error which corresponds to the sinlessness of Jesus falls apart by this concession.

DID JESUS HAVE A PROGRAM?

Thus we can only agree when Schleiermacher wants to have nothing to do with a "program which the Founder of the Christian religion sketched for the good of mankind,"[81] this true offspring of the eighteenth century which thought that also in the area of religion everything proceeded from a rational calculation. But when he bases this rejection on the following grounds: "Christ would at some time not have known what he intended, and that is unthinkable apart from sin"; indeed, even what is inherent in a program, the "contradiction of ends and means, so strongly bears within itself the trace of a moral imperfection that it is not possible to ensnare Christ in it." Also, the "reflection upon which would be better, this or that" he prefers not to ascribe to Jesus because "therein lies an inner uncertainty which puts Christ on the same level as other men, so that he would no longer be the object of worship" (p. 122). These are reasons which may suffice in a dogmatic because there one is not accustomed to something better, but they do not belong in a historical investigation, or they deprive its result of scientific worth. More fruitful is Schleiermacher's use of the comparison with the developing artist, which was available for him through the romantic circle in which he moved so long.[82] Let us think, he says, of an artist and his art, and

81. This is recognizably an allusion to the title of a book by F. V. Reinhard, which had first appeared in 1781 and become famous. [*Versuch über den Plan, welcher der Stifter der christlichen Religion . . . entwarf* (Wittenberg, 1830, 5th ed.).]

82. [For a discussion of Schleiermacher's participation in the romantic circle in Berlin see Redeker, *Schleiermacher: Life and Thought*, pp. 25–34, 59–69.]

ask, How did this art come into being? If one says that "he had a plan, and, for example, a painting is explained on the basis of such a plan; the artist wanted to present this or that idea, and this or that was his motif, then only an imperfect piece of art is explainable in this way." The true artist does not create according to a plan or from a thought, but according to an inner picture. "The more you think," Schleiermacher tells his hearers, "that during this work he had to make something which was not in the original inner picture, the more you think an imperfection into it; but if the picture presents the external as it was in the inner, then the picture is perfect" (p. 124). In a word, it is the concept of creative genius which Schleiermacher here applies to Jesus, and in consequence of which he conceives of his activity as one which proceeded out of an inner constraint more or less instinctively.[83] "The consciousness of indwelling power and the consciousness of external need (on the part of the world)—together both became for him a single impulse of constant self-impartation" (p. 126). But even the most creative artist needs, in addition to the inner picture, also aptitude in order to express it externally and this he must acquire. Still this is, in part, something totally different from that programming of which we spoke; in part, with respect to Jesus, the aptitude which he needed for his calling consisted solely in knowledge of men, and this developed in him entirely of itself, from the inner direction of his disposition. Here Schleiermacher expresses himself beautifully: "There is no true foundation of knowledge of men other than pure love and pure self-consciousness; the

83. [Strauss gives the reader no clue to the fact that he himself had used the category "religious genius" for Jesus, though in a different sense; see above, p. lxvi. Though making use of quite different categories, the "new hermeneutic" approaches Schleiermacher's conclusion that Jesus' use of language was not only authentic but spontaneous, the direct reflex of his perception of God, and not the result of a deliberate decision to speak in a certain way.]

former is the desire to identify with men, and if we assume the pure self-consciousness as it existed in the Redeemer" (to be sure, here the dogmatic presupposition insinuates itself again), "then it is *index sui et falsi* [the touchstone of what is genuine and of what is false], and was that from which the opposite in others disclosed itself to him" (p. 127).

JESUS AND THE MESSIANIC IDEA

"One question," says Schleiermacher here, "is not to be avoided: How did Christ come to apply the messianic idea to himself? And can it be explained as follows: that he applied the messianic predictions to himself in such a way that neither a self-deception nor an effort to deceive others with it is somehow tied up with the explanation?" (pp. 130ff.). Indeed, his aim was only "to transfer his life to men, that is, to make them also to be such persons as would be determined solely by the will of God, and to base a dominance of the divine will on his person." But in contrast, these messianic predictions manifestly concerned an external sovereignty; they understood the idea of theocracy in a political way. "Did Jesus then understand them to mean that in fact he was their object? Were they not understood differently from the start, and the whole conception of a political theocracy only a misunderstanding? That idea would be the simplest," Schleiermacher answers, "but I do not believe that it is right." We have no right to insist "that Christ was convinced that the prophets had thought of him as appearing the way he did"; rather, exactly as in regard to the conception of the world in general, as discussed above, so also here Schleiermacher says that "if someone occupying our standpoint had asked Christ, 'Is it your understanding that the author of Isaiah 61 thought of this as referring to the appearance of a single teacher?' Christ would have denied it; but he went farther and deeper into the truth of the idea," and then the application to himself which he made of similar passages is "perfectly correct" (p. 253). For Schleiermacher the first assumption is naturally forbidden because it would posit an error in Jesus; thus the dilemma which appears repeatedly in the Jewish line of interpretation is made dogmatically harmless by the beloved formulation that it is seen as the "adoption of concepts with respect to which Christ had no calling to develop a conviction" (p. 133). Still, apart from this, one can only applaud Schleiermacher's explanation.[84] According to him, Jesus regarded the religious element to be the true kernel of messianic prediction in the Old Testament, and he had a right to do this, for, precisely among the nation's most devout persons, the expectation of the higher place of the people of Israel among the rest of the nations was always at the same time the expectation of an expanded kingship of God among men. Thus,

in the same measure that his peculiar self-consciousness developed, this also could develop in him: that he is the focal point of the entire Jewish preparation, and also the one to whom all those institutions and sayings point which are to portray the consummation of the divine decree with respect to the Jewish people. That was neither a result which became fixed in him after all sorts of vacillations [again this is said dogmatically], nor must one see this conviction as a special divine revelation; rather it is his peculiar self-consciousness, only in relation to Jewish history and nationality. [pp. 113 ff.]

JESUS' BAPTISM

The starting point of the public activity of Jesus is customarily seen, according to Acts 1:22, as his baptism by John. Schleiermacher disturbs this ancient boundary

84. [It is one thing for Strauss to "applaud" Schleiermacher, and another to admit—which he did not—that he had also appropriated him in his *LJGP*. For details see above, p. lxxiv. Interestingly, Strauss never doubted that Jesus regarded himself as the Messiah; in this regard, subsequent criticism was more skeptical than Strauss.]

marker. The viewpoint of Jesus' gradual, natural development appears to require here also a gradual transition. "It lies in the nature of the case," it is judged, "that a rising development of a self-consciousness must proceed to its being shared, and an end of the one and a beginning of the other is not to be posited" (p. 134). That has, to be sure, a measure of truth in it; to that extent one could distinguish the still less definite activity of Jesus, which was provoked from time to time by individual occasions, from the definite and coherent activity as it was evidently characterized by the gathering of a special circle of disciples. Concerning the latter, one could assume that, while the former was not lacking previously, properly it began only after the baptism of Jesus by John. But if Schleiermacher, not satisfied with this, postulates also that the calling of the disciples occurred before the baptism, something special must lie behind this view. This is the first time, in the context of Schleiermacher's presentation of the life of Jesus, that a notice of his preference for John intrudes. This Evangelist indeed reports the witness of the Baptist and the subsequent attachment of some of his disciples to Jesus (John 1:26ff.) without mentioning a previous activity by Jesus. But when he further reports (2:1ff.) that a few days later Jesus went to Galilee because there was a wedding to which he and his disciples had been invited, Schleiermacher asks, How could anyone in Galilee know about these disciples who had just been acquired at the Jordan? If previously, on the other hand, Jesus had occasionally appeared openly in synagogues and elsewhere in Galilee, then it was natural that such relationships had developed and then one could assume that in Cana he now would have certain persons with him who were his disciples, and who thus were invited with him (p. 135). Elsewhere, too, Schleiermacher wants to find traces in the Gospels that "Christ had attained a certain fame before he was baptized by John." He cannot infer this from the Baptist's initial refusel to baptize (Matt. 3:14), since he regards this as an arbitrary improvement by a later narrator;[85] nor does it escape him that the deeds in Chorazin and Bethsaida (Matt. 11:20ff.) can be placed prior to the baptism only arbitrarily. Here, too, it is rather by means of John, with indefinite signs mentioned in 2:23, 3:2, and evidently 2:3, with the presupposition which appears to manifest itself in Mary's command to the servant in Cana, that Schleiermacher is confirmed in the opinion of such a prior activity on the part of Jesus. But that here an erroneous interpretation lies at the base can be seen in every commentary on the Johannine Gospel; besides, with a proper view of this Gospel every historical warrant from these passages disappears.

But how, then, did Jesus arrive at the point of allowing himself to be baptized by John? And what actually happened in the event? Above all, had there previously been a personal relationship between the Baptist and Jesus? It is well known that Luke 1 reports family relationships in consequence of which both men must have known each other; at the same time, according to John 1:31 and 33, the Baptist repeatedly asserts the opposite. Schleiermacher says, "I explain this momentarily," by saying that Luke's narrative "could not arise against the definite saying of the Baptist" in John (p. 137). He is fully right in not allowing a manifestly poetically inclined presentation, like that of the first chapter of Luke, to stand as a historical report; but he does not ask whether also the assertion put into the Baptist's mouth that he had not known Jesus previously could have its origin in the theological trend of the Fourth Evangelist.[86] That Jesus submits to John's repentance-baptism

---

85. *Über die Schriften des Lukas*, p. 59.
86. F. C. Baur, *Kritische Untersuchungen über die kanonischen Evangelien*, p. 105. See also my *Leben Jesu für das deutsche Volk bearbeitet*, p. 346. [Schleiermacher's point, that Luke's report which made John the

creates a contradiction with the presupposition of his sinlessness. Schleiermacher seeks to escape this by merely finding dispassionately in this act of Jesus the explanation that a share of the messianic kingdom is not due the Jews simply as preservers of the Law, but that they must make themselves worthy of this kingdom solely by the remission of sins.

With respect to the events at Jesus' baptism, Schleiermacher makes the report of the Fourth Gospel the basis of the presupposition that John received the story from the mouth of the Baptist himself, and that the deviations of the rest of the Gospels can be understood as additions to this original narrative. In the Johannine account, what is especially dear to him is that it refers the miracle solely to the Baptist. But when he goes so far as to say, "The miraculous in the story of Christ's baptism does not interest us, and it is no concern of ours to form a definite conception of it, since it did not pertain to Jesus but to the Baptist, and because it occurred only with reference to him and in his company, but did not originate in him, and he himself did not act in it at all" (p. 142), then this is an escape, since in any case the miracle is told as one which occurred for the sake of Jesus and for the advancement of the divine purpose with him, and since, in the context of the remaining
• miracles of the Gospel history, it may not be ignored in the determination of the character and value of this history. Besides, Schleiermacher does not keep to himself his surmises about the facts in the matter. The heavenly voice does not interest him, since John knows nothing about it; also, John has the Holy Spirit come like a dove upon Jesus, but only Luke, on his own authority, ascribes to this dove

---

Baptist and Jesus relatives would not have arisen in the same circles which knew the tradition that John the Baptist denied knowing Jesus, is sound insight into the pluralism of early Christian traditions. Yet he deprives it of all force by denying that the statement that John had not known Jesus was a piece of tradition. Strauss's view is the more likely.]

a bodily form; and if one combines the opened heavens in our Synoptic Gospels with the light in the apocryphal ones,[87] then according to Schleiermacher it "begins to look as though what John saw was an appearance of light which came from an opening in the clouds." The comparison with a dove refers to "the outline or the movement" of this light, and "the 'remaining' can be thought of only as its gradual disappearing from Christ" (pp. 141–44).[88]

Now it is remarkable to see how Schleiermacher's own acuity disturbs his satisfaction with this view of the matter. In the Johannine account, on which, of course, he builds everything, he concedes an "inconsistency." The divine promise to the Baptist (1:33) says only that he will see the Spirit come upon someone and remain on him; here there is no mention of a dove. So the remaining of the Spirit can even be understood as something "that could be perceived only by extended observation." That is, Schleiermacher wants to say that one could interpret the promise to mean that the Baptist is to become convinced of Jesus' messiahship by extended observation of his mode of action. The actual vision, on the other hand, in which he found the fulfillment of the promise made to him, the Baptist describes in John's Gospel in such a way that he definitely saw the Holy Spirit come upon Jesus as a dove and remain on him (1:32). Here one must think of something singular and perceptible, in which case one really does not know how he is to conceive of the "remaining." But if nonetheless the promise was so much more spiritual, then the Baptist, Schleiermacher thinks, "was perhaps wrong to think that it was fulfilled by an appearance whose connection with the

87. [The appearance of light at Jesus' baptism is mentioned in the Ebionite Gospel and in several manuscripts of pre-Vulgate Latin versions of Matt. 3:15; Justin Martyr (dial. 88:3) mentions fire.]

88. [John 1:32–33 has John the Baptist report, "I saw the Spirit descend as a dove from heaven, and it remained on him."]

divine voice rested only on his own interpretation" (pp. 141ff.). Indeed, since from Schleiermacher's standpoint the allegedly divine promise can be only an idea which emerged in John's mind, later he must have misunderstood his own previous thought, which is inconceivable. Rather, here Schleiermacher's sagacity, counter to his intent, actually exposes a feature which allows one to recognize the report of the Fourth Evangelist as a secondary one. John found the dove in the older Gospels and retained it; but while the others have it only descend upon Jesus, as is fitting for a dove, he has it remain over him—something that can be said only of the Spirit which continually rested upon him. This is indeed the constant procedure of the Fourth Evangelist: to take up the sentient miracle from the received tradition, and so to fill it with ideal content that the sentient form is at the point of rupture—yet not to let it come to this rupture, but to hold the sentient and the spiritual interlocked in each other.[89]

THE TEMPTATION STORY

The temptation story, as a real event, disappears from the start for Schleiermacher not only by the fact that John is silent about it, but also because the fixed scheme of calculating the days at the beginning of his Gospel definitely excludes the story with its "forty days." In a quite beautiful way, Schleiermacher then makes his students aware of the impossibility of thinking that the event happened as it is told. What would have been the purpose of a temptation

89. [Today we would formulate Strauss's point differently, though concurring with his observation. We would say that John regards Jesus' miracles as "symbols," but that he does not dissolve their actuality. But we would no longer assume that John knew the Synoptics, though he might have been familiar with some of the materials they used. In the case of the baptism story, it is quite possible that John used an independent tradition.]

of Jesus by Satan? If we take Jesus to have been like our-selves, then enough temptations meet us in ordinary life and they do not require a personal appearance of Satan; indeed, Jesus would have had it easier than ourselves if, in his case, temptation would have been dispensed with in those three acts which, with the exception of the first, could not even have had any attraction for him. And if Jesus recognized the devil, which is expressly stated in the account of the last event but probably is to be assumed also in the earlier ones, then doubtless all temptation disappeared—unless we think that fear of Satan would have been a possi-ble motivation for Jesus to ponder the former's suggestions—but this is foreign to the foundation of the story (p. 151). It is well known that Schleiermacher understood the temp-tation story as a parable which Jesus told his disciples, but which later, in the retelling, came to be understood as his-tory. This time he silently ignores the mythic interpreta-tion, against which in earlier years of the lectures he openly expressed himself;[90] instead, he repeats the opinion that "here Christ presents in the form of a story what occurred internally at the time when he began his career," and does so with the explanation that he was convinced that "this hypothesis permitted no faith in Christ at all" (p. 151). Here is one of the points where Schleiermacher's pupils softened the strictness of the master, and indeed took up precisely that interpretation which he had expressly ex-plained as being "the worst neoteric nonsense which was perpetrated against the person of Christ."[91] If they took as their point of departure the view that a place has to be made for the power of tempting thoughts and the possibility of inner struggles within Jesus—if one is to take seriously

---

90. See my *Leben Jesu für das deutsche Volk bearbeitet*, p. 22.
91. *Über die Schriften des Lukas*, p. 54.

his full humanity—then they were indeed right, in contrast with the master;[92] but if they thought that thereby they did not affect Jesus' sinlessness, then they made the same mistake which Schleiermacher, conversely, made when he held the sinlessness of Jesus to be harmonizeable with his true humanity.

92. [Strauss is sympathetic to the modifications introduced by Schleiermacher's followers because he himself had written in this vein in his *LJGP*; see above, p. lxxiii.]

CHAPTER FIVE

THE SECOND PERIOD: THE STORY OF JESUS' PUBLIC LIFE

If only a few individual stories about the first period of the life of Jesus, his childhood and youth, have been preserved for us, then even the second period, about which more ample reports are available to us, does not afford us a continuous account, due to the character of those reports. The first three Gospels, Schleiermacher judges, are only disconnected collections of materials; John indeed gives a running narrative, but ameliorates only slightly the possibility of solving the problem of a continuous account, because he tells only that which is significant for his theological tendency. This is "to make understandable simultaneously the catastrophe in Christ's fate and the proper nature of his activity," or to solve the contradictions of how, this nature of his activity not being perceived, he nevertheless could be rejected by the Jews (p. 159).

In general, this conception of the theological tendency of the Fourth Gospel is entirely correct. But why then does Schleiermacher speak only of the nature, that is, of the character, of the *activity* of Jesus, and not of *his nature* or of his being itself, as the content of the Fourth Gospel's presentation? Clearly because he will not admit that the Fourth Gospel speaks of a peculiar nature of Jesus, that is, of him as a superior, superhuman being. And yet the

Evangelist finds just here the key to the riddle of Jesus' rejection by his people. Had he been only the human Jewish Messiah, then the Jews would scarcely have refused him; but he was really the enfleshed Logos, the divine light-principle; hence it is no wonder that the children of darkness did not accept him. This speculative point of view from which the Fourth Gospel sees the life of Jesus is, to be sure, unthinkable for a disciple of Jesus; since Schleiermacher wants to hold onto the disciple as the author of the Gospel, he is not permitted to find that point of view in the Gospel.

THE EXTERNAL SIDE OF JESUS' PUBLIC LIFE

Schleiermacher distinguishes an external from an internal side in the public life of Jesus. In the former he includes the locality, the external circumstances and the external living arrangements; in the latter, the teaching of Jesus and his activity for the founding of a society (p. 156).[93] With regard to the locality, as has already been mentioned, Schleiermacher has perfect insight into the contradiction which is found between the first three Gospels and the Fourth, as well as into the fact that the contradiction is not to be solved if these authors all stood equally close to Jesus and the facts generally, but only on the assumption that

93. [The difference between the external and internal aspects of a person's life is important for Schleiermacher; indeed, he begins his *Life of Jesus* with a discussion of this theme. For Schleiermacher, a person is not merely the sum of actions and reactions, he is an inner center to which all externals must be related, but from which he is also independent. Schleiermacher illustrates his point by asking, Suppose Christ had not been executed when he was, but had returned to Galilee—what would he have done? Only if we know the inward aspects of Christ well enough to be able to answer this do we really know the person (p. 17). Furthermore, it is important for Schleiermacher that Jesus' teaching be regarded as his internal rather than external activity, because the teaching is his self-communication. Similarly, the founding of the church is grounded in the self-impartation of Christ, not on an externally prompted deed.]

either the first three or the Fourth Gospel are of later origin. Among the Synoptics it is a matter chiefly of Matthew—concerning which, says Schleiermacher, "many have made it doubtful whether in its present form it really comes from an apostle; and I believe," he adds, "that the matter will develop ever more negatively in this regard. Therefore," he concludes in his customary way, "the Gospel of John is to be made the foundation, and this really sees Judea as the place of the public life of Jesus, and sees all other sojourns as only momentarily occasioned by particular motives" (pp. 171ff.). But if this is the real fact of the matter, one must ask how the opposite view of the first three Gospels arose, in which Galilee instead appears as the true scene of Jesus' activity. John, even though he himself knew it to be otherwise, still has others give as the dominant understanding in Jerusalem that Jesus was regarded as one who was actually at home in Galilee. Where could this understanding have come from? From the fact, answers Schleiermacher, that Jesus had been reared in Galilee, that the majority of his disciples were Galileans, and that he, like they, spoke the Galilean dialect. "There were sufficient grounds for this view to develop among those who did not belong to Jesus' closest associates, so that it was the common one in Judea and in this way came into our Gospels" (p. 172). How? During his public life Jesus remained virtually always in Judea; but because of his Galilean dialect and because it was known that he had been reared in Galilee, the view developed in Judea, where he virtually always remained, that he had almost always been in Galilee. This explanation of the known conflict will satisfy no one; rather, one will find himself driven from this to the alternative where, with the foundation of the Synoptic view as the historical one, the deviating Johannine presentation is explained by the theological tendency of that Gospel to have the divine wisdom appear right in the center of its would-be possession; the light of the world appears precisely in the headquarters of darkness, in the heart of Judaism.[94]

With regard to the external subsistence of Jesus, Schleiermacher explains how it was not dependent on his family, with whom he no longer had a close relationship after his public appearance; rather, it depended partly on the earnings of the apostles to the extent that some of these earnings flowed into the common fund, partly on contributions of other adherents such as the certain women of means (Luke 8:2–3), and finally, partly on the hospitality which was highly practiced among the Jews, especially with regard to scribes and public teachers. The saying that he had nowhere to lay his head (Matt. 8:20) "is only the expression of the lack of a definite home, so that he always was led here and there by circumstances, not by actual poverty" (p. 180). Moreover, in the Galilean towns he attached himself to the households of his disciples who lived there, and likewise in the environs of Jerusalem he attached himself to those households which honored him as the Messiah or as a prophet; further circumstances are obscure for us (p. 175).

94. [There is a measure of truth in Strauss's point, but the whole question of how the Evangelists present the location of Jesus' ministry has become much more complicated. On the one hand, form criticism has alerted some scholars (under the influence of Old Testament study) to think in terms of local Christian traditions. On this basis, John would rely on chiefly Judean and specifically Jerusalemite traditions of Jesus, while the Synoptists, following Mark, would embody Galilean ones. On the other hand, the more the theology of the Synoptists has come into view, the more "Galilee" has been seen as a theological motif in Mark; see, for example, Willi Marxsen, *Mark the Evangelist*, trans. John Steeley (Nashville: Abingdon Press, 1969), ch. 2. While the latter motif has been overemphasized, both the Synoptic and the Johannine presentations are affected by theological considerations. Thus while the Synoptists locate Jesus' primary activity in Galilee (perhaps for theological reasons in part), they also portray the Jerusalem ministry from a theological standpoint; here Jesus confronts "the headquarters of darkness, in the heart of Judaism"—this is precisely the portrait which Strauss attributes to John.]

The living arrangements, or the way in which Jesus spent his time, were naturally different in those places where he remained customarily or even repeatedly from the arrangements in those to which he seldom came. In general, Schleiermacher conceives the daily life of Jesus to have been filled with solitary meditation and study of the Scriptures, with public teaching activity, especially in synagogues, with special instruction of the closer circle of his disciples, with occasional discussions with the people who turned to him, and finally with the social contacts which were based on hospitality and personal relationships (pp. 185, 188, 190).

JESUS' MIRACLES

Here, under the rubric of the disposition of time, Schleiermacher also puts Jesus' miracles. If one adds up the miracles largely passed over in silence in the first three Gospels, and especially in Matthew, such as those in Chorazin and Bethsaida, which are mentioned only in passing (Matt. 11:20–21), those which are reported collectively, as in the summary notices in Matt. 4:23–24 and elsewhere, and finally the individual miracles told in detail, then it begins to appear as if "the doing of miracles must have taken a great amount of time in the life of Christ" (p. 192). But if one wants to take all that in the Gospels literally and form a composite picture out of it, then, according to Schleiermacher, that is a difficult task. It presupposes a disproportionate number of sick people who after massive healings still repeatedly appear in the same areas and in the wilderness and are transported everywhere with Jesus. Things are somewhat different in the Fourth Gospel, since at the festivals in Jerusalem it is conceivable that "more such acts occurred, yet not so many that one cannot examine them singly" (p. 193). In fact, however, in this regard the Fourth Gospel has no advantage over the others since, apart from the individual miracles which it narrates in detail, it also points repeatedly to additional miracles, indeed to many, which Jesus did (John 2:23; 3:2; 4:45; 12:37; 20:30).

It is well known that in *The Christian Faith* Schleiermacher took a most liberal attitude toward miracles. According to him, "In the interest of piety there can never arise a necessity of understanding a fact in such a way that its dependence on God destroys its contingence on the continuity of nature."[95] Especially the miracles of Jesus, which Schleiermacher explains wholly according to Herder,[96] could doubtless make his contemporaries who saw them take note of him. For us who did not see them they no longer have such power, but are dispensable insofar as now into their place has stepped historical knowledge of the character, extent, and duration of the spiritual work of Christ, in which we have an advantage over his contemporaries.[97]

95. *The Christian Faith*, par. 47. [p. 178ff. The Mackintosh-Stewart translation reads: "It can never be necessary in the interest of religion so to interpret a fact that its dependence on God absolutely excludes its being conditioned by the system of Nature."]

96. [J. G. Herder (1744–1803) denied that the miracles prove the truth of Christianity, whether one understands it as a religion or as a teaching. He did not deny that the miracles occurred with regard to Jesus (e.g., the transfiguration) or occurred through him, and granted that they were necessary at that time to launch this religion in this particular way. "The miracles did not occur for our sake, but for Christ's contemporaries and for Christ himself; in that respect they achieved their purpose." We, on the other hand, cannot prove that they happened, and they in turn cannot prove the truth for us ("Vom Erlöser der Menschen: Nach unsern drei ersten Evangelien" [1796], *Sämmtliche Werke*, ed. B. Suphan [Berlin: Weidmannsche Buchhandlung, 1880], 19:235–39).]

97. *The Christian Faith*, par. 103, sec. 4. See Schleiermacher's *Predigten*, Sammlung 3 (1821²), p. 467. [Schleiermacher had renounced any appeal to external legitimation: "We must show, without recourse to compulsion by means of miracle or prophecy (which is a thing alien to faith) that Jesus possessed a sinless perfection and that there is a communication of this perfection in the fellowship founded by him" (par. 88, sec. 2). In the passage cited by Strauss, he says that "miracles can only direct the spiritual need to a definite object in virtue of their immediate impressiveness," but, like Lessing, he goes on to say that "this impressiveness . . .

Also, especially with respect to Christ, it is said to be a natural presupposition that he who exercised such a peculiar activity upon the spiritual side of human nature would also, on the basis of the general continuity of things, have exercised a peculiar power on the bodily side of man and on his external nature. Nonetheless, by no means can it be said that Jesus could not be acknowledged as who he is for Christian faith if such phenomena were absent from him.[98] For this reason, according to Schleiermacher, the acknowledgement of the miracles done by Christ belongs "less to our faith in Christ and rather more to our faith in the Scripture." Specifically, "we cannot bring these occurrences into the realm of nature which is customary for us without taking refuge in such presuppositions as would jeopardize the trustworthiness of the entire fabric of our reports about Christ."[99] This means that neither Schleiermacher's religious belief in general, nor his faith in Christ in particular, has direct need of miracles; but his belief in Scripture—and here this really means only his belief in John—needs it,

---

is lost in proportion as the person who is to believe is at a distance from the miracle itself in space and time." The history of Christ's influence serves the same function today—it directs our need to Christ. This gives moderns an advantage over those who saw Christ's miracles, because this "general spiritual miracle, which begins with the person of the Redeemer and is completed with the consummation of his kingdom" is a "witness whose power increases" with time, while that of the miracles decreases. That Schleiermacher speaks out of Christendom's self-confidence is clear at the end of his discussion, where he avers that preachers today do not need miracles "in view of the great advantage in power and civilization which Christian people possess over the non-Christian, almost without exception." Kierkegaard took precisely the opposite position: neither the eyewitness of Jesus nor modern man has an advantage, because Jesus is the Incarnate One. "If the fact in question is an absolute fact . . . it would be a contradiction to suppose that time had any power to differentiate the fortunes of men with respect to it . . ." (*Philosophical Fragments*, trans. David Swenson and rev. H. V. Hong [Princeton: Princeton University Press, 1962], p. 125; see also, p. 72).]

98. *The Christian Faith*, par. 14, postscript.
99. *The Christian Faith*, par. 103, sec. 4.

and accordingly even his faith in Christ needs it indirectly once again. For if there were no truth to the miracles of Jesus, then John's Gospel, which most definitely reports them, would no longer be trustworthy; but then the historical basis of Schleiermacher's Christ, which he appears to find in the Johannine portrait, would disappear.

Still this admission on the part of Schleiermacherian theology must purchase miracle at a high price. It must deny the accusation that a miracle is an absolute supernatural event, and be satisfied that it is not "pulled down into the realm of nature which is customary for us," especially if it is not assumed that Jesus worked his miracles "according to rules learned somewhere" or that he acted according to such laws of nature "as are known to us as being valid for all times."[100] Then, from the strict understanding of miracle, which he has excluded, Schleiermacher seeks to withdraw also biblical support. "We are not permitted to presuppose in the gospel stories our elementary contradiction between the natural and the supernatural," he explains, "because at that time there was no knowledge of nature. In the understanding of the time this contradiction did not mean much more than our contrast between the usual and the unusual or the exceptional" (p. 194). But also, we who live in the present can "nowhere determine the realm of the supernatural with perfect certainty, because we have not taken the measure of nature and have not reached its limits. And so we find ourselves, despite our knowledge of nature, in a situation quite analogous to that of those who were the immediate witnesses of these deeds of Christ: namely, we too cannot definitely distinguish the unusual from the supernatural on the basis of their differing qualities" (p. 204).

But on the other hand, the concept of miracle is repaid for this despair over absolute supernaturalness. What it

100. Ibid.

loses in dogmatic content it gains in historical compass. Because we "must agree that our knowledge of created nature is always in flux," we are to have *"no right to consider anything to be impossible!"* Rather, *"everything, even the most miraculous*, which happens or has happened must remain a problem for scientific research" in the hope of "attaining future knowledge." Especially because we "can neither determine exactly the limits of the reciprocal effect of the bodily and the spiritual, nor even insist that they are everywhere and always completely the same, incapable of development or of fluctuations," a possibility is said to be given precisely for the New Testament miracles, which for the most part lie in this indeterminable area.[101] One can say that Schleiermacher explains the miracle as such, as something absolute, to be impossible; but *the miracles*, the gospel miracle stories, insofar as they can be viewed relatively, he provisionally acknowledges as all possible.

In order to come to more definite results, Schleiermacher tries above all to classify the miracles in the Gospels. Classified according to the subject, he distinguishes miracles done *by* Christ, (from God) *through* Christ, and *to* Christ; according to the object, he distinguishes miracles done by him on living persons, on the dead, and on impersonal nature; according to the occasion, he distinguishes miracles which Jesus did purely out of his own impulse from those which he did in response to a request or even involuntarily; finally, according to purpose, he distinguishes benevolent miracles from those in which such a purpose is not recognizable—miracles for the good of others and miracles for the sustenance of himself and his followers (pp. 198–204). With regard to this differentiation Schleiermacher establishes the canon, "The more, first of all, such a deed can be understood as a moral act of Christ, and secondly, we can establish

101. *The Christian Faith*, par. 47, sec. 3.

an analogy between Christ's mode of acting and other human modes of acting, the more we can conceive the acts to be
actual ingredients of the life of Jesus" (p. 205). "But the
less"—this is the obverse of Schleiermacher's canon—we
first "can understand those deeds as moral acts of Christ,"
and secondly, "the less we can discover such analogies, the
less we are in a position to trace the narrative to any sort of
definite conception and to assert what is factual in it" (p.
205).

In both respects, physical as well as moral, the marvelous
healings of Jesus are most understandable to us. From the
moral standpoint it makes no difference whether Jesus is
asked for help or whether he almost insists on giving it,
whether he comes to the aid of strangers or cares for his own
convenience and that of his followers—for Christ, says
Schleiermacher, "had these powers at his disposition the way
every man, according to moral laws, has disposition over his
powers" (p. 207). On the physical side there appears "an
effect which comes from man and goes to man, not as an
absolute supernatural one" insofar as in it both "the agent
and the effect are natural ones." In Jesus' healings the
effect was "the healing of a diseased organic state"; the
agent was "predominantly a spiritual one, namely, the will
of Christ." Still, a mediating physical factor was added: the
articulation of this will, with which occasionally touching
and other external acts were combined. "Natural science is
full of examples of sudden effects on the human organism of
the presence of another who exercises a certain mastery, a
spiritual and physical superiority over people—effects which
are not yet traced back to definite natural laws." Christ,
then, as the man of the absolute, powerful God-consciousness according to Schleiermacher, acted "with a completely
different potency of spiritual superiority" than others, even
the most important others. To this extent, the effects which
he brought about in this way were in fact "supernatural,"

and we can "set no limits" to what he could do on the basis of his peculiar dignity. Nevertheless we can and must seek out analogies for it, always with the reservation that these are to be seen only as similar, not identical, cases (p. 204).

If, by regarding the healing miracles in the same way as we previously regarded miracles in general, every barrier between the conceivable and the inconceivable is torn down in advance, and in principle all Gospel stories of this kind are admitted to be possible, then the subsequent distinctions of different classes of such miracles can still be of only subordinate significance. One difference is based, according to Schleiermacher, above all on the kind of malady which was healed. The more "the malady lies in a vital function which is in constant connection with the psychic, the more we can think of it as healed by a psychic effect." On "disturbances," then, "which are associated with the conceptualizing capacity (demonic states), the dominating influence of a superior spirit must be able to produce a psychic effect which is analogous to this superiority." But also, where the malady is a purely organic one, a psychic influence on the organism remains conceivable, for "there is nothing in the life of man which is totally cut off from the connection with the psychic" (p. 206). As true as this generalization is, it is still much too indefinite to bring miraculous healings, like those of the possessed, the blind, and those with dropsy, in any way closer to conceivability.[102]

If, according to Schleiermacher, the analogy of the healing miracles reaches its limits in those cases where the healing occurs at a distance, then it abandons us completely in Jesus' miraculous effects on external nature. Still, ac-

102. [Strauss appears to forget that in his *LJGP* he himself had tacitly made the same move, for he granted that people who expected to be healed by Jesus probably were healed. See above, p. lxxv. More important, in the third edition of the *Life of Jesus* he cited Schleiermacher (the same text cited in note 85) and agreed with him. For details see Hodgson's introduction to *LJCE*, pp. xlii–iii.]

cording to Schleiermacher, among such the following are at least morally intelligible: the stilling of the storm in which Jesus rescues himself and his followers from mortal danger, the miracle in Cana, where to be sure he does not remedy a need but a social embarrassment, and Peter's catch of fish— where, however, the concept of miracle is said to be debatable. If, on the other hand, the physically unintelligible acts are not to be understood morally either, "then we find ourselves in the greatest dilemma." Here Schleiermacher puts above all the story of the fig tree, which strikes us physically as magic, and morally as having proceeded from a totally baseless rage on the part of Jesus. The same is true of the miracle of the coin, which must have physically occurred through the supernatural knowledge of Jesus concerning the nearness of a fish which had swallowed the coin, and which must have occurred by magical activity through which the fish bit precisely Peter's hook; morally, however, it has a difficulty, in that the coin, particularly since the matter was not urgent, certainly could have been acquired in a natural way. Equally, there was no case of need in the miraculous feeding, since Jesus had only to dismiss the crowd in good time to make it still possible for their hunger to be satisfied in a natural way; neither was a demand made of him. Jesus' walking on the lake appears to be totally pointless, "which to be sure," comments Schleiermacher, "occurred at nighttime and in a situation in which perceptions were uncertain" (p. 220).

Without physical point of contact are the raisings from the dead, "for here we cannot say, if we assume that death really occurred, that the psychic is the mediating factor between the influence of Christ and the result, because the psychic is no longer present" (p. 217). Here, as is well known, Schleiermacher definitely sees in the case of Jairus's daughter only a coma; he finds the case of the boy at Nain at least "problematic" in view of the custom of prompt burial among the Jews; but for the raising of Lazarus he devises the previously mentioned category of miracles worked not by but through Jesus. If in a sermon "On the Miracles of the Redeemer" he says Christ "could restore bodily life out of its innermost, hiddenmost recesses when it appeared to have completely died already,"[103] then he betrays clearly how he thinks of all so-called raisings of the dead done by Jesus. "Concerning Jairus's daughter, Christ says explicitly that she has not died but that she sleeps; one cannot," concludes Schleiermacher, "view this as a true raising of the dead without contradicting Christ's own words" (p. 217). Accordingly, the disciples caught his meaning when they understood his words, "Lazarus, our friend, sleeps," to refer to natural sleep, and John contradicts Jesus' words when he insists that Jesus rather spoke of Lazarus' death (John 11:12ff.). With regard to someone dead, Schleiermacher continues, an appeal to the corpse would also have been superfluous; "On the other hand, if we assume that the girl was not dead, then the voice could bring about an effect, and then it is useful to recall the experience of those in a coma who say upon returning to life that they had not lost their hearing during the extinction of all other signs of life" (p. 218). That here Schleiermacher permits himself to occupy the same ground as the most banal rationalism in the interpretation of Scripture, or rather the distortion of Scripture, and that he actually ignores a Christian fundamental-linguistic usage to oblige a natural explanation of miracles, I have set forth already elsewhere.[104] Still more miserable, if possible, is the information which he finds in the miracle of Lazarus: "In that Christ bids God to hear him, he does not ascribe the effect to himself, but accepts it as a divine act which occurred in response to his prayer; then Christ actually

103. *Predigten*, Bd. 3, p. 450. [*Werke* 2, part 3.]
104. See my *Leben Jesu für das deutsche Volk bearbeitet*, p. 482; cf. pp. 464–65.

leaves the realm of miracle, with the exception of the firmness of conviction that what he asked would also be done by God" (p. 218). Now one must remember that, according to Schleiermacher, proper prayer is only "the presentiment which developed out of the total activity of the divine spirit,"[105] and the more it rests on a particular content, "the more necessary it is that this is thought of in agreement with the original divine order."[106] How, then, can Jesus have assumed so definitely that the reawakening of Lazarus lay within this original divine order, particularly if, according to a comment of Schleiermacher's, it must remain unclear whether Martha was right or not in thinking that her brother had already passed into decay?

Through this miracle, which exceeds every natural analogy, Schleiermacher, despite the license he contrived for "everything, even the most miraculous" at the beginning, finds himself transplanted into a not unimportant dilemma at the end. In it he points out how in many cases the narrative is such "that one cannot recover the sentient facts of the matter" (p. 214). Thus in the case of the miraculous feeding it must necessarily have been visible how the provisions multiplied themselves; but in the Gospels nothing is said about it. In the stilling of the storm a command is placed in Jesus' mouth, which would have been totally without purpose "since the elements have no ears" (p. 216).[107] Jesus' walking on the water appears to be utterly without purpose (p. 220); hence one must reconstruct the events

105. [*The Christian Faith*, par. 147, sec. 2.]

106. *The Christian Faith*, par. 47, secs. 1, 2; par. 147, sec. 1.

107. [Theodor] Keim (*Der geschichtliche Christus* [Zürich, 1866³], pp. 123ff.) explains the miracle of the rescue of Jesus from the storm as an immediate intervention of God by means of the provision which he is said to have reserved for himself, so that in cases of an unfavorable confusion of finite causes he could rescue the highest aims of the world. A nice idea for children, but one which would have amused not only the "immanentist" Spinoza but also the transcendentalist Leibniz.

differently. If we consider that in the case of the feeding it was already evening, hence dark, and that Jesus' alleged walking on the water occurred on a stormy night, who will vouch for the correctness of the observations? Likewise, in the case of the transfiguration, the disciples, according to the explicit assertion of Luke, were very drowsy. "But once it proves necessary in several cases to blame the narrative, then one has the right to assume the same thing also in other cases where the ethical factor is not to be grasped in a clear way" (p. 220)—or also, we must add, where the physical goes far beyond every analogy. When Schleiermacher describes such cases by saying that "it is permissible to supplement and transform the narrative in order to exhibit the fact" (p. 216, 222ff.), he appears to have in mind a crossbreed between a natural and a mythical explanation, and he is indeed correct when he admits that "even with that we do not get out of the difficulty" (p. 210). Therefore he even anticipates an answer to this point: "If in time an explanation of the genesis of these narratives were to be found in which the miraculous were to disappear, that is, if those effects on external nature would disappear which lie totally beyond the visible limits of human power, then that would be no disturbance of faith; to the contrary, it would be the most desirable outcome of our investigation" of this point. "But we can set aside as a task for us that which is only to be fulfilled when we have a completely certain theory about the origin of the first three Gospels." (On another occasion he speaks of the Gospels in general.) Still, it is "not necessary that it be solved" (p. 221).

If we ask, Why should that not be necessary? then Schleiermacher's admission is illuminating: "Also, a theory about the first three Evangelists which would have more leeway does not help, because we retain the Cana story in John" (p. 210)—that is, a miracle which, while morally not unthinkable, physically nonetheless goes as far beyond any analogy as any other. In this concession, one does not know what to think of Schleiermacher's insistence that, in the case of those Gospel miracle stories which remain obscure for us physically and morally, we are to seek the blame for this obscurity in the character of the narratives exclusively on the side of the Synoptics, with two exceptions—but only apparent ones—in John. Namely, he first makes the Lazarus story into a merely apparent exception by means of the previously mentioned interpretation, which does not harmonize with his own principles; secondly, he does so with the feeding story, by means of the comment that here John, by using Jesus' word (6:26) that the Jews followed him not because they saw signs but because they had eaten of the loaves, himself substracts the multiplication of bread from the sum of miracles, and suggests that it was something natural (p. 219). Schleiermacher himself still concedes that the narrative presents the matter as a miracle; then John, despite the suggestion given by Jesus and noted by him, would have to have deceived himself crudely about the nature of the event, and his narrative would just as much require a correction as those of the other Evangelists. But the third, real, exception (of which Schleiermacher remarkably makes no mention here) would certainly be the miracle in Cana, which is peculiar to the Fourth Gospel and which, together with the Lazarus miracle, is decisive against the insistence that there is less difficulty in John's miracle stories. On the other hand, that also a number of Synoptic miracles are absent from John is not to be reckoned as an advantage for this Gospel as long as one cannot make more intelligible the absence of the transfiguration story than can Schleiermacher.

"If one considers the story" (in the first three Gospels), he judges, "then first of all one finds the miraculous in the two figures who are designated as Moses and Elijah; then also one's own impression of the figure of Christ, who appears to suggest a state which is not to be harmonized with a perfect human body." Now if such a portrayal of the occurrence on the mountain was in circulation, and if John did not consider it true, but "had an entirely different conception, then he could," Schleiermacher thinks, "deliberately have declined to mention it because he could believe that in this way it would disappear sooner" (p. 468). But a biographer who discovers a widespread false conception of an event in the life of his hero would act very inappropriately if for his part he completely bypassed the event; the only appropriate thing, rather, is to oppose the false presentation with the true one. That is also what the Fourth Evangelist really did here, except that for him, that which he offers appears to be correct, not on historical but solely on dogmatic grounds, as I have demonstrated elsewhere.[108] Concerning the event itself, Schleiermacher is satisfied this time with the comment, "The report actually does not require us to assume anything miraculous in it, because we see very clear traces of evidence that the disciples were not in a perfectly wakeful state of mind but were half-asleep and half-awake, a state from which they momentarily roused themselves. The fact that Christ said they were not to speak of the matter could have had its basis in the fact that of course they had not grasped it fully" (pp. 468–69). But what was so difficult to grasp here that it could not have been cleared up by a few words employed by Jesus if, as Schleiermacher explained in previous years of his lectures, the transformation of the figure of Jesus were only a natural "optical appearance," if the heavenly voice were only the subjective interpretation of this phenomenon on the part of disciples in the misunderstandable reports of later Hellenistic narrators, and if what was taken to be Moses and Elijah were but two secret adherents of Jesus, such as Nicodemus?

108. See my *Leben Jesu für das deutsche Volk bearbeitet*, pp. 549ff.

This occasions the general comment that in the last year of his lectures Schleiermacher dealt with the individual Gospel miracle stories more briefly than he did in previous ones —if we do not want to assume somehow that the well-meaning hand of the editor here and there excised several things which permitted an interpretation which was disadvantageous to his master. If we had to censure the latter sternly, we could not praise the former either. The less historical worth the narratives under discussion have, the more worth they have critically.[109] What we generally have in the Gospels is nowhere more apparent than in their miracle stories. Whoever wants to get to the root of the former must subject these exact parts to a precise consideration; whoever does not do so awakens the suspicion that he does not really seriously undertake to get to the root of the Gospels. Especially with regard to the Fourth Gospel does a fundamental discussion of the single miracle of Lazarus yield a greater elucidation than every other consideration. On this, as on the miracle in Cana, Schleiermacher this time is very brief; other miracles, such as the healing of the man born blind, he silently bypasses. It is, in fact, only general points of view which he expresses in order to make Jesus' miracles conceivable—a graduated series from the easier to the more difficult on which he places them. But the more this difficulty increases and in the end becomes identical with incredibility, the more pressing becomes the task of explaining where such narratives came from, and how the inconceivable and thereby the unhistorical arose in them. Here the mythical point of view is intimated: the Gospel miracle stories are to be understood only on the basis of the confluence of the historical moment given in the person of

109. [Strauss's dictum has been substantiated. That is, narratives which do not recount solid history are important for the critic's concern to account for the narrative's existence. Precisely the "unhistorical" narratives about Jesus tell us most about the beliefs of those who created the stories.]

Jesus with the ideal moment given in the messianic expectation, and subsequently in the concepts and efforts of the new community. Schleiermacher sees this road, but he sees it as a road which leads to destruction, and therefore he guards himself from entering it. "Since the Gospels," he said in an earlier year,[110] "which are our sole historical sources about Christ, narrate miracle stories about him with more or less emphasis, our judgment concerning miracles must be such that through it the credibility of the Gospels is not injured; for otherwise our faith in the person of Christ would be ruined, and he would become for us a *mythical* person!"

But although for Schleiermacher, as a result of his aversion to using the right key, surely far too many Gospel miracle stories remain unlocked, afterwards he still tries a false key, with an "auxiliary line," as he calls it, which can still be used here. The two extreme points with regard to the Gospel miracles are said to be, on the one hand, those in which Jesus initiates effects on other persons with perfect certainty of success; on the other hand, those which he does not derive from himself but views only as an answer to his prayer on the part of God. "Between both points, however, we find also such miracles in which the miraculous in the result appears to be qualified by foreknowledge." If, then, we find it necessary in a miracle story to construct a hypothesis about how the elements in the event may have cohered differently from the way they are presented in the narrative—which is the case in all miracles which go beyond the scope of influence on persons—then (here I improve the poorly edited text, p. 225) "the difficulty is less if we must deal only with such foreknowledge and are able to suppose such a transformation of the narrative that this becomes the main point; for here we come upon an area in

110. [Strauss evidently is relying on his own excerpts from student notebooks of Schleiermacher's lectures. See above, p. xxiv.]

97

which we also have analogies again." Specifically, "there are experiences of just such knowing of the unobserved, and yet a knowing which has a certain reliability and which also authenticates itself." Schleiermacher here thinks of the appearance of magnetic clairvoyance which for him, as we know from his letters, was a settled matter.[111] In this perspective he then places, at least presumably, the stilling of the storm (p. 226) and, it also appears, Peter's catch of fish, when he says that "the possibility of Christ's human knowing of the location of the fish cannot be disputed" (p. 220); but in this case an ordinary sense of perception is not thought of at all. Similarly, in the story of the coin, according to Schleiermacher, "the miraculous lies in Christ's knowing of something accidental which is distant from him and (sentiently) not perceptible," namely, "that the fish was at that place and that it had swallowed the coin" (p. 225). But nonetheless if, according to Schleiermacher's own previous avowal, the fish's biting precisely Peter's hook could be the result only of a supernatural influence, then here already that pitiful expedient is insufficient. And then Schleiermacher himself restricts it even more by the remark that we can ascribe such a foreknowledge of Christ only to results which, though accidental and rare, were still possible in a natural way, such as those situations with the fish, but not to results which, like the multiplication of food in the feeding story, "lay outside the laws of a natural phenomenon." One sees that Schleiermacher has tried his lock-pick also on this feeding story, which is especially fatal for him, and that there it broke off for him.

An unusual light falls on Schleiermacher's view of Jesus also from two questions which he puts forward at the end of his observations about the miracles of Jesus. "Why," he asks, "did Jesus make no use of his miracle power in that

111. [During his early days in Tübingen, clairvoyance and spiritualism were "settled matters" also for Strauss. See above, p. xxi.]

moment when his life was in danger, up to the last catastrophe?" (pp. 210, 226). We naturally answer, Because he did not possess such a miracle power at all. But actually, in our purely human view of the person of Jesus, such a question cannot occur to us at all. That it occurs to Schleiermacher and is answered by him in a farfetched moral argument shows precisely that he does not view Jesus as a true man. The other question concerns "Christ's capacity for foreknowledge." Why did he not put it into effect in order to find "those persons who, perhaps living at a distance, were most receptive to his influence, in order that, passing over the more obtuse near by, he might turn exclusively to these and thereby attain a much greater result?" (pp. 227–28). To be sure, this admits a more natural understanding; yet in connection with that other question and with surmises about how Jesus' life would have turned out had he put this higher capacity to work, it reminds one of the scholastic problem, How would things have turned out if it had pleased the Son of God to come upon earth as a pumpkin?

JESUS' TEACHING ACTIVITY

From the external aspect of the life of Jesus Schleiermacher goes directly to the inner, and here treats in turn his teaching and his community-forming activity. This could easily be the best passage in Schleiermacher's lectures, since here, apart from his acuteness from which the smallest differences do not escape, his penetration is confirmed which, supported by a lively power of imagination, knows how to picture the remotest relationships and achieve fruitful results therefrom. Yet at the same time, even here the dogmatic-critical bias curtails those advantages, but not so much that it puts them into the background, as in the parts we have just perused.

Regarding the teaching activity of Jesus, Schleiermacher contests with more basis the distinction between an exoteric and esoteric teaching manner than he does the distinction between the teaching *of* Christ and a teaching *about* Christ which appeared only later, insofar as he seeks to invalidate the later contention primarily by the fact that he presupposes the Johannine discourses of Jesus. Of the distinctions which he himself makes with reference to Jesus' teaching manner, two are especially important. Specifically, concerning the origin of what was said, that which Jesus expounded as his own is distinguished from that which he appropriated as given in the dominant conception, and merely qualified in his own way; in this case one must note very carefully where the "given" ends and Jesus' own teaching begins. Related to this, in reference to the intent of Jesus' discourses, is the distinction between direct and indirect presentation, that is, whether in his discourse Jesus purely intends only to put forward what is in his inner life, or whether he aims at something at hand, something he contests or defends himself against. Here this canon results: "The more the discourses of Christ are apologetic or polemical, the less certain it is that we can take his own conviction directly from his discourse; on the other hand, the more Christ's discourse proceeds from his inner life without reference to the ideas of others, the more it must be the expression of his innermost truth and conviction" (p. 242).[112] With these distinctions and the rule of interpretation which is drawn from them, Schleiermacher provided himself with two contrivances whereby it cannot be difficult for him to set aside every part of what the Gospel gives as Jesus' teachings which is undesirable for him. At the same time he

112. [This criterion is clearly an expression of Schleiermacher's high estimate of the artist whose work is a spontaneous, immediate expression of his inner life (see above, p. 69). On the other hand, Joachim Jeremias has recently argued that many of the parables, the most genuine element in the Synoptics, were Jesus' responses to criticism (*The Parables of Jesus*, trans. from 6th German ed. by S. H. Hook [New York: Scribner's, 1963], pp. 38–42).]

knows how to derive by these distinctions new advantages
for the Johannine Gospel, since the direct presentation pre-
dominates in it just as the indirect, especially the polemical,
does in the Synoptics; furthermore, by means of the precision with which John, especially in comparison with Matthew, gives every occasion for Jesus' discourses, John makes
it essentially easier to decide the extent of what is Jesus'
own teaching and what is merely appropriated. The insight
to which Schleiermacher closes his eyes—that the direct
teaching manner in the Fourth Gospel only serves the development of the Logos-dogma of the Evangelist, and that
both the discourses and all their occasions are freely composed[113]—naturally gives the matter a different cast.

With regard to the content of Jesus' teaching, Schleiermacher distinguishes the teaching concerning his person
from the teaching concerning his vocation. That he puts the
former first is already an effect of the dominance which the
teaching manner of the Fourth Gospel has for him. And
when he then, first of all, explains how Jesus presented
himself as the promised one, it is a manifest mistake for him
to take his point of departure mainly from Johannine
passages. Here is the very first opportunity, which on
closer examination he takes, to put into motion his dredging
machine for ridding the exegetical channel of obstructive
items. Concretely, in John 5:45–46, Jesus says that Moses
wrote of him; so if one wanted to take that literally, then
every investigation of the genuineness of the Pentateuch
would be quashed, since Jesus speaks of it as a work of
Moses. Nevertheless, according to Schleiermacher, "Christ
could say that without having undertaken an investigation
concerning the author, since he made use of the general
common designation of the book; he does not speak of the

113. [Today, critics agree with Strauss in saying that the Johannine discourses are not genuine Jesus' words, but disagree with him by viewing
them as end products of complex tradition-histories.]

man but of the book, without having any kind of conviction about the critical question of the author of the books" (p. 247). Here Schleiermacher confuses investigation and conviction throughout; in any case, Jesus did not undertake a critical investigation concerning the genuineness of the Pentateuch—rather, what is at stake here is only the Fourth Gospel—and therefore he could have had a very firm conviction that Moses was the author of these books, and he must have had it, since otherwise these books could not have had the high prophetic authority for him which he ascribed to them. How Schleiermacher in general understands Jesus' attitude toward the Old Testament prophecy, and the extent to which we can agree with his understanding, has already been discussed.

In addition, in the Gospels Jesus presents himself as one sent by God. This is also developed by Schleiermacher primarily on the basis of the Fourth Gospel, where above all he seeks to do away with the sayings about a preexistence in the manner which we have already illumined, while he translates a number of amenable Johannine passages directly into the language of *The Christian Faith*. If the Johannine Christ says in 5:19 that the Son can do nothing of himself, but only what he sees the Father doing, then this means, "His God-consciousness is constant, and apart from it he is nothing." That in 3:13 and 6:46 he designates himself as the one who is with God or in heaven is "only the constancy of the God-consciousness" (p. 263). Jesus' explanation in 6:41 that no one can come to him if the Father does not draw him means that "the acceptance or nonacceptance of his call depends on the manner in which man is affected on the natural side as well as by the way he is determined by the other social relationships which proceed from the governance of the world" (p. 284). Jesus does not trace his mission, like the prophets of the Old Testament, to a single call which once came to him. Even if he claims to be one sent by God, "we cannot," according to Schleiermacher, "understand it differently than that it belongs with the natural development of his self-consciousness" (p. 264). However, the Gospels at least do not see the matter this way, least of all the Fourth. The born Son of God, the incarnate Logos, did not need any further call; but his consciousness was from the start different from that of all other men.[114] It has already been shown that inferring a gradual human development of Jesus' self-consciousness from a Johannine passage (5:20) rests on a virtually deceptive exegesis. If Jesus designates himself as the Son of God, then Schleiermacher thinks of the contrast asserted in Hebrews 3:5–6 between the (grown) son as the one who is intimately related to the Father's will and the servant who stands outside it (pp. 101, 269). And if Jesus presents God above all as his Father, but in a derived sense also as the Father of those who believe in him, then according to Schleiermacher he replaces "the concept of a sovereign state with the concept of the household, and this has a decisive influence on the presentation of the whole relation between God and man" (pp. 278–79).

Schleiermacher formulates Jesus' vocation in a completely Johannine way (5:26; cf. 15:4ff.) as the sharing of the assumed divine life in him, whose acceptance on the part of man is faith. But since the individual can accept this life which proceeds from Christ only as a member of the community founded by Christ, two sides or elements differentiate themselves: "The first, the vital communion of each person with Christ, we shall call the mystic element; the other, the communion of the believers among themselves, the ecclesiastical" (p. 291).

With regard to the latter, the community founded by Jesus himself is said to be not of a political kind but one

114. [In *LJGP* Strauss had asserted that the New Testament is docetic, but we are ebionitic. See above, p. lxxii.]

which is compatible with every political community. With regard to Old Testament theocracy, he indeed completely separated his followers from the theocratic form, but did not intend to do away with the Mosaic Law; that is, according to Schleiermacher's interpretation, it is not to be done away with by an arbitrary act done by Jesus or any other individual until that condition commenced which of itself would make the observance of the law impossible—the destruction of Jerusalem and of the temple. While Jesus and his community at first still remained within Judaism, he nonethel ss explained this initial form to be only the first stage of velopment which must be followed by another, whose beg nning he thought to depend on the collapse of the Jewish theocracy as a result of the destruction of Jerusalem. But also, for that interim condition, he interpreted the law on the basis of its original form and explained all the pharisaic additions to it as corruption, partly because they suppressed the popular spirit through the impossibility of fulfilling them, and partly because they were accompanied by an orientation to the external (pp. 292–97).

What was imparted by the Founder to the Christian church, namely, what according to Schleiermacher is called the mystical side, is eternal life; according to the Johannine-Schleiermacherian presentation this is to be thought of not only as something future but equally as something already present (p. 337). Just as Jesus is the unifying principle of the community founded by him, so one often finds sayings of Jesus in which he appears to ascribe also to the world, which is hostile to this community, a similar unifying principle—the "prince of this world" or the devil, with whom is also associated a circle of subordinate demons. It is understandable that against this conception, which is dogmatically contrary to him, Schleiermacher would set going all his mechanisms in order to destroy it even in its exegetical roots. Jesus, when he speaks of the devil and demons, is said to speak only hypothetically (Matt. 12:26ff.); now he only makes use of a current conception without himself advancing a doctrine (Matt. 13:19, 35ff.; 25; 41; John 8:43–44). If, taking as his point of departure the demons, he goes on to speak of the devil, this is said to be conversion of the former concept into the latter (Matt. 12:25ff.); and if once, after Satan has been mentioned, he speaks of "the whole power of the enemy" (Luke 10:19), then this is said to seem as if Jesus intended to interpret the concept of Satan on the basis of a more general one of hostility against the kingdom of God (pp. 309–21). In a similar way, where the expansion of Jesus' community and his death as its precondition are being discussed, he works against the presentation of this death as an atoning death. That Jesus came to serve and to offer himself as a ransom for many (Matt. 20:28) is said to mean only that his entire life proceeded with service and also finally will "focus" on this, and that liberation was the thrust of his life to the point of death, but not a special effect of it. Likewise, with respect to the words of institution, chicanery is practiced with Matthew's addition to the words about the blood, "shed for the remission of sins" (26:28); one does not know whether the point of "this" concerns the chalice of wine or the blood (which are identical since they are equated), or why this is said only of the wine and not equally of the bread. Jesus is also said to declare (John 13:10) that the disciples are "clean" even before his passion, which they could not have been if only his death brought forgiveness of sins (pp. 325–26). In such exegetical maneuvers Schleiermacher is not even original; all this is found to excess from the Socinians to the rationalists.

With respect to the conclusion of the present world order, Jesus found among his compatriots the concept of a judgment on all nations, associated on the one hand with the appearance of the Messiah and on the other hand with the resurrection of the dead. Now Schleiermacher maintains that in numerous passages the latter conception is spiritualized by Jesus (in John), but that his discourses on judgment partly (in Matthew 25) have a predominately parabolic character, and partly (in John) present judgment as a continuous one. "And so," Schleiermacher explains,

> there emerges for me no kind of certainty from Jesus' discourses that he had a definite conviction about such a general judgment which was bound up with the end of human affairs; therefore he did not have such a conviction about his personal return, which we find expressed only in Christ's parabolic discourses. Rather, as a definite conviction of Christ, I find expressed only this ongoing judgment which occurs in the development of the Kingdom of God itself. [p. 335]

This is saying too much even for the Johannine Christ, inasmuch as he lets stand the future bodily resurrection and the last judgment alongside the spiritual resurrection and the continuing judgment.[115]

JESUS' ACTIVITY IN FOUNDING THE CHURCH

In the activity through which Jesus formed the community, insofar as he developed it during his lifetime, Schleiermacher includes baptizing as well as calling disciples, and does so for the sake of the well-known Johannine passages (3:22; 4:1–2); accordingly, the command to baptize (Matt. 28:19) which was given after the resurrection is seen as the ordaining of baptism also outside the Jewish area (p. 341). But with regard to the selection of the

115. [Strauss has clearly seen the problem to which Bultmann offered the more drastic "solution"—that the references to the future (John 5:28–29; 6:39, 40, 44; 12:47–48) were interpolated into John's text by a later traditionalist seeking to harmonize this Gospel with the prevailing view. This view has not won general acceptance (Rudolf Bultmann, *Theology of the New Testament*, trans. Kendrick Grobel, 2 vols. [New York: Scribner's, 1955], 2:39).]

disciples, everything that Schleiermacher advances is determined by an unusual scrupulousness, on account of the betrayer. That Jesus did not select the Twelve at the same time, which is believable on the basis of passages such as Mark 3:14 and Luke 6:13, is evident already from stories of individual callings, such as those of both pairs of brothers (Matt. 4:18ff.; 9:9–10); for Schleiermacher it is even more evident from the corresponding narratives in John (1:35ff.). But he goes so far as to insist that the number twelve was accidental, and that only after Jesus' death did the disciples begin to attach significance to this (p. 347). In support, virtually all kinds of things are adduced. A reference to the number of the tribes would presuppose an all-too-Jewish thought pattern in Jesus; moreover, after the exile the tribes no longer existed, and so on. All the more did "twelve" become something ideal, and thereby achieved the possibility of providing a numerical foundation for a spiritual Israel, more broadly conceived. But these are not Schleiermacher's real reasons; as already implied, they appear to flow from the choice of the betrayer, Judas. If one visualizes a definite choice of apostles on the part of Christ, then there is the dilemma: either he did not know what was in Judas or, if he did know it, he himself drew Judas into ruin. For us there would be no hesitation with respect to the first assumption, since history teaches how many an exceptional man deceived himself about individuals among his closest associates, and since, furthermore, we do not know how extensively or how long Jesus deceived himself about Judas and what reasons he may have had, when once he perhaps did see through him, for still not promptly dismissing him. But Schleiermacher cannot assume this. For, he says, "it would not agree with the exceptional degree of precise knowledge of what is within man which we must necessarily posit in him, just as John also actually says (2:25)" (p. 345). But Schleiermacher is required to posit in

107

Jesus this knowledge of human nature, which is to be seen as an absolute one which excludes every error, only because of his dogmatic presupposition, which has no validity in a historical question. Thus, in the attachment of the apostles to Jesus he assumes differing degrees of participation on Jesus' p rt; that is, some were called more by Jesus himself, others were more permitted to come on their own, and especially in the case of Judas "the circumstances must have been such that Christ would have had to refuse him in a very definite way if he were not to join the Twelve; but his knowledge of human nature would not have been a sufficient basis for doing so, since this would not have been understandable to everyone" (p. 346). One could ask Schleiermacher, on his own grounds, whether such a passive attitude in such an important matter as the choice of the Twelve is to be harmonized with the "peculiar dignity of Christ." Actually, however, such an odd explanation, to which Schleiermacher finds himself pressed by his presupposition about the person of Christ, can only be an additional reason for us to reject this presupposition.

Regarding the mission of the Twelve during Jesus' lifetime, Schleiermacher sees himself prevented from attributing to it the aim of preparatory training because such a mission is also mentioned for the Seventy, which he cannot regard as a closed circle with a special destiny like the Twelve. This moves him to surmise a different aim for both missions, namely, "the more the total impact on Christ's relationships was one of quiet development, the less occasion he could have had of undertaking a change in his usual practice of having the apostles accompany and surround him in his teaching activity; but if the development seemed to him to be threatened, then he could easily have had the desire first to bring the proclamation itself to a certain stage before the catastrophe occurred." There could come times "when his own personal activity was not enough, when he wished that the business of proclaiming the Kingdom of God could be carried on simultaneously at several places in the total environment of the Jewish countryside, and when he thus desired an accelerated result. In this way the missions can be explained in agreement with everything else, but it is impossible to say anything more definite about the matter" (pp. 360–62).

In this passage Schleiermacher poses several interesting questions pertaining to Jesus' intentions and mode of action. His pragmatic and psychological observations such as these are always excellent, full of insight and historical perception as well, just as generally everything is excellent when dogmatic prejudice or bad exegetical habit does not come on the scene. We cannot insist, he says—rather, the contrary is probable—that already during Jesus' lifetime there existed an organized community of his disciples. The question remains of whether even with a longer life he would not have given real form to what had been preparatory. As reasons which prevented him from doing this during his lifetime we can imagine that he wanted to accelerate neither his own catastrophe by founding a formally organized society, nor the national catastrophe by the disturbance which such a founding would have aroused. If one assumes, however, that Jesus did not have these reasons for refraining from doing so, what would he then have done? What did he have in mind with reference to the community founded by him? Schleiermacher answers, "He did not want to destroy the law, so he did not want to destroy the temple worship either; consequently he would have also allowed his followers to attend the temple service just as he himself participated in it." His followers would have had to be satisfied first of all with following the synagogue regulations, as they subsequently actually did; and if Christianity had made progress without the rupture with Judaism which lay in the execution of Jesus, then the temple proper in Jerusalem would also have been partly Christianized. "The peculiar spirit of this community must have consisted in seeing the ritual, the legal, and the ceremonial as a purely national thing and in basing religion on the foundation which lay in Jesus' person." In this way the matter could have organized itself even during his life, and had he not wanted to avoid the catastrophe, indeed the national even more than the personal, he would also have instituted it this way (p. 362).[116]

EVENTS LEADING TO THE PASSION

The question which Schleiermacher immediately asked, In what way was the catastrophe of Jesus' fate brought about? (p. 362), designates one of the most important points for the decision between the Synoptics and John, and therefore everything hangs on not assuming in advance something in favor of one of them, but solely on seeing which presentation allows the actual event to be conceived more naturally. Let us see then how Schleiermacher says that the first three Evangelists give us in this section both too much and too little: they give us too little, because "no one could arrive at a view of the actual situation if we did not have the Fourth Gospel," especially since they "know of only one sojourn of Christ in Jerusalem;" but they also give us too much, because "their reports cannot be coordinated into the threads of John's Gospel, since too little of the chronological data in those Gospels is established" (p. 362). Thus it is clear that he presupposes the historical trustworthiness of the Johannine report, since only on this presupposition does the Synoptic one appear as incomplete. Since then, it has been demonstrated convincingly by Baur[117] that the presentation which the first three Evangelists give

116. [It is strange that Strauss did not comment on this hypothesis. Was it because he never saw his way clear to a historical reconstruction of the relation of Jesus to the church? See above, p. civ.]
117. *Kritische Untersuchungen über die kanonischen Evangelien*, pp. 189ff.

of the development of Jesus' relationships are of themselves entirely satisfactory, and that not only can they dispense with every supplementation from the so-called pragmatism of John, but that by his supplement the natural sequence of the Synoptic presentation would only be distorted. Here Schleiermacher points to John as the only true "guide" because the others, "where the delineation of an intensification" (of the tension in Jesus' relationships) is concerned, can scarcely be used because of the lack of chronological order; "in contrast, in John a pragmatic tendency in this regard is undeniable" (p. 355). But here also Baur made it clear how in the presentation in the Fourth Gospel, instead of such intensification, right from the start the relationships rather appear to be so deliberately tangled that, on the one hand, one does not understand how Jesus can repeatedly succeed in eluding the hate of his enemies, while on the other hand, one must say that just as he succeeded repeatedly, so he could also continue to succeed. This is why an indeed very exceptional, but historically inconceivable, event—the raising of Lazarus—must bring about the catastrophe. Schleiermacher sees himself induced to ask why, in view of the fact that Jesus knew the consequences of that act (namely, the decisions made by the rulers of the capital to plot his ruin), he did not, as frequently before, evade the danger and remain absent from the forthcoming Passover (p. 380). John's answer is, Because he knew that his hour, the time of his death and of his glorification, had now come. Still Schleiermacher will have nothing to do with the idea that Jesus himself "plotted his death in any way" (p. 362). Rather, also in Galilee and Perea Jesus is said to have been increasingly in mortal danger from the Pharisees and Herod, and so, being equally in danger on all sides, he went to where his place was during the festival, namely Jerusalem (p. 384). The artificiality of this combination is obvious, and if one must once ignore the views

111

of the Fourth Evangelist, then making the Synoptic presentation the foundation results in the far more natural view. Also for the Synoptists, Jesus goes to Jerusalem in order to die; but since it was his first and only time there since his prophetic-messianic appearance on the scene, we can naturally imagine how he could have found it necessary, after suitable preparation in the countryside, to make the decisive effort in the capital; though the effort was dubious, the city had not been hostile during previous visits there.[118]

For all the prejudice which Schleiermacher has for the normative place of the Fourth Gospel, he still hesitates to reject the harmonious tradition of the first three altogether. As is known, the so-called cleansing of the temple is located by the Johannine Gospel during Jesus' first visit to Jerusalem, and by the Synoptics during the one which ended with his death. Likewise Jesus' festive entry into the capital is presented by both in such essentially different ways that it is difficult to combine both accounts. With regard to the latter event, contrary to his former custom in such cases, Schleiermacher has already in his book on Luke[119] relied on the expedient of understanding it as an event that could easily be repeated, an expedient which he now wants to use in the lectures for the cleansing of the temple also (pp. 364–85).

118. See Baur, *Kritische Untersuchungen über die kanonischen Evangelien*, pp. 126ff; Strauss, *Das Leben Jesu für das deutsche Volk bearbeitet*, p. 252.
119. *Über die Schriften des Lukas*, p. 245.

CHAPTER SIX

THE THIRD PERIOD: THE PASSION AND RESURRECTION STORY

THE LAST MEAL

In the third and final period, concerning the passion and resurrection story, Schleiermacher's attention is called first of all to the difference between the first three Evangelists and the Fourth with reference to Jesus' last meal. The chronological divergence he treats as a merely apparent one in that he puts the meal (with John) on the day before the Passover, but still regards it (with the others) as a Passover meal on the assumption that strangers, because of the excessive crowding, surely could celebrate one day ahead of time (p. 401). He considers the assumption that John speaks of a meal other than that of which the Synoptics speak to be excluded, because both have the betrayal by Judas predicted at this meal (p. 393). All the more seriously does Schleiermacher take John's silence concerning the institution of the Lord's supper, "in view of the great detail in which John treats the last days of Christ" (p. 393). Schleiermacher finds it impossible to explain John's silence on the basis that his Gospel intended to be a supplement—that because the matter already stood in the others, he bypassed it. The story of the hint of betrayal at the same meal of course is found also in the others, and yet John does not think it superfluous to repeat it. Thus, if he does not narrate the story of the institution of the Lord's supper, one must look for another reason. If he had had the first three Gospels, which tell it, before him, then he would have had to say to himself that by his silence he would mislead his readers, and accordingly would at least, if he did not want to give a detailed report, have had to suggest that also this act of Christ occurred at this meal. The matter appears differently on the supposition that the others were not available to John when he wrote his Gospel, since their contents were assembled only later. Therefore he was free to select, from the incidents of that evening, those which appeared to him as the most important (p. 393).

However, although he is silent about the Lord's Supper, he reports the foot-washing undertaken by Jesus; it is at least clear that this must appear more important for him than the Lord's Supper, just as he also regards it as an act which is to be repeated by the disciples. That "forms a remarkable contradiction to the fact" that the Lord's Supper rather than the foot-washing "was introduced as an institution in the church" (pp. 393ff.). The other apostles must have understood the words spoken by Jesus at the distribution of the bread and wine as a command referring to this institution. The words themselves, according to Schleiermacher, do not contain such a regulation for the entire scope and future of the church; they could be taken to refer only to the circle of the apostles. Still, "though we cannot guarantee that we have the actual words of Christ," since they read differently in different reports, we can nonetheless assume "that the apostles were right in understanding him this way." In this case it indeed remains problematic why John should have regarded the matter differently. One sees that if only the four Evangelists are involved, Schleiermacher, as virtually always, will decidedly ascribe a misunderstanding to the first three and a correct understanding to the Fourth. But this time the former are reinforced by the apostle Paul and the practice of the church from the oldest times onward; hence he does not dare to declare himself as unconditionally for John as usual, but is content, also in *The Christian Faith*,[120] to leave it undecided whether Jesus himself intended the Lord's Supper to be a permanent institution or whether it was only that the apostles later believed they had reasons for understanding his words in this way. Schleiermacher can say this "all the more, since it is sufficient for us," he had added to his lecture in a previous year,[121] "if it was only the conviction of the disciples that in the institution and repetition of this act they were acting in accord with the will of Christ."

GETHSEMANE, THE TRIAL, AND CRUCIFIXION

The same difficulty, the silence of his major Evangelist, immediately meets Schleiermacher with regard to the Gethsemane scene, but is resolved by him here with much more openness, though one may ask whether with equal success. Furthermore, this time it is more than mere silence, since rather the one story excludes the other, as Schleiermacher rightly sees. If one were to imagine that after the Farewell Discourses and the high-priestly prayer in John there followed the soul-struggle in the garden the way the Synoptics describe it, then, Schleiermacher judges, "one must concede that in Christ there was a force of darker concepts or unspecified feelings, which are difficult to ascribe to him because they follow precisely such a considered, firm situation of agreement with the divine will" (p. 395). Concerning the Synoptic narrative, he then says that we "evidently do not have it any longer in the original form; one need only observe the threefold repetition in order to be convinced that this is no literal report, because such a solemn number must

120. *The Christian Faith*, par. 139, sec. 3.
121. [Strauss is again relying on his own notes. See p. xxiv.]

arouse the surmise that the narrative is structured for a definite purpose (in order to be truly exemplary)." The strengthening angel in Luke is "another special addition; so we cannot say what we are to regard as the true fact; perhaps the historical foundation belongs to an earlier time" (p. 395). One can only announce his agreement with these judgments of Schleiermacher as a whole.[122] Nevertheless, even the latter surmise—that the historical element in the matter perhaps belongs to an earlier time—shows us which way the wind is blowing for Schleiermacher, namely, from John, whose narrative in 12:27 he appears to regard as the foundation of the soul-struggle in Gethsemane. And immediately we also recognize how just in this part lies one of the reasons why Schleiermacher prefers the Johannine Jesus to the Synoptic one. Concretely, when he deems "a depression of the soul" such as the Synoptics portray for us "to be part of the garb which the report has received, so that thereby the example of Christ is the more applicable to others in whom this could occur as well," he puts himself on the side of those for whom "the difference between weakness and a sinful state" appeared to be one which "could not be maintained" (pp. 395–96).

Earlier, during the departure to the Mount of Olives, there occurs the saying, peculiar to Luke (22:36ff.), about the swords which Jesus commands his disciples to buy, and Jesus' explanation, in response to their report, that the two which they already had were enough. Schleiermacher seeks to explain the contradiction between this narrative and the rebuke which Jesus expresses subsequently about Peter's sword-thrust by this assumption: should the high priests

122. [Current criticism sustains these judgments. See Eta Linnemann, *Studien zur Passionsgeschichte*, Forschungen zur Religion und Literatur des Alten und Neuen Testaments 102 (Göttingen: Vandenhoeck and Ruprecht, 1970), pp. 11–40, and the literature cited there. I do not find Linnemann's own reconstruction convincing, however.]

have wanted to have Jesus captured by persons without official standing, Jesus was determined to resist; but since it was men from the temple guard whom they sent, he did not want to oppose legitimate authority (p. 391). An ingenious surmise, but with regard to the solitary and problematic report in Luke, nothing more is accomplished.[123]

In the last printed lecture Schleiermacher passed lightly over all these incidents, from the entry to Jerusalem to the death of Jesus, presumably because time was pressing. This is why we want to supplement the lectures here and there with material from previous years.[124] With regard to the capture, he is very indebted to John because he appears to rescue him from Judas's kiss, which he finds "remarkably repugnant"; naturally we also find it so, and the whole man as well, but without seeing therein a reason for doubting it historically. Whether the falling down of the arresting officers at Jesus' "I am he!" in John is equally welcome to Schleiermacher, and whether he tried to deduce it from the "dignity of Christ" or to soften it exegetically, we could not ascertain. The report about the cross-bearer, Simon of Cyrene, remains uncontested, the silence of the Fourth Gospel going unnoticed (pp. 418, 426, and in the earlier notebook); what is more striking is that Schleiermacher seeks to obviate the conclusion which is commonly drawn from this substitution, that it was due to the physical weakness of Jesus, by raising the possibility that it may have occurred in order to distinguish him from common criminals.

If, furthermore, the first three Evangelists have Jesus brought before the actual high priest Caiaphas, but John

123. [These passages continue to elude persuasive explanation; they inevitably figure in discussions of Jesus as an insurrectionist. See, for example, S. G. F. Brandon, *Jesus and the Zealots* (Manchester: Manchester University Press, and New York: Scribner's, 1967), pp. 340–42.]
124. [See note 121.]

has him brought before Caiaphas's father-in-law, the old high priest Annas, then naturally for Schleiermacher John is right, and the "awkwardness" of his narrative is even appealed to as evidence of truth. The matter is explained, presumably, by the fact that the old man did not appear in the assembly late at night, and yet wanted to give his own opinion. The later Evangelists then took the two high priests for one, and thus spoke of two hearings before Caiaphas. What went on before Caiaphas, although this was Jesus' actual official trial, is not reported in the Fourth Gospel; "hence John must not," Schleiermacher concludes very lightly, "have been present" (p. 395). That he puts equally little weight on the testimony concerning the saying about the destruction and rebuilding of the temple, and thinks "there was nothing to be made of this" (pp. 395, 399, 401), will not appear to us as a fortunate critical judgment. For us it is not a matter of further interest to see how Schleiermacher combines, pragmatically and critically but always with the foundation of John as the norm, the Gospel stories of the trials of Jesus before the high priest, Pilate, and Herod. Only this is to be noted: that, like the recent compilers of the story of Socrates, he shows himself concerned with presenting the opponents and judges of Jesus as more human and to a certain extent more credible historically. According to him, the Sanhedrin had "no personal animosity against Jesus, but was guided only by concern for what might result from his activity for the general situation." But Pilate, after the competent Jewish court had given its verdict about a matter which lay within his jurisdiction, "could confirm the decision with full right without violating his duty"; nevertheless, having once personally participated in Jesus' case and having tried to rescue him, he allowed himself to be driven into a corner by the Jews' threat of defaming him before Caesar; this "was cowardice, and here he acted actually against his conviction" (p. 410).

As soon as Schleiermacher begins to speak of the crucifixion he immediately takes up the question of the reality of Jesus' death.   In order to substantiate this—since most crucified persons otherwise remain alive much longer than Jesus did—circumstances have been sought and collected which are to make a more speedy death in Jesus' case explicable.   One especially appealed partly to his delicate constitution and partly to the exhausting circumstances which preceded his crucifixion.   Neither appeal is regarded favorably by Schleiermacher.   Against the former he objects that no trace of such a constitution can be found in Jesus' prior life; no case can be adduced "in which Christ would have been hampered in his spiritual activity by something defective in the bodily aspect of his appearance."   If one already feels the dogmatic breeze, then it becomes even more undeniable in Schleiermacher's comment, "If someone puts the question of whether Christ, with respect to his bodily constitution, is to be seen as a delicate creature, and one who borders on weakness, then his question is not a matter of indifference to him" (p. 417).   Naturally, since according to *The Christian Faith*,[125] from the prototypicality of Christ one must infer a healthiness "which is equally distant from exclusive strength or mastery of individual bodily functions and from sickly weakness."   Neither does Schleiermacher want to hear of any special debilitating incidents which preceded the crucifixion.   The scene in Gethsemane to which an appeal is made is not strictly historical, and what is true in it is probably to be put earlier; the scourging was administered to everyone to be crucified and could not have been the basis of anything special in Jesus' case.   As true as this

125. *The Christian Faith*, par. 98, sec. 2.

119

is, here too for Schleiermacher a dogmatic interest lies in the background. Not only will he not have his Christ be generally weak, but he will not have him in a weakened condition before death, either. He has "an interest in the steadfastness of the picture of Christ which we have made for ourselves, namely, that it remain pure up to his last moment" (p. 417). The man of the absolute, powerful God-consciousness, which of course could actualize itself only in relation to his physical consciousness, must have been in a state of full strength up to the end, as far as physical consciousness is concerned.

Schleiermacher leaves elbowroom only for the accidental dissimilarity which lay in the nature of the execution. The crucifixion, he says, being carried out by the ignorant, was a crude operation by which the organism could be damaged to a greater or lesser degree. The bleeding depended on how the nails were driven in, and the stretching of the body on how the limbs were situated. In themselves the nail wounds were not mortal; "there may have been two or four." But according to how they were used, the arrival of death could be hastened. "It is known," Schleiermacher adds, with reference to the number of nails, "that recently Canon Hug in Freiburg has insisted on a defense of the four wounds of Christ" (p. 419).[126] Indeed! Why this sharp tone if the number of the nails is so unimportant? It was not unimportant for old Paulus in Heidelberg. Against Hug's demonstration he wrote his "Two Nails Less for the Coffin of Rationalism";[127] he therefore saw in the number of nails a vital question for the entire theological standpoint whose representative he was. But Schleiermacher surely is

126. [J. L. Hug, *Einleitung in die Schriften des neuen Testaments*, 2 vols. (Tübingen, 1808), 1:40.]
127. [H. E. Paulus, *Exegetisches Handbuch über die ersten drei Evangelien*, 3 vols. (Heidelberg, 1842), 3:664–754.]

not a rationalist.[128]   How can this question concern him? Presently we shall see why in more detail.

THE REALITY OF JESUS' DEATH

In fact, Schleiermacher first approached the question, Was Jesus' death real or not? with the assurance, "For me it seems to be something quite unimportant whether one says the one or the other." But he adds, "At the same time, I insist that there is no means at all for demonstrating the one or the other" (p. 415). And then he shows quite aptly how neither the necessity of Jesus' death can be confirmed dogmatically nor its reality confirmed exegetically/physiologically. With reference to the former, he says that "it could make no difference for divine justice whether Christ's death was a real one or a deathlike condition; as soon as he had merely completed the act of dying in its spiritual significance, when his consciousness had been reduced to zero, when he had passed through the pain of death,"[129] then divine justice was satisfied, according to the churchly presupposition. Whether then also the "physical" aspect of death "reached its completion or not" is said to be "unimportant for this significance of the matter" (pp. 415–16). But physiologically it is certain that "there is no more certain sign of death than decay": that is, "the resurgence of the chemical process which in life is curbed by vital power" (p. 416). But it cannot be demonstrated exegetically/historically that decay began in Jesus' case. On this basis Schleiermacher then mocks the churchly exegetes in that he tries to demonstrate from the letter of Scripture itself that Jesus could not have been really dead. According to Peter's words in the Pentecost sermon (Acts 2:27, quoted from Psalm 16:10) the holy one of God, that is,

128. [This is surprising, since Strauss repeatedly accuses Schleiermacher of rationalism, especially in his exegesis. See below, p. 160].
129. See also Schleiermacher's *Festpredigten*, 1:297.

Christ, was not to see decay. If he had been dead for but a single moment, decay would have set in, since no interval is conceivable between death and decay (p. 416); or, as Schleiermacher elsewhere says, "to die and to begin to decay are the same thing."[130] Even in a sermon[131] Schleiermacher can conclude, "If the apostle took his words in their strict and proper sense, he must have thought that the life of the Redeemer had not completely departed, because otherwise he must have seen decay, even if only in its initial stages." Very likely, therefore, he quietly assumed that the apostle did not take the words in their strict sense, that is, not in the sense of our present-day natural science but in the sense current in his time, which is still found today in popular notions, according to which a man can indeed be dead for a while, and even be really dead, without decay setting in.[132]

Still, Schleiermacher's contention was that neither the one nor the other, that the death of Jesus was real nor that it was not real, can be demonstrated. But now he shows only the former, the nondemonstrability of a real death. Where, if his position is so impartial, is the evidence that the unreality of Jesus' death is equally impossible to demonstrate? The proposition that the single sure proof of the reality of death is decay should have been compared with the alternative, that the sure sign that death is *not* real is that the one thought dead comes to life again. According to the New Testament reports, this is what happened in Jesus' case. Thus, it would have proven that his death was not a real one, if his revivification had not been an absolute miracle. That it is not a miracle for Schleiermacher is evident already from the way he conceives its result, Jesus' new

130. *Predigten*, 3:257. [Werke 2, part 3.]
131. Ibid.
132. See my *Leben Jesu für das deutsche Volk bearbeitet*, p. 27.

condition. For whomever the resurrection is a miracle, also its result, the new life, must be a miracle; that is, the new corporeality of Jesus must be a supernatural one. Whoever is so zealous, as we shall see in Schleiermacher's case, as to present Jesus' condition after the resurrection as a perfectly natural one and as a pure continuation of the previous one, thereby confesses, more clearly than with words, that for him also the resurrection itself is but a natural resuscitation.

Even the Johannine spear wound, understandably for Schleiermacher an incontrovertible fact, gives him no more security about the reality of Jesus' death than do the two nails. The spear-thrust surely did not have the aim of killing Jesus if he were still alive, for in that case one would have broken his bones, as was done to the others; rather, its aim was to test whether he would still show signs of life. Consequently one would have found a sensitive spot, but one where the thrust, if it did not go deep, would not have been mortal. "That blood and water came from the wound was for the soldier one more sign of Christ's death, for if Christ had still been alive, lymph and blood would not have been separable. Consequently there was a chemical disintegration of the blood." Still, later a limitation is given as a variant explanation: "Lymph and serum had already separated, though not completely, for otherwise no blood could have flowed" (p. 427). One sees that Schleiermacher here is seeking a middle way between death and life, something which cannot be found. It was said better, because it was more decidedly rationalistic, in an earlier year of the lectures that the "blood and water" cannot be understood on the basis of the decomposition of the blood, for that would have been the decay which, according to Acts 2:27, Jesus was not to have seen (put correctly: for in this case a revival would no longer have been possible). Rather, out of some vessels there flowed blood; from others, lymph. "Therefore, the only thing we can say here," he says at the end, "is that, also for those who had the task of bringing about the death of the crucified one as directly as possible, Christ really appeared to have died, and indeed contrary to expectation, since this was the object of amazement. We need not go farther into the fact, because nothing is to be ascertained about it" (p. 428). That sounds like an excuse, but is a warning, like a skull erected at a dangerous swimming hole: here one must not think farther, because otherwise faith could easily be damaged. That is, from Schleiermacher's standpoint; from ours, the danger for faith lies in a totally other place than where the authentication of Jesus' death is concerned.

Let us go back a few steps. Schleiermacher's comments about Jesus' words from the cross, what he says about the cry "My God!" and so on, in Matthew and Mark, is indicative of his position, which is more dogmatic than historical. He could not, he explains, conceive of Christ's whole frame of mind in this last part of his life otherwise than in the way it manifests itself in the Farewell Discourses in John; therefore, a relapse into such a distress of spirit as would be contained in that saying is not probable for him. "To the extent to which I try to conceive of that as an expression of Christ's self-consciousness, I cannot come to terms with it. I can conceive of no moment when the relation between God and Christ would be changed; it must always be the same, and the unity with the Father can never have been destroyed; but in such a cry it appears to be destroyed" (p. 423). The explanation that the words are to be understood only as part of the entire psalm (Psalm 22), which concludes with a most joyous affirmation, is common to Schleiermacher and to the older, partially or completely rationalistic theologians.

John's silence affords Schleiermacher elbowroom for a free attitude toward the miracles at Jesus' death. Two of them, the rending of the temple veil and the resurrection of the saints, he has already, in his work on Luke,[133] derived partly from older examples of poetic-symbolic presentations like those allegedly customary in Christian hymns. "The necessary symbolic interpretation," he comments also now on the former miracle, "points pretty clearly to the origin of this story in the sort of saying by which the relation of the old covenant to the new could be specified, and hence one can easily conceive how in Christian speech, and even more in Christian hymns, it was said that the veil of the temple was torn at Christ's death; we find the sense of this expressed very similarly in Hebrews (6:19–20; 9:6–12; 10:19–20). The symbolically expressed doctrine was then interpreted as a fact" (p. 421). Also, the resurrection of the saints, according to Schleiermacher, cannot be construed as a fact, especially as it is not known what happened to these saints during the time from Jesus' death, when their graves were opened, to his resurrection; during this time they are said to have gone into the holy city and appeared to many. Here also we must conclude a similar origin in Christian speech and hymns (p. 422). In connection with these Schleiermacher finally confesses that he is inclined to surmise that the darkness during Jesus' death hour "most probably came into the straightforward story from a poeticizing presentation" (p. 426). Originally he had tried to take it as an actual fact and, in a naturalist explanation of the paltriest style, sought to support it with comments such as this: such atmospheric darkenings are something "which we often experience for a while," and if we "do not conceive of them in those three hours as a continuum," which

133. *Über die Schriften des Lukas*, p. 293–94.

is not all necessary, "but in frequent repetition, then the miraculous disappears completely" (p. 420).

In the story of Jesus' burial, Schleiermacher above all gives up Matthew's narrative of the guard as improbable and untenable on all counts. With regard to the particulars of the burial, what is especially important for him is the divergence in accounts: according to the Synoptics, the grave into which Jesus was laid belonged to Joseph of Arimathea, while in John there is no hint of this; rather, John says (19:41–42) that at the place of crucifixion there was a garden, and a new tomb in which Jesus was placed because it was nearby and haste was necessary. "From this report," Schleiermacher observes, "it definitely appears that one must conclude that the grave in which Christ was laid did not belong to Joseph, for otherwise this motivation (its proximity) would not have been necessary" (p. 429). In this contradiction between the Synoptics and John, "one could not," he thinks, "avoid granting that John is right"; he appears to be the one who was more accurately informed, while the others easily assumed that the grave in which Joseph placed the corpse would also have been his property. The burial was done in haste, probably without an agreement with the owner of the garden and the tomb. Here Schleiermacher now sees a double possibility: either Jesus' corpse was only temporarily deposited in this grave, and Joseph wanted to have him brought after the Sabbath to his family burial place, possibly to Arimathea; perhaps, since nothing more is divulged about Joseph, he also turned over the further care of the corpse to Nicodemus. Or, on the other hand, the corpse would have and should have remained in the grave according to an agreement with the owner; "which is correct," Schleiermacher judges, "can no longer be decided" (p. 429). Nevertheless, later we shall discover that the former alternative, the merely interim burial, was the more probable for him.

126

THE RESURRECTION AND THE STORIES OF THE EMPTY TOMB

Concerning Jesus' resurrection, Schleiermacher teaches in *The Christian Faith*[134] that, like the miracles, it belongs less to the doctrine of the person of Christ than to the doctrine about Scripture. The disciples perceived the Son of God in him before they could surmise anything about resurrection, and so also in us proper faith in Christ can be present without any reference to his resurrection. But it is reported in the Scripture, and therefore we accept it. And yet, there is an indirect connection with faith in Christ himself. If because of the miraculous (that is, so as not to have to accept the resurrection as a literal fact) one would rather assume that "the disciples deceived themselves and took what was internal to be something external," then one attributes to them such a spiritual weakness that their entire testimony about Christ becomes unreliable; furthermore, then also Christ himself, when he chose such witnesses, would either have been a poor observer of human nature, or else, if he chose them deliberately, his sincerity would have become suspect. Already we see here how the point of Schleiermacher's polemic in this passage is directed only against assuming that sort of deception which takes the internal to be the external, that is, against the view that Jesus really died but did not really come to life again, but that the first disciples, like Paul later, took subjective appearances to be objective ones. He leaves untouched the other conceivable case, that the disciples took a mere coma to be a real death, and took one who revived again naturally to be one who was miraculously resurrected—as if that would not be just as much a deception, and a much cruder one at that.

"The narratives," he says accordingly also in the lecture, "about that which took place between Jesus and his dis-

134. *The Christian Faith*, par. 99.

ciples after his crucifixion are, according to my judgment, attested in such a way that I cannot make room for the thought that either they were later inventions or that self-deception of the disciples prevailed" (p. 474). And, almost somewhat irritatedly, he says elsewhere, "If one says, 'All these narratives about Christ being together with his disciples after his crucifixion are deceptions,' then all narratives about Christ are deceptions; these narratives present themselves as reporting something actually observed. Either give up the whole thing or accept this also; everything else is of no consequence" (p. 442). It is not a good sign for the thing which he defends when a man otherwise known for being circumspect now falls victim to a heated exaggerating rhetoric. If I do not believe someone who tells me that a dead man entered through locked doors and immediately afterwards ate and let himself be touched, may I not believe him if he tells me completely natural things about the man's death and previous life? It is not possible to make the aphorism, "One can no longer trust a man who fibs once," as vague as it is, into a principle of historical criticism, and it is definitely not possible to say the reverse, that because he certainly did not fib about certain things he is to be trusted with other matters also. Rather, one must first ascertain what had to have been fibbed because it is historically impossible; then one must observe where the narrator falls into fibbing as a rule, and on this basis one can undertake to sort out the true from the untrue in the narrative. He can do so with the reservation that one certainly can reach a clear decision about what must be necessarily untrue, while about what in itself might well be true, but still might not be, there will always remain an uncertainty. The point which regularly takes the Evangelists off the historical track (apart from the more negative influence of distance in time and place, the passage of their reports through oral traditions, and the coloring and transforming influence of party rela-

tionships among early Christians)[135] is their Messiah-con-
cept, which increasingly moves toward the supernatural as
it applies to Jesus; the immediate result of this appears in
their narratives as the miraculous. The miraculous element
in the resurrection constitutes the apex because it designates
the reflex against the strongest negation of that Messiah-
concept which lay in Jesus' death; this negation was overcome by his first adherents by means of that intensely
heightened condition of spirit whose results were the visions
of Christ.[136]

Completely in accord with the meaning of his quoted
declaration, Schleiermacher tries to put the contradictions of
Acts, which have served the opponents of Christianity as a
main weapon all along, on the same level with the contradictions which are found in the earlier parts of the Gospel
reports about Jesus. He points especially to the difference
between the first three Gospels and the Fourth, which goes
through the entire story of Jesus; but in the resurrection
story it is worse. There, one can say, everyone contradicts
everyone else and even himself.[137] In general, Schleiermacher has a quite correct attitude, namely, that which already Lessing had, when he candidly admits actual contradictions—only supposedly soluble—in the narratives, yet
pleads that such contradictions "occur everywhere where
details are narrated by eyewitnesses, which are then repeated by others, and in which someone supplements the

135. [The inclusion of "party relationships" reflects Baur's advance beyond
Strauss's first *Life of Jesus*, in which Strauss had regarded myth as the
natural precipitate of common early Christian beliefs. See above, p. lx.]
136. [In this way, Strauss avoids explaining the resurrection as deliberate
deception, which had been advocated by H. S. Reimarus. See *Reimarus:
Fragments*, ed. Charles H. Talbert, Lives of Jesus Series (Philadelphia:
Fortress Press, 1970), pars. 53–55.]
137. [Reimarus's compilation of these divergencies in Gospel accounts of
the resurrection remains unsurpassed. See *Reimarus: Fragments*, pars.
10–31, especially 22–31.]

deficiencies of the narratives from other narratives or from his own conjecture" (p. 433). But certainly Lessing would have shaken his head had Schleiermacher then pushed forward with his "maxim" that also here John must be our guide, since his Gospel is "a report of an eyewitness," and since what he himself did not see nevertheless "came from the report of eyewitnesses directly into his own" (pp. 432–33, 435).

In Schleiermacher's criticism of the Gospel history the premises, divergences and contradictions in the report are always rightly presented, and the dilemma, where there is one, is sharply put. But the decision as a rule is not made according to the real facts of the matter, but according to a preconceived judgment. Thus Matthew knows nothing of appearances of Jesus which the disciples would have seen in and around Jerusalem; "Luke at various times has different information about the matter," and at the beginning of Acts gives a "correction" of his report at the end of the Gospel. (In the Gospel everything actually takes place on the same day, and the last thing of all, the ascension, "appears to follow immediately Christ's meeting with the disciples on Easter evening; in contrast, at the beginning of Acts, Luke makes up for this and mentions a time span of forty days during which Christ appears to the disciples, and now tells of the ascension as an occurrence distinctly separated from that first evening after the resurrection.") The thrust of Matthew and Mark in this passage is not at all a truly historical one, that is, one aimed at a coherent presentation of individual incidents. The former is concerned only, on the one hand, besides with making intelligible the first announcement of the resurrection, with making intelligible the disbelief of the Jews and the origin of the fable about the theft of the corpse, and on the other hand, with basing the preaching activity of the apostles on Christ's command. Similarly the individual narratives in Mark (Schleiermacher has no critical reservations about Mark's ending, just as he has none about the twenty-first chapter of John)[138] have the sole aim partly of portraying the disbelief of the disciples and their being rebuked by the appearing Christ, and partly of tracing the success of the Gospel to the command and promise of Christ (pp. 432–34). Into all such contradictions and deficiencies of the reports Schleiermacher sees as sharply as anyone. But already, when he ascribes "a purely historical tendency" to Luke, whose dogmatic thrust is virtually tangible by his using as proof Jesus' eating and being touched, then one promptly notes how things will fare with John, who is said to be totally concerned with nothing else at all but a faithful reproduction of what he himself experienced or heard from eyewitnesses (p. 435).

But Schleiermacher once again posed in the sharpest way the dilemma which results from the general view of the Gospel resurrection accounts. We have "on the one hand the fusion of the entire affair, as it were, into a single act, with which the resurrection life begins and also ends," namely the Galilean meeting in Matthew; on the other hand "the multiplicity (of appearances) in John, together with the mention of the fact that much more of the kind could have been offered, and besides, the definite assertion of the time span" of forty days in Luke. According to Schleiermacher:

Two opposing explanations are possible. One can imagine that gradually, various elements attached themselves to a simple narrative, but one which is not factual in itself— rather, one in which the miraculous has been elaborated. The opposite explanation is that the facts were transmitted in their multiplicity from the beginning, and only the way in

138. [Strauss refers to Mark 16:9–20, which is absent from the best texts and is clearly a later ending with a complex history of its own. That John 21 is an appendix is now accepted by virtually all students of this Gospel.]

which our Gospels arose in time and place, which we can no longer determine, prevented their being appropriated together. [p. 435]

On behalf of the view that in this dilemma one is to decide for the latter alternative, Schleiermacher appeals to the apostle Paul who, being one of the oldest witnesses, "in the Corinthian letter (1 Cor. 15:8ff.) mentions even other cases of Christ's appearances before the disciples which are not found in any of our Gospels." What quickly becomes undeniable by this means is what otherwise was to be surmised even from the nature of the case: already, in earliest times, one told not of one but of several appearances of Christ, which occurred in various places. Thus it appears to be no less evident from the correction which, according to Schleiermacher's expression, Luke brought about in his previous presentation, that the course which these narratives took generally was not at all that of allowing the additional elements to disappear; contrariwise, as the individual stories were collected, one tried to make room for the ever-mounting number of appearances by extending the time in which they were to have occurred. Consequently Matthew's conception of the matter must have a different basis, as Schleiermacher thinks, than the conception at the time of the writing of this Gospel; "much of that sort of thing had already been lost." And we need only remember how, in the discourses of Jesus, the First Evangelist has the habit of pulling together into a few great blocks of discourses what was spoken separately on various occasions; thus we see immediately that also here, at the conclusion of Jesus' earthly career, he went to work in the same way. The various appearances of the resurrected one about which stories were told could no more have been unknown to him than to the apostle Paul or to the author of the corresponding passages of the Gospel of the Hebrews, since they certainly belong to the most discussed parts of the early Christian tradition.[139] Of these, he rejected the Jerusalemite tradition, with the exception of the appearance to the woman, being faithful to genuine historical memory; but according to his literary characteristics he combined the Galilean traditions into one concluding appearance. His concern was to make an announcement which attests to the crucified Messiah not only as the resurrected one but at the same time as the one exalted into world-dominion as well, and who is the Lord who remains present with his community until the end of this age; the announcement was also to portray the proclamation of the gospel in the whole world as his direct command. It could achieve both aims only if the appearance was the first and the last.

If, according to this, there surely was a fusion of an original plurality into a unity in the case of Matthew, in comparison to the older Pauline report, as Schleiermacher asserted—only not as a result of the extinction of the original information, but as a literary compilation—then, if we compare the presentations in Luke and John with the Pauline report, the progression from the simpler to the complex, which Schleiermacher rejected, emerges nevertheless. To be sure, it is not numerical, since in any case Paul adduces more appearances than any one of our Evangelists; but rather it is a progression with respect to quality. Paul speaks of appearances absolutely; he knows nothing of proofs by touching and eating such as are found in Luke

139. [Strauss's judgment has not been sustained. Today one no longer assumes that all the appearance stories were known throughout earliest Christianity. For an excellent set of essays which reveal the current stage of the critical discussions see C. F. D. Moule, ed., *The Significance of the Message of the Resurrection for Faith in Jesus Christ*, Studies in Biblical Theology, Second Series (Naperville, Ill.; Allenson, 1968), vol. 8. See also R. H. Fuller, *The Formation of the Resurrection Narratives* (New York: Macmillan, 1971).]

and John. Likewise, even in the narrative of Acts, which is no longer the original one, concerning the appearance of Christ which occurred to Paul, light and words are mentioned, but there is no mention of flesh and bones or of broiled fish and honeycake. And this corresponds completely to the nature of the case. Once there was a disposition for visions, then it certainly did not end with *one*; and if several visions occurred, then one did not need to provide for the early origin of yet many more narratives of such appearances. Originally these narratives said what they had to say right from the start: they presented as something viewed externally what was perceived inwardly, as something actually heard. With the awakening of misgivings and with the circulation of the objection, however, that this was not yet sufficient proof of the reality of those appearances, the stories of the tangible proof were added; accordingly, they indicate the latest stage in the development of these narratives.

With reference to the individual narrative pieces, primarily those which contain the first news of the resurrection even before the appearance of the resurrected one himself, Schleiermacher not only analyzes the differences among the various reports with his customary acuteness, but overdoes a good thing when he produces a difference which does not even exist. The Evangelists are said to diverge from each other not only in that some speak of one angel and the others of two, and in that some have the appearances occurring within the grave, others outside it; but "in Matthew and John they are expressly called angels, in Mark it is a young man, and in Luke it is men; the differing view of each personality is the reason for this" (pp. 438, 440). That is, Schleiermacher thinks that one is to understand that in the mind of these Evangelists Luke's "men" and Mark's "young man" were, in fact, only men. That again this is a piece of the worst rationalistic exegesis needs several demonstrations today only because Schleiermacher made himself responsible for it. In Judges 13 the narrator has both Manoah and his wife speak only of a man of God whom they also treat as a man; but he who knows better calls him an angel (similar cases are found in Judges 6:22 and Genesis 18:19). In exactly the same way, here Matthew and John designate the appearance on the basis of its essence, namely that of angels, but Mark and Luke designate it on the basis of its external appearance, that of men or youths, without it occurring to them that they could be misunderstood by anyone. When Schleiermacher asks, "What is more probable, a man or an angel?" (p. 441), we must say that this question is badly put. If we are to understand it on the basis of reality, then unquestionably men are more real than angels; but if we are to ask for the understanding of the Evangelists in this story, then the opposite is equally certain. Thus when Schleiermacher answers, "In such a historical time as that one, an appearance by angels was surely no longer in place," such wisdom is almost funny. And when he goes on to ask, "What is more probable, that someone claims an angel to be a man, or that he claims a man or youth to be an angel?" and naturally finds the latter more probable, one should rather answer that it is not at all a question of various claims or of a different view of the nature of the appearance, but that the diversity pertains only to the expression, and that Mark as certainly had angels in mind as Matthew did, and Luke as John.

Still, Schleiermacher occasionally is severely punished for his rationalistic obduracy by the dilemma into which his angel-men bring him, and even precisely with respect to his main Gospel. In the first three Gospels the women found the man or men at or in the tomb; when afterwards, according to Luke's narrative, Peter went to the tomb in response to the women's message, he found no one. Naturally, in the meantime the men had departed. In John, however, Magdalene sees at first only the stone rolled away, and runs to the disciples in the city without having observed an angel or a man. Thus far it could well be that the men certainly are in the tomb into which Magdalene seems not yet to have looked. But now she comes back with Peter and John, and while she remains standing outside, the disciples enter the tomb one after the other, without observing the slightest thing apart from the empty clothes. But they have hardly gone when Magdalene, as she looks into the tomb, sees two angels in it—that is, according to Schleiermacher, men. How they are to have gotten into it is indeed puzzling, since immediately before that they had not been found therein by the two disciples while Magdalene stood watch before the tomb. That John puts him into this dilemma almost offends Schleiermacher. "One must wonder," he says, "that he did not question Magdalene more carefully about the relation between what she had seen and his own visit to the tomb" (p. 441). That is, he would like very much to be able to imagine that the sequence of the two incidents was the reverse, namely that Magdalene previously had seen and spoken with them and that Peter and John began their walk only afterwards and found the tomb empty, after the men meanwhile had departed. But since the narrative of his eyewitness (John) restrains him, he says "something is left obscure here." Something obscure remains, in any event, namely, how such an explanation was possible for a man of intellect and taste.

But that is how it fits together, even though one can get a fleeting glimpse now and then into the actual background of the view only through narrow fissures in the lecture.[140] "Joseph of Arimathea," Schleiermacher summarizes the story up to now, "had put Christ only temporarily into the tomb, but could not complete the burial until the Sabbath

---

140. [Strauss sees that Schleiermacher's view of the resurrection must be pieced together, because his lectures did not really do this.]

was past; therefore, persons instructed by Joseph could have found the tomb already empty" (p. 442). To this scheme, according to Schleiermacher, Magdalene was privy to the extent that she knew of the aim to put the corpse into Joseph's tomb after the Sabbath; therefore the stone's being rolled away made her think immediately that the corpse had been taken away, but she did not know *where* Joseph's tomb, as well as the corpse now, was to be found. We thus learn who the angel-men were: namely, persons instructed by Joseph. And since the discovery of the emptiness of the tomb is combined with their coming, they, or rather those who came with them, must have been the ones who took Jesus' body, in whatever condition, out of the tomb, and went away again before the arrival of the women. That this is Schleiermacher's real understanding is confirmed when he promptly designates the circumstance that when the women came "someone was already in the tomb" to be "a trace found in the story which can explain the fact of the resurrection" (p. 442). And in such a conception he can find so little deceit that he seeks to repel only the conclusion that the problematic men were somehow "secret associates" of Christ. Please, not Bahrdt and Venturini too![141] For the rest he intends to be responsible.

But this time he still comes very near to the precipice. For if it was only Joseph's people and not emissaries of an Essene society who took Jesus' body from the tomb, the surmise still lies close at hand that it was the care of these adherents which brought him completely back to life. But in previous years of his lecture course this appeared unacceptable to Schleiermacher, because in that case Jesus must have known what had happened in his resuscitation and his exit from the tomb. If he had known, it, then he must have

---

141. [Karl F. Bahrdt and Karl H. Venturini viewed Jesus as a member of the Essene society and held that his fellow Essenes resuscitated the half-dead Jesus. See note 78.]

told it to his disciples, if he were honest. But manifestly he did not do this, for otherwise the reports before us would contain something of it. Therefore, Schleiermacher had the resuscitation of Jesus take place while he was yet in the tomb, in a way unknown to us—and probably also to himself—and without human cooperation; and at least without deliberate human cooperation he also had the stone moved from the grave. The new tomb in the garden, which belonged to a Jerusalemite landown r probably not known to Jesus, had doubtless stood open ntil Friday evening (in order to dry out better, we can imagine). Then early in the morning, after the Sabbath, the owner's servants entered the garden and saw the stone rolled up to the door, and thought, What is the stone doing there? They too it away, not in order to let Jesus out—they did not know that he was in the tomb—but because the stone did not belong there now. Thus Jesus could come out, without human intention being involved, without himself knowing the connection of events —by a pure course of providence.[142] Whether this combination subsequently appeared too artificial for Schleiermacher or whether something else brought him back from this path, in the printed lecture it is no longer the servants of the unknown owner of the garden but, as observed, "persons instructed by Joseph" who took the stone from the tomb and took Jesus out of it—it is not said whether he had already revived or still appeared to be dead. And that he did not explain to his disciples what had happened is no longer the consequence of the fact that he himself did not

142. See my article "Schleiermacher und die Auferstehung Jesu," *Zeitschrift für wissenschaftliche Theologie* 6 (1863): 391ff. With reference to this article, Keim (*Der geschichtliche Christus*, p. 128) says that I was the first to "unveil the secret of Schleiermacher's theory of Jesus' apparent death and to ransack it." I find the latter expression witty but inappropriate. Only that is ransacked which it is a duty to keep secret; but where is that to be found in this case? Moreover, Keim's judgment on Schleiermacher's view agrees with mine.

know but of the fact that the disciples did not ask him about it. "If they had done so, then it is not conceivable that Christ should not have told them how he had come out of the tomb" (p. 467). Certainly. But it is equally inconceivable that they should not have asked him about it. Schleiermacher speaks of a "praiseworthy hesitance which they had about burdening Christ with inquisitive questions" (p. 442). We can no more find such hesitance to be praiseworthy than we would reproach a question of the disciples concerning the actual course of events in the resurrection as being inquisitive. Schleiermacher further specifies the former as the hesitance to "ask Jesus about something that was not essential with reference to faith" (p. 467). Now we know that from that point on the apostles built precisely their entire faith on the resurrection of Jesus; hence there was no question which had a closer relation to faith than just this one which they are to have been too hesitant to ask about. "But if they did not ask him," Schleiermacher thinks, "then he also had no interest in telling them." We think that if from the start Jesus had only answered the disciples what they asked him, then they would have learned very little from him which was intelligent. But how, precisely according to Schleiermacher's view of Jesus' condition after the resurrection, he had the most pressing occasion to instruct his disciples about the course of these events, we shall see presently.

JESUS' POSTRESURRECTION LIFE

With reference to Jesus' condition after the resurrection there are, according to Schleiermacher, "two opposing indications" in the Gospel narratives, namely, first of all, "the indication that one is to think of his condition as a complete restoration of his life to the previous one" (p. 444). With this belongs the fact that he is recognized, and therefore has his previous form; that he shows limbs and wounds, moves about, and takes food like a natural person. In contrast with this we find secondly, however, "other indications which occasion the conception that a continuity in Christ's existence is not to be believed, but that the whole thing manifests itself more as an apparition." Here, by way of an exception, we must blame Schleiermacher because he has put even the dilemma falsely in order to shrink back from one alternative. The disappearing, the entry through locked doors, and especially "the isolatedness of Jesus' appearances which occur without reference to his sojourn in the interval" are by no means intended in the Gospels to mean that the "existence" no longer was a continuous one; rather they mean only that the appearance of Jesus after the resurrection was no longer a continuous one. Far from this alternative meaning that "the whole thing manifests itself as an apparition," in the minds of the Evangelists the existence of the resurrected one rather is a real one in the highest sense: he lives, and lives uninterruptedly, a new higher life, even if only occasionally and for brief moments he thinks it proper to show himself visibly to his own.

Nevertheless, opposing indications always remain: in a real situation we cannot coordinate eating and disappearing, tangible limbs and coming through locked doors. Whoever wants to imagine Jesus' postresurrection condition as a real one must choose between the contradictory characteristics. So then Schleiermacher thinks that upon closer examination he discovers that the indices of one kind, namely, those which point to something supernatural in Jesus' new condition, are found exclusively on the part of the disciples and their prejudiced understanding; while on Jesus' part an endeavor is manifest throughout "to present to the disciples his life after the resurrection as completely human" (p. 466). "He wants to be regarded as an appearance which does not deviate from common human life; he wants to be touched for proof that he has a real human body like everyone else; he causes the signs of what he experienced to be seen; he eats in their presence" (p. 449). Thus Schleiermacher advances the canon for the reports of Jesus' appearance after the resurrection: "One is to keep to that which Christ deliberately does and says, to how he wants himself to be conceived; and everything miraculous, such as how he appeared to the disciples, one is to ascribe to the judgment of the disciples" (pp. 447, 469). This canon would be entirely correct if we only had the real Christ somewhere. In our Gospels, however, we have first of all only the Christ of the Evangelists, and whether their conception corresponded to reality is most in question precisely in this part of the Gospel history. Therefore, what they have their resurrected Christ expressly explain and specifically explain and specifically undertake, such as the reference to flesh and bones and the eating, has no greater validity than what they tell on their own about him and the impression which his appearance made on the disciples. Rather the one, like the other, is an element of their conception of Jesus' existence after the resurrection, and if these elements contradict each other, then we have no choice except to explain that we cannot conceive of such an existence. In addition, these endeavors of Jesus to convince the disciples of his natural corporeality do not belong to the earlier formations of the resurrection story in Paul and Matthew, but to the later one in Luke and John.

Now, according to Schleiermacher, Jesus took great pains to convince his disciples that his life after the resurrection was exactly like his life beforehand, and that absolutely nothing supernatural was in the picture. But he did not prevail in this; they could not rid themselves of the conception that he was no longer a natural man as before. So we must say that he had himself to blame that he did not achieve his aim, for he did not use the very means which most certainly would have brought him to it. This was telling them how he came out of the tomb, namely, in a totally natural way. According to Schleiermacher's printed lecture Jesus knew this, but made the telling of it depend on whether the disciples asked him about it, and they did not ask him. In fact, however, in their stubborn foolish belief that he was a ghostlike being, there lay such a pressing challenge for Jesus to correct them on this point that it could not require an explicit question first.

Still, we must also see in detail how Schleiermacher came to terms with the features of the Gospel narratives which appear to speak for something supernatural in the condition of the resurrected one. Immediately on resurrection morning we find that Mary Magdalene takes Jesus for the gardener and addresses him as such. That seems to point to something strange in Jesus' figure; but Schleiermacher thinks it could also have been due to his changed clothing; in the tomb he had only the clothes which he left there, so after coming out he must have acquired strange clothing (probably that of the gardener who lived nearby). That is what it says in an earlier notebook. In the printed form of the most recent one I have not found this feature. Then follows the appearance of Jesus on the way to Emmaus, where both disciples recognize him neither by the form nor, in the extended discussion, by the voice, by which Mary Magdalene had recognized him in the morning, but only at the breaking of bread, whereupon he immediately disappears from them. Now Schleiermacher finds the extended lack of recognition to be explicable by the fact that neither disciple thought at all of the possibility that the executed one could be alive; "during their astonishment, then, after they once recognized him, he could easily have slipped away from them and they only perceived it after it had happened" (p. 445). When subsequently both walkers were engaged in reporting their experience to the disciples in Jerusalem, among whom Peter had also seen an appearance, Jesus, according to Luke, stood so suddenly in their midst that they thought they were seeing a ghost. To be sure, Schleiermacher concedes in the earlier notebook, that clearly looks like a miraculous appearance. But if we compare it with John, where he tells of the same experience, then we read that when the disciples were assembled and the doors were locked, Jesus came and stood in their midst. "True, one naturally thinks that the entry and the locked door are invented." The fact alone that in Luke nothing is said of an entry and of the door, Schleiermacher thinks, makes the matter in Luke appear docetic. In the printed lecture he tries using the expedient of distinguishing between the outside door and the room door. "If the apostles were together in the evening, then doubtless the house was locked, but there would also have been someone who had the responsibility of opening it; that the room must have been locked would have gone beyond custom and would also have been without purpose" (p. 445). Indeed, as far as the doors are concerned, one can take them to be the outside doors or the room doors or both; it says they were locked, but that they were opened is not said, and may not be added mentally to the situation as self-evident since rather, according to the thrust of the narrative, what is to be seen as the miraculous in the matter is precisely that the opening of the door was not necessary.

Schleiermacher thinks that he is able to conclude that there was nothing supernatural in Jesus' condition after the resurrection from the following feature as well. On resurrection morning, when Jesus says to Mary Magdalene that he has not yet ascended to the Father but that he is to do so, and that she is to go to the disciples and to announce it to them, then according to Schleiermacher "this seems as if Christ had no definite conception of the duration of this renewed life" (p. 443). Also his appearance in the evening, when he imparts to the disciples the Holy Spirit by breathing on them, as well as their authority to forgive sins, "very much has the character of a last commission, and there we find no trace that Christ thought of remaining longer with them, and no word to the effect that they were to expect him again" (p. 464). But now Schleiermacher thinks that he discovers in Jesus' consciousness a further development with respect to this point.[143] At the very first he doubtless "was not certain about a definite duration of his continued life," but when he later orders the disciples to Galilee, "then this expresses the consciousness of a longer duration of his condition than in the first moment." Thereupon he must have returned to Galilee himself, "completely restored to the course of a perfect life, because there he acts entirely, and under the same circumstances, as before" (pp. 465, 469), namely, he is now with individuals or with several disciples (John 21), now also with greater crowds (the five hundred brethren of 1 Cor. 15:6).

With reference to this journey to Galilee, Matthew—when he has the angel and Jesus himself give the command as early as resurrection morning—must surely be wrong, according to Schleiermacher, because according to John,

---

143. In the well-known Easter sermon "Christi Auferstehung ein Bild unseres neuen Lebens" (*Predigten*, Sammlung 5; *Festpredigten* 1 [*Werke* 2, part 2, pp. 55–68]) Schleiermacher finds this development not only in Jesus' consciousness concerning his state, but he speaks in an entirely rationalist way concerning Jesus' life after the resurrection, saying that "it gradually grew stronger and gained powers. When the Redeemer," he continues, "first appeared to Mary, he said, as if his new life were still as fearsome as it was sensitive, 'Do not touch me . . .' But in a few days he showed himself to Thomas and summoned him to touch him firmly, to put his hand into that of his master and his fingers into the scars which the nails of the cross had left behind, so that he was not afraid of being touched in even the most sensitive places. But also on the first day, as if he actually wanted to strengthen himself by this means, we see him walking from Jerusalem to Emmaus and from Emmaus back again to Jerusalem, just as later he went ahead of his disciples to Galilee and then led them back again to Jerusalem." To be sure, given the allegorical cast of this sermon, we do not know the extent to which these events can be taken historically.

even eight days later the disciples are still in Jerusalem and experience an appearance of Christ there. But even Schleiermacher clings to the journey itself because of John 21, only he has it follow somewhat later, however, also upon an instruction from Jesus. If we ask about the purpose of this journey, then Schleiermacher makes the following disclosure for us: once he had decided no longer to have anything to do with the world outside the circle of the disciples, the resuscitated Jesus could no longer remain at one and the same place, especially in the environs of the capital, lest he "bring those who shared in the secret of his resurrection into an all too suspicious situation." Now in Galilee he had numerous adherents, and could at the same time "be more isolated and be more unobserved with his disciples than was possible in and near Jerusalem" (p. 455). And if we consider his meeting with the five hundred brethren, which in all probability took place in Galilee and hardly had the purpose of merely attesting his resuscitation, then, according to Schleiermacher, the surmise lies close at hand that "Christ went to Galilee and there met with them for precisely this purpose: together with his disciples he could lay virtually the first foundations for an organization of the Christian community" (p. 462).

But now Luke shows Jesus with his disciples finally again in Jerusalem ("again" only if one combines Luke with the others, for Luke himself of course has the disciples "not depart from Jerusalem," in accord with Jesus' explicit prohibition). What, then, is to have been the reason that Jesus once again returned there? Possibly, Schleiermacher answers, the same which moved him previously to take the journey to Galilee: that also here his presence gradually began to be known in circles from which danger might arise. Besides, he of course chose the capital of his nation as the point where the preaching of his disciples was to commence after his departure. If he now led them to this place, "then it was

145

the presentiment of the impending end of his second life which moved him to return from Galilee to Jerusalem" (p. 469).

Now, should we regard this presentiment of his end as a feeling of bodily weakness, of exhausted vitality? If one views Jesus' death as a coma and his resurrection as an awakening from this, then in any case this conception is the most natural. At the same time, Schleiermacher comments rightly that if one imagines the body of Christ with the wounds from the crucifixion and his condition as that of a sick man with weakened vitality, then the journeying to Galilee and back again has something improbable about it. Besides, already on the first day during the walk to Emmaus, and from there back into Jerusalem, he appears rather as an entirely healthy man for whom neither wounds nor fatigue cause concern. In any case, from this it follows that our Gospel writers did not think of Jesus' condition after the resurrection in that way. But now Schleiermacher volunteers, "Manifestly, part of the picture of his condition is that by no means may we present Jesus as do those who stop at the concept of a coma, that is, we must not see him as passing this time with weakened vitality" (pp. 455–56). We do not know what we are to say to this. Does Schleiermacher not conceive of Jesus' death as a coma? If not, our entire presentation of his view up to now would be incorrect. Surely he conceives of this entire "second life" of Jesus, as he calls it, as a perfectly natural one, as the restored earlier life. But a natural life would doubtless also have been restored in a natural way, and its natural restoration is conceivable only if it was not really destroyed, if the destruction—death—was merely an apparent one.

But Schleiermacher expressly explains that in the resurrection of Christ things are the same as in his entire appearance on earth: "The former is a miraculous event, but what follows was a perfectly natural one" (p. 445). In earlier years of the lectures he maintained only that one should not want to reduce the resurrection of Jesus to the common limits of nature, so that we lack only the knowledge of certain circumstances in order to grasp the entire process; such an endeavor to reduce the miraculous, which is part of this unique moment of development of humanity, might easily also be accompanied by another endeavor: to reduce this moment itself, even with respect to its spiritual context, to the ordinary. If someone only demurs, "If there was still a trace of life in Christ I do not need to regard his resurrection as an absolute miracle," then Schleiermacher finds that harmless. We cannot even say in general what an absolute miracle is, since we can neither discern the limits of nature nor know how many extraordinary things may still fall within these limits. It appears that among the properties of the normal man, on the basis of which Schleiermacher conceived his Christ, he reckoned also such power to restore corporeal life; in turn, he regarded this power as supernatural insofar as it was connected with the absolute strength of God-consciousness in him—but he simultaneously regarded it as natural insofar as its efficacy was limited to the laws of the influence of the spiritual on the corporeal. But now this power must not merely have restored life but must also have healed the wounds and overcome the loss of strength. In the first place, we do not know how to conceive of such a restorative power, and in the second place, even if we wanted to assume it, we would not be in a position to understand the body in which it functioned, and the life which it renewed, as a natural human one.[144]

144. Also Keim's brief and opaque hints (*Die geschichtliche Würde Jesu* [Zürich, 1864], p. 46–47) appear to lead to something similar, or to a Weissian influence from the spirit world. Now he expressly identifies himself with belief "in an appearance of Jesus in a transfigured, newly-constituted corporeality" (*Der geschichtliche Christus*, p. 139). That means sheathing the weapons of thinking, and fleeing to the ground of miracle; hence the question emerges, Why only at the end and not right

Therefore from the physical, as previously from the moral side, here we conclude that Schleiermacher's conception of Christ as well as the church's, rather than finding the right middle ground between the ebionitic and the docetic, as he endeavors, is subject to the latter folly. This is also completely natural since there is no such middle ground, nor can there be any. The ebionitic conception of Christ is of course precisely that which perceives him as a true and real man. Hence every conception of him which goes beyond this must necessarily land in what is still merely apparently human, or the docetic.[145]

Still, in spite of this mysterious point of departure and, as we shall soon see, also in spite of such an outcome, Schleiermacher insists on the perfect naturalness of the course of this second life of Jesus, and does not retreat from any counterevidence. One such consideration concerns the question of where Jesus stayed during the long intervals which separated his individual appearances. Why did he not either show himself openly or at least remain with his disciples? According to Schleiermacher, the former had its basis in the fact that he was through with the world and wanted to have nothing more to do with it. If one asks what could have caused him, or more specifically, could have justified him, to come to this decision, then Schleiermacher surmises that if Christ had openly shown himself as the resurrected one, this would indeed have had a greater effect,

---

away at the beginning? What displeases the Zürich theologian concerning our view is mainly the enthusiasm [*Schwärmerei*] in which it appears to implicate the early church. The sober Christian consciousness of today resists the desire to derive the resurrection from the heightening of visionary circumstances—as if our planet, now so thoroughly cooled off, had not also been a glowing mass, and as if we did not know approximately as much about the time and manner of the cooling off of early Christian consciousness as we do about the process of the cooling off of our earth.

145. [See note 114.]

but as a result there could also "have broken out a tendency toward an external messianic kindgom" and already this consideration suffices fully to explain why he isolated himself in this way (p. 459). Still, if he wanted to have nothing more to do with the people, why did he not remain continually with his disciples, for whom now he wanted to be present exclusively, as Schleiermacher also assumes? One thing depended on the other, Schleiermacher answers. If Jesus wanted no longer to become involved with other persons, then he would have had to avoid notice completely, which would have been impossible had he remained the entire time with his disciples (pp. 444–45).

But where, then, was he in the intervals, and why do we find no explanation at all about this in the Gospels? "We have no report about where he actually stayed, because of the disciples' reluctance to ask him"; in an earlier notebook it said that Jesus himself had reasons for keeping his whereabouts secret from them so that they, when questioned, could say with clear consciences that they did not know where he was. "But if one wanted to say," Schleiermacher continues, "that that clearly presupposes other relationships which Christ had, then I would agree, but I would not find them outside the circle of disciples which is constantly discussed" (p. 445). But since he appeared only temporarily to the Twelve as a whole, and to individuals among them, what does Schleiermacher understand by the group of disciples, known independently, with whom Jesus is supposed to have stayed permanently? The mention of Bethany at the end of the report in Luke lets him remark that here an analogy emerges between the whereabouts of Jesus before and after the resurrection: previously, when he came to Jerusalem during festivals, he customarily stayed in Bethany; so it is probable "that also after the resurection he stayed here" (p. 453). However, in Bethany the family of Lazarus was, according to John 12:10–11, specifically exposed to hatred and persecution from the Jewish authorities; therefore Jesus could have found secure refuge among them least of all.

But now, the more the few and brief meetings of Jesus with his disciples shrink to a minimum, in contrast with the extended times of concealment during the forty days, and the more enigmatic he is about his whereabouts during these intervals, the more pressing there repeatedly arises, on the one hand, the surmise that this behavior is no longer natural but is more ghost-like; on the other hand, there emerges the suspicion of those secret associations. But ever since Bahrdt and Venturini, this assumption has been deemed ridiculous. This is why Schleiermacher strives to multiply as much as possible the number and duration of those meetings. Of course, none of our authors undertakes to report all appearances of the resurrected one. To the contrary, at the conclusion of his Gospel John points to many other signs which Jesus had done in his disciples' presence but which are not in his book, among which one is to understand especially signs from the time after the resurrection as well (p. 458). That there were still more appearances of the resurrected one than those which our Gospels mention we see also from the Pauline passage in 1 Corinthians 15: 5ff.; conversely, since Paul equally omits some which are attested in the Gospels, he could have also bypassed others. From all this Schleiermacher draws the conclusion that the life of Christ after the resurrection nonetheless was not as interrupted and fragmentary as it appears to have been, and that this time "must have been taken up more fully by Jesus' association with his disciples" (pp. 453, 457). Especially if we combine on the one hand both "Galilean incidents" and the meeting with the five hundred brethren, which doubtless was one of a number of similar occasions, and on the other hand, that which John narrates in his appendix, "then we see," according to Schleiermacher, "two things:

150

first, Christ's association with his disciples in a greater crowd, and second, his association with a part of the apostles and with individuals. This appears to us as a regular continuation of his life and of his activity" (p. 463). However, the fact that Schleiermacher speaks of an association and of meetings which Jesus attended is already a distortion of the stories which always speak only of a momentary appearance; where one must think of a little more extended presence of Jesus the stories treat the matter in such a way that Jesus disappeared again soon after he was recognized or had said what was necessary.

Still, the most dangerous instance with which Schleiermacher must come to terms is the way the apostle Paul speaks of the appearances of the risen Christ in 1 Corinthians 15. "There," he admits, "it is very remarkable that Paul combines, and therefore evidently equates, the way Christ appears to him and the way he appeared to others (the appearances before the older apostles)" (p. 451). Here there appear to be only two possibilities: either the appearance of Christ which Paul experienced was like that of the earlier appearances as Schleiermacher conceives of them—that is, the natural encounter of a person physically alive so that "one assumes with the notorious Mr. Brenneke that Christ still lived when Paul was on the road to Damascus"[146]— or conversely, those earlier appearances were "also only the same as his"—that is, according to the apostles' understanding, appearances of a supernatural being, but according to ours, images of aroused fantasy. Still, Schleiermacher gives us reason to reflect on the fact that in the context of 1 Corinthians 15, Paul had a dogmatic purpose. He intends to illumine two things: first, the resurrection of Christ and its attestation by means of all sorts of appearances; second, also

146. [J. A. Brenneke, *Biblischer Beweiss, dass Jesus nach seiner Auferstehung noch siebenundzwanzig Jahre leibhaftig auf Erden gelebt, und zum Wohle der Menschheit in der Stille fortgewirkt habe*, 1819².]

the exalted status of Christ after the ascension as a model of our future state after the resurrection. Consequently,

> for him the difference between them, the resurrected and the exalted Christ, virtually disappears; he conceives of the resurrected Christ in such a way that no further change in him is necessary in order for him to pass into the state of exaltation, with the result that the ascension does not appear as a special point. He could do this since he conceived the relationship in Christ's case the way he conceives of it generally, namely, that the germ of the transfigured body already lies in the present one.

But from this it does not follow that "Paul did not conceive of Christ's state [this negative must be supplied here] as a truly human one and that he saw no difference between the appearances of Christ before the ascension and that which [later] occurred personally to him" (p. 452). All this chatter basically amounts to nothing other than this: the apostle Paul indeed made no differentiation between his own Christ-appearance and these of the earlier apostles, but we must make one; he conceived of the appearing Christ in both cases as a superhuman being, as belonging to a higher world, but we, or rather I (Schleiermacher) can no more regard Christ at Damascus as a man still physically alive (with Mr. Brenneke) than I can regard him who appeared at Jerusalem and in Galilee and to the Twelve and to the five hundred to be a higher being or a pure image of fantasy. That especially the apostle Paul shared with the two middle Evangelists the conception of an ascension between earlier appearances of Christ and the appearance to himself is presupposed here by Schleiermacher without any basis whatever;[147] if he did not share it, but if he conceived of Christ

147. [Only in the secondary ending of Mark (16:9–20) is there an ascension in this Gospel. Strauss does not accept this ending (see note 138). Moreover, Strauss is also correct in seeing that Paul knows nothing of the ascension story reported by Luke 24:50–51 (not found in all MSS); Acts 1:9–11.]

as already exalted to heaven with the act of resurrection and as appearing from there, then for Schleiermacher, every basis and every possibility itself that Paul could have conceived Jesus' state before and afterwards to have been different collapses.

When Schleiermacher then approaches the Gospel reports of the ascension, he is aware that by means of the standpoint occupied thus far he has not made it easy for himself to come to terms with these items. "If one presents the time of Christ after the resurrection as fully human," he says, "then it is more difficult to attach the ascension to it afterward; conversely, those who view it as already a supramundane state have it easier" (p. 466). If we start from the assumption of a truly human life, then the question arises, How could this state have come to an end? If it was the previous body which was vivified then he was also mortal, "and this would include the necessity" (and not simply, as another reading has it, the possibility) "of a second death of Christ after the resurrection as fully human," he says, we did not have the report of the ascension in Luke (for Mark's, according to Schleiermacher, is partly too indefinite, partly so constituted that we cannot trace it to an eyewitness). It would not be unacceptable, from the standpoint of Christian faith, for "the spiritual exaltation of Christ, his sitting at the right hand of God, has no connection whatever with the way his human body came to an end" (pp. 470–71). Nonetheless it would then be difficult, Schleiermacher thinks, to explain why every report of this second end of Jesus' life is lacking from the Gospels. One could try to explain it somehow on the basis that "Christ had deliberately withdrawn into total concealment." Motives which could have moved him to do this are readily conceivable; he had finished with the world and he would only have delayed the independent appearances of his disciples by more extended association with them. What is to be rejected is only the conception of "secret relationships with those who were not disciples"; they are, Schleiermacher assures, "historical fantasies" (p. 471). But precisely the fact that these fantasies repeatedly concern Schleiermacher like nightmares shows that he did not go to bed properly.

In any case, this is how it is without Luke. But now we do have him and his double report of the ascension. What is the effect of this? If we view what he tells us of the removal of Jesus as an external event, and if we have conceived of Jesus' life until then as a natural one, then according to Schleiermacher we must necessarily inject an event—a change in the body of Christ so that it lost weight and altogether ceased to be a human body. But does Luke's report really give us Jesus' ascension as an external event? According to Schleiermacher, what he says at the end of his Gospel—that Jesus departed from his disciples and was raised to heaven—no more requires us to conceive of the matter as an external visible event than when Mark has him taken up to heaven and seated at God's right hand. Rather, one can understand it in the same way as when previously Jesus spoke of his exaltation and his going to the Father. Surely this is not even true of the report in Mark; for if Mark says that after Jesus had spoken with them he was raised to heaven, then this can be understood only of a visible removal which is indicated more specifically in the words, "He departed from them and rose to heaven," at the end of the Gospel of Luke. The same thing is merely amplified at the beginning of Acts. "There," says Schleiermacher, "Christ is with his disciples, speaks with them, and gives them a task, and after he has completed his speech he is raised aloft in such a way that they see it, and a cloud removes him from their sight." On this basis, how does the phenomenon take place? They could see that Christ was raised aloft, one could say; but now "a cloud takes him away from their sight; it therefore veiled him and they no longer saw him; what they could still see was the cloud in which they knew Christ was enveloped; now they look at the sky, whence the cloud moved (and surely upward) and with their eyes they follow the motion of the cloud which had veiled Christ" (p. 472). If one wants to construe this as a real event, then "an event must have a beginning and an end; here, however, in the nature of the case, the end is not at all perceptible." Or it is completely different from the beginning: "The movement begins as a corporeal one"; its end is "the sitting at the right hand of God; but that cannot be regarded as the end of a corporeal, spatial movement, since it is a spiritual conception" (p. 473). It was not quite this way for the Evangelists; for them heaven as God's dwelling place was actually a *place,* and the way to it led upward through the sky. But Schleiermacher is quite right when he says that we cannot construe the passage as a real event whose end does not fit the beginning. "If we ask," he says, "Is this a necessary beginning for that end? then we must say *no,* because we cannot demonstrate the connection between the two." That is, even if we were to find the exaltation of Jesus to a superhuman state acceptable, according to our current world view we would still not be able to imagine that an elevation in clouds was the way to it.

Nevertheless, if the report were strictly attested it would have to be respected. Now according to Schleiermacher, Acts, which is most concerned here, is indeed an authentic book based on documentary-type reports about the first church. "But that does not prevent the existence of individual passages where one must doubt whether something which is told as factual is also to be understood as really factual" (p. 474). Among them Schleiermacher reckons the story of Peter's vision, the narratives of events on Pentecost, and other things. It is probable that "some of the poetic elements were transmitted as fact"; traces of this are found also in the other biblical books. "If we must then say," Schleiermacher continues, "that such things occur in

155

Acts, and if we include also the character of this narrative—first, the forty days which, being a formal number, suggest that it is not an exact account; further, the way in which (in the description of the ascension) what was perceived moves into what is not perceptible; and the instruction which the apostles received from the two men who stood before them in white garments" that this Jesus would come again in the same way—then we cannot know "how much of these narratives rests on actual definite reports and how much in them is taken up as fact from explanations and conceptions which were not properly meant to be factual" (p. 476). In addition, Luke stands alone with this narrative. In the time when Matthew and Mark (and John?) wrote, Schleiermacher thinks, such narratives of a definite, observed ascension must not yet have been in circulation, for otherwise they would have mentioned the matter, even if but with few words. Therefore in the narrative of Acts we have "a composition which gained less circulation, composed of actual historical elements and of other presentations which have been drawn into the historical elements" (p. 477).

After also the report at the beginning of Acts is thereby set aside as a historical account, the question returns again, How then did this second life of Jesus come to an end? It must have ended, Schleiermacher thinks, before Pentecost, that is, before the fiftieth day. For on Pentecost the Apostles show no expectation of a further meeting with Christ; also, the fact that they pray to him presupposes that they no longer think of him as on earth. But can the apostles have been witnesses of his end? If this end had been death, surely. But then it would not be intelligible, as has been already said, why no report of it whatever had been preserved. "Therefore, that the disciples knew that Jesus died again is a hypothesis which we must exclude." But at the same time, in their speeches or writings the apostles do not allude to "a different end of his life which they had observed" but always only to the resurrection and the subsequent appearances. In any case, Jesus appears to have designated a particular meeting as the last, "but what they further perceived sentiently about the end of his life is something of which we cannot make a definite conception on the basis of the extant narratives." According to Schleiermacher, we can conceive a "natural end" of his life only in such a way that it could not be perceived, but only its negative side, namely, Christ's no longer being on earth, could be perceived (p. 478). Hence, it was a pure disappearance, an act of becoming invisible. That is not the "natural end" of a human life, or else the life which ended thus would not have been a natural human one. With this presupposition about Christ's end Schleiermacher himself annulled his entire conception of Jesus' state after the resurrection. To be sure, there is also a natural way of becoming invisible. Schleiermacher had excluded only the hypothesis that "the disciples knew that Jesus died" again. Therefore he could in fact have died, although his disciples learned nothing of it. This would have been possible if he had withdrawn himself into a seclusion from which no report of his further fate could any longer reach the disciples. Such a turn of events Schleiermacher himself had not found unthinkable; he thought only that one must reject the concept of Jesus having secret relationships. But that is easier said than done; throughout Schleiermacher's stance toward the miraculous in Jesus' life he always finds himself grinned at by the masks of Bahrdt and Venturini. A disappearance of his hero either into the spirit world or into an Essene society is the dilemma in which he leaves us.

PART THREE

CHAPTER SEVEN

CONCLUSION

What comes to light in this dilemma is only the division in the view of Jesus, and the fact that Schleiermacher's attempt to heal it is unsuccessful. The New Testament authors have an idea of the person and of the life of Jesus which cannot be harmonized with our concepts of human life and the laws of nature. They tell especially the supernatural about him, but we can accept only the natural in him. Do perhaps their narratives permit an interpretation according to which he truly was a natural man and did only natural things? This is what rationalism asked, and it knew how to treat those narratives in such a way that it thought it could answer *yes*. But only the exegete said *yes*. That the Gospel narratives said *no* loud enough to this he did not or could not hear. Schleiermacher's ear was more sensitive; he let a part of the narrative—to be sure it was the smaller part—keep its miracles, but in turn surrendered it as unhistorical. He sought to support the greater part by extending the concept of nature and of the natural. By substracting from the narratives what is to be substracted and by adding to this concept what is to be added, also he believed himself able to answer that question *yes*. But now we have seen in a host of points that it cannot be done this way either. A far greater number of Gospel narratives than he wants to admit contain the supernatural, and this supernatural element is not to be understood as something natural again by an extension of the concept of nature, however forcefully it is distorted.

Schleiermacher, we can say, is a supernaturalist in Christology but in criticism and exegesis a rationalist. His Christ, however many of the miraculous attributes of the old confession may have been removed, still remains essentially a superhuman, supernatural being. In contrast, his exegesis, as far as it pertains to the miraculous in the Scripture, is distinguished from that of Paulus[118] only by somewhat more spirit and subtlety—a difference which precisely in the main points, such as the resurrection story, becomes imperceptible. The one appears to contradict the other; rather, however, the one is the basis for the other. Because Schleiermacher wants to remain a supernaturalist in Christology he must be a rationalist in criticism and exegesis. In order not to lose the supernatural Christ as a historical personality he cannot surrender the Gospels as historical sources. But in order to avoid a supernatural Christ in the sense in which the supernatural is unacceptable to him, he must remove exegetically from the Gospels the supernatural which offends him. Indeed, he retreats to one Gospel, the Johannine, and appears to let the other three go. However, they still have too much in common with John, with regard to content and standpoint, to be separable in this way. Whoever thinks that in the miracle stories of the Fourth Gospel he has the facts in the report of an eyewitness will also assume facts in those of the first three, even if in more indirect tradition; and since he no longer believes in actual miracles, apart from the miraculous personality of his Christ, he will have to explain also these in a rationalist way.

148. [The reference is to H. E. G. Paulus, the most famous rationalizing interpreter. See note 127.]

Therefore it comes to the same thing: whether one formulates the doctrine which results for theology from the failure of Schleiermacher's attempt as requiring it to cease viewing Jesus as a somehow supernatural being, or whether one says that it must cease viewing the Gospels as historical sources in the strict sense. For with the former the latter disappears, and with the latter the former. The positive element in both negatives is that Jesus is to be regarded as a person, as a great—and as far as I am concerned, the greatest— personality in the series of religious geniuses, but still only a man like others,[149] and that the Gospels are to be regarded as the oldest collections of the myths which were attached around the core of this personality. Not that they do not simultaneously carry with them much historical material; but the medium in which they transmit this to us is thoroughly the mythical, that is, the concept of Jesus as a supernatural being. This determines also the character of those writings in relation to history. We will harbor no reservations against conceiving of the Gospels in this way as soon as we have rid ourselves of the idea of needing a supernatural Christ; conversely, only if we are able to view the Gospels with open eyes can we convince ourselves that their authors, and the circles for which they wrote, could not conceptualize their Christ supernaturally enough. But precisely the more impartially we bring to consciousness the arbitrary element in their whole standpoint, the less we will feel ourselves tempted to make their modes of understanding our own.

In a word, the point is that the Christian world must *come to terms* with the faith of the church and its foundation, the gospel history. Conversely, Schleiermacherian theology, and especially also Schleiermacher's *Life of Jesus*, was a last attempt *to make us agree with it*. We find that

149. [For Strauss's use of the category "religious genius" see above, pp. lxvi, lxxiv, lxxvii.]

this last attempt, like all previous ones, has failed. Once and for all, it cannot be done anymore. Nowadays we view all things in heaven and on earth differently from the New Testament authors and the founders of Christian doctrine. What the Evangelists tell us we can no longer take to be true in the way they tell it; what the apostles believed and the way they believed it we can no longer hold necessary for salvation. Our God is another, our world is another; also Christ can no longer be for us who he was for them. To admit this is the duty of truthfulness; to want to deny or cover it up leads to nothing other than lies, distortion of the Scriptures, and hypocrisy with regard to faith. Officious attempts at mediation where two things can no longer go together lead only to deeper embitterment; but if they come to terms in such a way that they are free with respect to each other, then henceforth probably even a friendly relation is possible. As soon as we no longer expect to treat the Scriptures as other than a human book we will be able to treat them with full respect; as soon as we take courage to really put Jesus in the ranks of humanity, our reverence, or love, cannot fail.[150]

But indeed we must be serious and honest about this humanity. We may no longer ascribe predicates to him which had their full meaning in the old system but which from the standpoint of the current world view are but empty, indeed deceptive, words. We may no longer, like Schleiermacher, speak of a redeemer after we have given up the God-man who offered himself as a sacrifice for the sins of the world. We may no more call Jesus the light of the world than any other single person, if we no longer regard him, with the Fourth Evangelist, as the Word become

150. [In *The Old Faith and the New*, Strauss abandoned this appreciation for Jesus. See above, pp. lxxvii–lxxviii.]

flesh.[151] A Christ who, without knowing himself to be the God-man in the strict sense, had called himself the light of the world would have been a braggart.[152] Whoever calls

151. [At this point Strauss provided a long footnote concerning his recent polemics with Schenkel. See pp. xliii–xliv. In criticizing Schenkel he became a bedfellow of his old enemy, Hengstenberg, who was even more critical of Schenkel. This, in turn, provoked H. J. Holtzmann into an attack on Strauss. Now Strauss bitterly counterattacks Holtzmann. I have inserted bibliographic data, supplied from Geischer, into the footnote.]

As already known, Dr. Schenkel, at the conclusion of the foreword to his *Charakterbild Jesu*, assures us that precisely in the development of this book which, especially in regard to the Fourth Gospel, also occupies a rather free critical standpoint, he became more certain than ever that Christ is and remains the light of the world. I find it appropriate to repeat as a supplement my judgment of Schenkel's book in general, as I published it at the time in the *National Zeitung* [Sept. 21, 1864, no. 441; Strauss included his review with *The Christ of Faith*]. If I here admit as well that from my standpoint I agree largely with the article in the *Evangelische Kirchenzeitung*, "Dr. Schenkels Apostasie" (I would only say, excesses), then here Dr. Holtzmann will find anew the congeniality with Hengstenberg which he (here also he is only a representative of the great scholar of Göttingen [H. Ewald, another bitter opponent of Strauss]) thinks to have discovered in me (Schenkel's *Kirchliche Zeitschrift 5*, part 5, p. 34). In any case, (according to Rev. 3:15–16) the decisive standpoints of right or left have always been preferable to me over spineless mediations, because in the former case a complete and full conviction is at least possible, while in the latter the inner contradictions can remain hidden only to him who consciously and deliberately closes his eyes. On the contrary, in the passion with which Dr. Holtzmann decries my *Life of Jesus for the German People* as "a program against all faith in the transcendent world," and as "a potion, subtly mixed, of poison and gall," I would have the right to see an affinity with the fanaticism of the *Evangelische Kirchenzeitung*. This is the famous "liberal mentality" of this mediating theology, the attack on which, occasioned by Schenkel's book, is so offensive to Mr. Holtzmann!

152. It is an entirely different matter when he calls his disciples, as the firtsborn of the true community of God on earth, the light of the world and the salt of the earth (Matt. 5:13–14). That the Fourth Gospel makes the "you are" into "I am" without further ado (John 8:12; 12:46) comports completely with the manner in which this Evangelist reworks the material transmitted to him from the first three Evangelists in accord with his basic idea. [Strauss will make a similar observation about Jesus in

him this without taking him to be such is a flatterer (or, if he is less concerned with Christ than with third persons, a hypocrite); he would be repudiated by the real Jesus in a quite different way than was that rich young man who addressed him as "good teacher." If no one is good save the one God, then even less is any individual the light of the world. He may be the star which surpasses the others in brilliance, as the apostle says, but none of them is the sun.[153]

But once this view has penetrated as the right one, what

The Old Faith and the New; see above, p. lxxvii. Having surrendered the idea that John knows and uses the Synoptics, today one no longer regards the "I am" discourses of Jesus in John in this way. The origin of these materials is still in dispute, some arguing for an ultimately pre-Christian Gnostic Revealer source which has been Christianized (Bultmann), and others for an Old Testament origin. For a convenient recent survey of the problems (and an attempt to trace the formula to the Septuagint) see Philip B. Harner, *The "I Am" of the Fourth Gospel*, Facet Books (Philadelphia: Fortress Press, 1970).]

153. Concerning a similar explanation in my new *Life of Jesus*, Dr. Keim says, "That is only his old philosophical presupposition concerning which, completely apart from Schleiermacher, we must first hear historical experience" (*Der geschichtliche Christus*, p. 100). Now to begin with, we do not need to ignore Schleiermacher; rather, in my previous work I have dealt critically with Schleiermacher in detail. In the next place, I am fully ready to listen to experience; but since it persistently keeps silent, that is, since in another area it does not know how to say that a figure was the greatest in the absolute sense—I am reluctant to view Jesus as such a one in the religious sphere, and to do so on the basis of historically uncertain sources which actually say something totally different. In the third place, I want to honestly wish the author of the lectures on the historical Christ that his present presuppositions, once they have become thirty years old, will have survived this test of time just as well as those of my old *Life of Jesus*.

While Keim blames me for staying with old convictions, the reviewer in the *Theologische Studien und Kritiken* (38 [1865]: 71–126) [C. Beck, "Kritische Anzeige von Strauss, *Das Leben Jesu für das deutsche Volk bearbeitet*"] on the contrary seeks to oppose my views by demonstrating all kinds of changes in them, and the Dean goes so far in tastelessness as to cite as evidence against me a sermon which I gave as a student. Are not the gentlemen like the boys in the marketplace, according to Matthew will become of Christianity, of the Christian church? This also, like many other things, Schleiermacher saw much more clearly and had more sharply in view than most of his successors. "The Christian faith," he says in our lecture, "rests totally on the person of Jesus; if this" (as prototype and as absolutely perfect) "cannot be maintained, then also Christianity as such will be surrendered, and only that in it which is true in itself will remain; that is, the task then would be so to consolidate the religious fellowship which is the church with everything true which it contains, that the conception of the person of Christ would be something irrelevant" (pp. 22, 24). In a sermon Schleiermacher once expressed the same thing this way: for a long time there circulated among men a fable, concocted by "Unfaith" and taken up by "Little Faith," that there would come a time, perhaps even the present, "when also about this Jesus of Nazareth what is just would be said—the human race owes much to him, and God accomplished great things through him; but nonetheless he was only one of us, and his time to be forgotten must also come. If it had been his concern to make the world completely free, then it must also have been his will to make it free from himself so that God could be all in all."[154] Throughout his life Schleiermacher summoned himself and others to guarantee that this fable would not come true. His main evidence, however, always was only what he speaks right out of the depths of his heart in the same sermon: "No, without this abundance of vitality and joy which the existence of the redeemer gives, I would not want to live!"[155]

11:16-17 [an allusion to Jesus' rebuke of his contemporaries who declined to play funeral or to play wedding]? But not quite. They all would certainly have been content with one thing—that I not write on the subject again.

154. *Predigten*, p. 10. [*Werke* 2, part 3.]

155. Ibid., p. 9.

The Redeemer was for him "the pure image of man, one who lived on earth without sin, the image of a soul constantly at one with God"; but we can have this image, he thought, in no other way than from him, the historical Jesus of Nazareth. But at the same time he says that even if "the text of the Gospel report about Christ were to disappear, which is sacred only because it preserves this image for us, the image itself would still remain forever; it is too deeply buried in man for it ever to be able to disappear."[156] Certainly this picture would not disappear with the Gospel texts; but only because it does not originate with these texts either. The image of the man without sin, of the soul at one with God, is the ideal of humanity which has its origin in human nature and its ethical-religious foundation,[157] which develops, refines and enriches itself with it. The ideal of humanity was refined and enriched especially through Jesus but it also underwent further development after him and will continue to do so. Schleiermacher's Christ-image, far from simply being taken from the New Testament, is to a great extent of modern origin; not a single apostle would recognize his Christ in it, but on the other hand Plato and Spinoza, Kant and the author of the *Speeches on Religion*[158] could reclaim individual features of it.

According to Kant, the idea of a humanity well-pleasing to God, which we make visible in the image of an irreproachable individual, of a moral son of God, has its reality

156. Ibid.

157. [It is not clear whether this rather general statement is grounded in Kant's claim that the idea of a humanity well-pleasing to God is given with moral consciousness, or in Feuerbach's idea that all religion is grounded in human needs and wishes. At any rate, Strauss goes on to speak of Kant.]

158. [Strauss refers to "the early Schleiermacher"; for a discussion of the *Speeches* in relation to his development see Redeker, *Schleiermacher: Life and Thought*, pp. 34–59.]

practically complete within itself and needs no illustration from experience to make it an obligatory example for us, since as such it lies in our moral lawgiving reason. For Schleiermacher, on the other hand, it all depended on whether this idea once lived as an actual man on earth; without that existence, the historical occurrence of such a redeemer, he would not want to live. This passion—as we can aptly call it—for a personal Christ who existed historically is an anachronism in Schleiermacher's otherwise thoroughly modern spirit; this remnant of the old faith ruptures his thoughts, which live in the ideas and strivings of the most recent present, and indeed, of the yet unborn future, like a rare idiosyncrasy. He himself feels a contradiction; he senses the danger which, coming from the power of the modern ideas which he permitted to permeate himself, threatens the fragment of faith which he has carried over from the past and does not want to give up for anything. This explains the diligent, and one virtually wants to say anxious, activity of his mind, so amply endowed with resourcefulness, to make peace with both parts—to make the believed Christ acceptable to thought, and to make thought agreeable to faith at least at this one point. For him this was not a matter of a certain amount of sophistry in details, but one of utter seriousness concerning the whole. But true reality is lacking from his own Christ; he is only a memory from a long-forgotten time, like the light of a distant star which still strikes the eye today although the body from which it shone has been out for years.

So long as one saw in Christ—as was the case in the first Christian centuries—the one who had ascended to God's right hand and who would soon return from there in order to awaken the dead, sit in judgment, and bless eternally his believing adherents in a renewed world, or after this expectation gradually faded, so long as one viewed him—as the reformers still did—as the one who satisfied divine justice by his death on the cross, as one who had offered himself as bloody expiation for the sins of the world, then so long naturally everything depended on the fact that one's Christ is no mere thought, but had actually lived on earth and still lives in heaven, for only such a being could have really made the sacrifice and could actually have brought to pass the expected transformation of all things. But if Christ, as he is for Schleiermacher, is only the image of sinless humanity and the soul at one with God,[159] then one cannot see at all what difference it would make whether this image had been there as an actual man under completely extraordinary conditions or not. Anyway, the rest of us men assume that no one really compares with Jesus, because in our case the conditions are absent which made him the sinless and completely perfect one to start with; his perfection therefore remains equally strange to us personally, whether he actually lived or whether he is but the image of our idealizing imagination. Or conversely, that the ideal of humanity increasingly forms itself in the whole race in the process of history, even if never perfectly, is a truer reality of the same thing than if it had once existed in a single person, the like of whom was never there before or afterwards.[160]

Redemption, says Schleiermacher, consists in the fact that sin is expunged from our consciousness; therefore, sinlessness must become visible to us in the person of Christ. Only when we appropriate his sinlessness in the most intimate fellowship with him, "the way everything is common to friends," will we become participants in redemption and in its fruits.[161] This is, as Schleiermacher furthermore ex-

159. [This represents a serious misinterpretation of Schleiermacher. See note 35.]

160. [One is somewhat surprised to find Strauss still retaining the view which he announced at the end of *LJCE*, and which he surrendered by the time he wrote *The Old Faith and the New* seven years later.]

161. In the sermon "Dass der Erlöser als der Sohn Gottes geboren ist," *Predigten*, Sammlung 5; *Festpredigten* 1. [*Werke* 2, part 2.]

presses it also as God's seeing the redeemed in Christ,[162] only the old doctrine of the vicarious atonement, even if weakened to a mere manner of speaking. His whole theory of redemption can be conceptualized to a certain extent only if one surreptitiously substitutes once more the dissolved church dogma for it. It is like a sheet of transparent paper which, when laid on an old picture, shows the outlines of a figure, but which appears blank when removed from it. Schleiermacher's zeal for the personal Christ-ideal who existed was precisely only a personal one; it changed nothing in substance. The ideal of the dogmatic Christ on the one hand and the historical Jesus of Nazareth on the other are separated forever. That, independently of one another, the one is to be evermore basically and relentlessly researched, while the other is to be ever deeper and more perfectly recognized and made ever more fruitful for human life—therein consists the task of theology for the immediate future, and therein lies the summons which humanity, in its present struggles to develop, awaits from it. It remains to be seen whether it awaits in vain.[163]

162. *The Christian Faith*, par. 104, sec. 3.

163. [Strauss does not have in mind the Christ of faith as being fruitful for mankind, for that is superseded; rather he has in mind the ideal Christ figure. *The Old Faith and the New* indicates that Strauss later decided that such waiting would be in vain.]